# LULU

## I DON'T WANT TO FIGHT

A *Time Warner* Paperback

First published in Great Britain in 2002
by Time Warner Books

This edition published in 2003
by Time Warner Paperbacks

Pictures reproduced by kind permission of Lulu and: Aquarius
Library (p. 2, top and middle; p. 3; p. 4, middle and bottom; p. 15, top
left); Alpha London (p. 14, top; p. 16, middle left; bottom left)
Mirrorpix (p. 2, bottom; p. 4, top; p. 5, bottom; p. 6, bottom; p. 8,
middle; p. 9, bottom; p. 12, bottom; p. 16, bottom right); Retna (p. 5,
top); Popperfoto (p. 6, middle; p. 7, bottom; p. 9, top; p. 15, bottom
left); SKR Photos (p. 7, top right); Redferns (p. 16, middle right); Rex
Photos (p. 10, top; p. 15, bottom and middle right)

A CIP catalogue record for this book
is available from the British Library.

ISBN 0 7515 3371 8

Typeset in Fournier by M Rules
Printed and bound in Great Britain by
Clays Ltd, St Ives plc

A Time Warner Paperback
An imprint of
Time Warner Books UK
Brettenham House
Lancaster Place
London WC2E 7EN

www.TimeWarnerBooks.co.uk

# Contents

To ma mammy and ma daddy. This would not have been possible with you here, but would never have been possible without you. I love you.

# 1

# *Mrs McClean and the Offal Dresser*

In the Glasgow of my childhood I woke to a symphony of glass, metal and steam, 'Shhhhh-chk-chk! Shhhhhhh-chk-chk!' It was the sound of milk bottles being dropped into crates and loaded on to lorries.

The depot was less than 100 yards along Soho Street, and from the third-floor window of our tenement I could just see over the iron gates to where the lorries stood.

My father, Eddie Lawrie, woke to the same sound at 5.30 a.m. He slipped away from my mother's side, tiptoed across the room and made himself a cup of tea. As the kettle boiled, he pulled on clothes that were stiff with dried blood.

In the wintertime he wore either two jumpers or three. First came a shirt, then two cardigans, and finally a thick sweater my mother had knitted him. Layers were the best way to fight the cold.

He always wore good shoes, polished to a brilliant sheen (even the arches). When these became too stained by sawdust and blood he threw them away and wore his next newest 'old' pair. A man could be penniless and hungry, but 'it costs him nothin' to polish his shoes,' my daddy would say. He judged a man on things like this and expected to be judged the same way.

I drifted back to sleep and woke to the sound of a metal shovel scooping coal into a bucket. Crouching on the floor, still shivering, Dad arranged the bigger lumps in the centre of the grate and the smaller pieces around the outside.

There is an art to lighting a coal fire. My father had a special way of creating his own firelighters. He rolled sheets of newspaper diagonally into long tubes and fashioned each one into a tight knot with one end left sticking out as a wick. These would burn slowly, generating enormous heat. Another of his tricks was to hold a sheet of newspaper over the fireplace, helping to draw the flames up the flue.

None of this was for his benefit. He was off to work. But by the time we woke in an hour and a half the fire would be blazing and the rooms would be toasty and warm.

Eddie walked to work every morning. The trams hadn't left the terminus at that hour. He worked in the Glasgow Meat Market for the Glasgow Corporation, one of the biggest employers in the city. He spent nearly thirty years there – leaving only once or twice for a year to work on the shipyards when big orders needed filling.

The Corporation always took him back. Officially, he was an offal dresser, although he liked to call himself an offal merchant because it sounded grander. He worked in a huge, echoing chamber the length of a soccer field, divided into cubicles with concrete floors and gutters. There were skylights above, with pulleys and chains suspended from the ceiling.

A freshly killed beast would be hoisted with a hook and chain. My father would take a knife, reach up and disembowel the animal with a few flicks of his wrist. All the important organs would fall into drums at his feet – with an extra container to catch the portions he was stealing. A little into this bucket, a little into that bucket . . .

Even now people talk of Eddie Lawrie as being like an artist with a knife in his hand. He could take a liver out of a beast in seconds and at the same time cut it into three perfect portions – one for him, one for the Corporation and one for his boss.

He wore a huge rubber apron and wellington boots, to stop him drowning in blood, but it made little difference to his clothes. I hated the way they smelled, but I still proudly held his hand when he occasionally took me to work of a Sunday. He didn't take me many places.

There was no petting the animals and I avoided seeing them killed. Growing up in the east end of Glasgow I had no real connection with sheep or cows. Farm animals were something from books and nursery rhymes and the only places I saw trees were the public parks.

Condemned beasts were immersed in foul-smelling disinfectant before being killed. Dad would bring the same liquid home and we used it to scrub the stairs to stop them smelling foosty (damp and musty).

Most days he would also arrive home with a bloody package under his coat. I would open it and pick off the sodden bits of newspaper that clung to the meat. Sometimes he would have swapped a piece of offal or sweetbreads for prime Scottish fillet or lamb chops.

'Yer'll never go hungry in this hoose,' he'd say, proudly.

I preferred beans on toast but wasn't game to tell him. Sometimes Mum would secretly give the meat to neighbours who couldn't afford it. Dad would say later, 'How was that steak?'

'It was smashin',' I'd lie, licking my lips.

*

There are very few photographs of me as a baby. I was small and fair, with a round face and dimples. And I didn't seem big enough to warrant such a long name – Marie McDonald McLaughlin Lawrie.

My mother had suffered at least one miscarriage and had started to fear that she might not have children. I kept her in suspense for a long time and then arrived on 3 November 1948 at Lennox Castle in Lennoxtown on the outskirts of Glasgow. It wasn't really a castle. Somebody told me it had once been an asylum for the insane, before becoming a hospital.

My mother's relief was enormous. At last something good had happened to her – something that couldn't be taken away. I belonged to her and I was going to be with her for ever, she thought. She became completely obsessed.

To understand these feelings, you need to know a little about her. Up until the age of fourteen she was Betty McDonald, the daughter of Nellie and Wullie McDonald, who lived on the corner of the Gallowgate, Fielding Street, in Glasgow's east end. She had brothers Frankie and Robert and sisters Jeanie and Annie who loved her. Betty felt the same way about them.

She was a cheeky and confident girl, with her own little gang of girlfriends who had secret catchphrases and passwords. They roamed the streets, looking for adventures and pretending to be tough.

My mother has a keen eye for a bargain and as a child she used to go around the middens (dustbins) collecting anything that might be useful or of any value. These were called 'luckies'. Once she found a carpet in almost mint condition. She took it home to the tenement and called up from the street, 'Hey, Mammy, look what Ah found.'

My grandmother leaned out the window and scolded her, 'That's terrible! You put that back where yi found it, Betty McDonald.'

Later, when the neighbours weren't watching, Betty was sent out to collect the same carpet. It graced the hallway of my grandmother's 'hoose' for years afterwards.

One day a girl came to the school gate during playtime and asked for Betty McDonald.

'Who wants to know?' said my mother, cocky as can be.

'Do ye know who Ah am?' said the girl.

'Who are yi?'

'Ah'm yer sister.'

'No ye'r not. Ah've got two sisters already.'

'Yeah, but Ah'm yer *real* sister.'

Betty didn't believe her at first. She went home and asked Nellie and Wullie if it was true. Despite their denials she saw the panic in their eyes and heard it in their voices. Slowly the truth came out – never cleanly, but in dribs and drabs.

Betty discovered that her real name was Elizabeth Kennedy-Cairns and that her natural family lived in Glasgow.

Deep down inside, my mother had always suspected that she was different . . . that she didn't belong. Even so, it came as a terrible shock to learn the truth. It played on her mind. Why had they given her up for adoption? What was wrong with her?

Slowly but surely all the fight went out of Betty. She lost her confidence and cockiness. She became quiet and withdrawn.

I have never been able to discover exactly why she was given up for adoption. I have only theories. Almost inevitably it comes down to religion. The Cairns were Catholics and the Kennedys Protestant in a city divided by sectarianism, violence, gangs and two rival football teams.

The Kennedys weren't just members of the Orange lodge – they were leaders. And when their daughter, a great beauty, took up with a big, handsome Irish peasant, it was a scandal. Both families tried to break the couple up, but somehow they stayed together.

Maybe it was true love, but it certainly didn't run smooth. My grandmother, who seemed to be permanently pregnant, was forever leaving her husband and going back to her family. The

Kennedy clan would embrace her and raise her children, until her husband turned up and she went back to him.

They had five or six children. One of them – their blue-eyed boy – died during the war, but they managed to raise the rest . . . all except for my mother. As a baby, Betty was given to Nellie and Wullie McDonald, who were apparently paid an annual retainer to look after her.

This wasn't a case of a family giving up for adoption a child that it couldn't afford to feed. Nor was it about keeping the boys and giving away the girl. And the McDonalds weren't a childless couple desperate for a baby. They had their own children before and after they adopted Betty.

I have one other theory. When he was drunk and fighting with my mother, I sometimes heard my father call my grandmother 'a whore' and 'a slut'. I don't know why he chose those insults. But what if there was some truth in them? What if my grandmother had been unfaithful to her big, handsome Irish husband? Maybe she fell pregnant and he couldn't be sure that he was the father. He was willing to raise his own 'flesh and blood' but not another man's child, so he decided to have nothing to do with the baby.

This would explain why they found another home for Betty. The McDonalds raised her as their daughter and never stopped loving her. To this day they refuse to accept she isn't a blood relative. All the same, I don't think anybody realised the impact the truth had on my mother. Her sense of abandonment never left her and she would never entirely trust anybody again.

She married my father when he came out of the navy in 1947. She was nineteen and he was three years older. Eddie Lawrie was small, with dark, curly hair, slicked down with Brylcreem. He was very handsome, although you might not get that from his photographs.

Like a lot of men of his generation, Eddie was very fashion-conscious. He wore his money 'on his back' and would never be seen in the same shirt two weekends running, or something that went out of fashion last Thursday.

When he walked down the street he wanted people to see a successful man. He wanted women to fancy him and men to envy him. Making money had never been difficult for him, although I don't think he realised quite how much my mother could spend when she put her mind to it.

She had her dresses tailor-made from photographs that she'd cut from magazines like *Woman's Realm* and *Woman's Own*. She bought fur coats and new shoes. And she had her hair done every week at a salon.

At times she went too far and spent all the house-keeping money. Then she'd visit the pawnbroker with a pocket-watch or my father's best suit or her engagement ring. Later, when he was asleep, she'd sneak more money from his wallet so she could redeem them.

Dad would have been horrified if he'd known the truth. As a child he'd watched his mother pawn family heirlooms to put food on the table. It had affected him deeply. That's why he was so proud of the fact that he was a good provider. He'd say to Betty, 'You'll no have to do what ma mother had to do, hen.'

According to the stories, the Lawrie family had once been quite wealthy, but the fortune had been lost by my grandfather, a former boxer. Eddie Lawrie senior was a mean, hard bastard who tortured my father as a boy, making him run miles without shoes and cutting off all his hair. 'Ah'll make a man out of 'im,' he'd said, when his wife tried to intervene.

At some point he abandoned the family and drank himself into oblivion. There was a shambling drunk I used to pass sometimes on my way to school, lying in a doorway, clutching a bottle. I knew he was my grandad, but I was ashamed to say hello to him.

His mind had gone. He was punchy and soft in the head. Dad used to give him money to go to the Salvation Army hostel in

Duke Street. That's where he slept every night. At one point, when I was very small, my mother took him in. She kept him off the bottle for weeks, but one day he took money from her purse and went back to his old ways. He wet the bed and she found him lying in sodden sheets. After that she wouldn't have him under her roof.

There were a lot of family secrets when I was growing up. Some of them were only mentioned in whispers or in the heat of an argument. The most scandalous was that my father had had a child with another woman before he married my mother. I don't know how she found out, but it hurt her deeply. Here again was proof that she was second-hand. Nothing was truly hers – not even her husband.

I often wondered if she ever really loved my father. He certainly worshipped her. When she was pregnant with Billy, three years after I was born, Dad would often run all the way back from work at 8.30 in the morning with hot rolls and cream buns from the bakery. He'd arrive home sweating, having taken the stairs two at a time.

Mum would be in bed. The fire had warmed the rooms. He'd dash in, put on the kettle and butter the rolls, bringing them to her in bed.

'Here yi go, Betty,' he'd say, giving her a peck on the cheek. Then he'd run all the way back to work. He was the most handsome and romantic man I had ever seen.

My abiding memories of my childhood are the tenement buildings and the greyness . . . grey buildings and grey skies. We lived on the third floor of 55 Soho Street. Each floor had three flats with a shared lavatory on the landing. Waterfalls of algae stained the outside walls where the downpipes leaked, sometimes forming great puddles that would block the close entrances.

I didn't regard my family as poor. We were like everybody

else. And I had no idea that Glasgow's slums were considered to be the worst north of Naples.

The tenements had been built to solve a chronic housing shortage in the nineteenth century, when Glasgow was one of the great workshops of the world. Tens of thousands of highlanders and Irish immigrants flooded into the city, escaping famine and looking to share in the economic miracle. They needed somewhere to live, so speculative builders went to work and created street after street of flat-fronted tenements.

A city that produced a third of the world's merchant fleet by 1914 built its own slums to solve a housing crisis and created a completely new set of problems – deprivation, squalor and hopelessness. By the 1950s, Glasgow was still seven times more crowded than any city of corresponding size in England and Wales.

A lot of these streets have been bulldozed in the past thirty years, but Soho Street is still there. They don't have white strips painted down the sides of the steps any more. And you don't see children scrubbing them with hard-bristled brushes and tin pails.

Our 'hoose' consisted of two rooms. The main one had a sideboard, a big pull-out table and four dining chairs. There were two armchairs on either side of the coal fireplace and a pull-down bed in a recess where my parents slept. The second room had a wardrobe, a dressing table with lamp, and a three-piece leather suite, which included a fold-up bed. Each new baby had a cot in the recess.

The main room had a sink, which was boxed in to make a sort of a scullery. This was where we cooked and washed the dishes and ourselves. There was no hot water and we shared a lavatory.

There were nine families in our building and all of them had children. We'd play on the stairs and out in the street, or we'd go climbing the dykes (brick walls) that divided each close.

I always wore beautiful sticky-out frocks – a different one every day – with matching ribbons in my hair, pristine white ankle socks and fancy knickers. I also had buckskin white Clarks' sandals, which had to be washed every day and then coated with Meltonian whitening cream.

I would look picture-perfect when I left the house at the start of every day. It wasn't necessarily how I looked at the end.

Summer evenings were spent playing on the street with the neighbourhood kids. We'd play 'Kick the Can' and 'Red Rover Cross Over', or circle games with wonderful songs like:

> *Be baw babbity,*
> *Babbity, babbity,*
> *Be baw babbity,*
> *A lassie or a wee laddie?*
> *I widnae have a lassie o,*
> *a lassie o, a lassie o,*
> *I widnae have a lassie o.*
> *I'd rather have a wee laddie.*

Girls would choose boys, or boys would choose girls. As we grew older the chasing games became kissing games.

I loved playing outside in the long twilights. I remember busting to go to the toilet, but not wanting to go upstairs because I knew Mum would keep me inside for supper or for bedtime. Once I wet my pants rather than miss out on any of the games.

When Billy was born he was too pretty by half. He had gorgeous blond, curly hair. Mine was mousy and kept in bunches with big, colourful ribbons, tied in bows.

I was jealous. I wanted Billy's hair and the attention he received from everybody except my mother (she was still obsessed with me). 'He looks daft,' I told her. 'He looks like a wee lassie. You should get his hair cut like a boy's.'

She did just that, taking him to the barber that afternoon. By the time his hair had been trimmed and plastered to his scalp with oil, he looked completely bald. My father came home and said, 'Are yi off yer fucking heed woman? Yi must be mental.'

'Well, Marie said he needed a haircut.'

'And you'r listening to a four-year-old, for Christ's sake! What's wrang wi' yi?'

Despite my jealousy over his hair, I fell madly in love with Billy. I dressed him and changed his nappies. I fed him his bottle and sang him to sleep.

Mum loved her children, but she wasn't particularly domesticated – a fact which sometimes drove my father crazy. The navy had given him many rules to live by, including tidiness and a pride in his appearance. That's why he preferred it when I ironed his shirts, because he knew the collars and cuffs would be perfect.

When we moved from Soho Street, across the railway bridge to Garfield Street, it was only a couple of hundred yards, but mentally it was a lot further. We had edged slightly up in the world because we now lived closer to Duke Street and further away from the Gallowgate. There weren't so many poorly dressed kids or runny noses.

Twenty-nine Garfield Street was a three-room tenement with an inside toilet. My mother treated the main living room like some grand drawing room. It was only big enough for a three-piece suite, a table and the radiogram. Mum and Dad had a bedroom to themselves for the first time and Billy and I slept in the second bedroom.

There was no bathroom so we washed ourselves in the sink, or in a tin bath in front of the fire. Filling the bath was a palaver so I preferred to use the tiny sink in the scullery, which had a hot water geyser. I had to raise each leg into the soapy water and use a flannel to wash my entire body. Dad used to call me 'Mrs McClean' because if I wasn't washing myself, I was scrubbing my shirts and rinsing my socks.

Every week we trooped down to the public baths, which were above the local swimming pool. There were two long corridors off the main entrance, with cubicles running down each side. The women were on the right and the men on the left. Once you turned on the taps, steaming water whooshed out, filling the bath within seconds. There were big back brushes and you could buy shampoos and all sorts of lotions to cleanse your body.

Not every family could afford the public baths, so the Scottish education authorities made sure all schoolchildren had mandatory showers. Once a week a mobile shower unit would arrive and park in the playground. It had a pipe system surrounded by heavy tarpaulin that created ten cubicles. Every class would have half an hour – fifteen minutes for the boys and fifteen minutes for the girls. We stripped off and each child was handed a towel and a bar of soap.

'Right, in yi get!' yelled the teacher.

We had five minutes to wash and another five minutes to mess about. Each bar of soap had to be handed back and carefully examined for signs of use.

For the first few years I went to Campbellfield Street School. It was typical of most state schools, with a grey and red sandstone building, three storeys high, overlooking a large playground. The youngest kids were on the lower floor.

When we moved to Garfield Street I changed to Thompson Street Primary School. It was much smaller, with separate playgrounds for girls and boys. These were marked out with the lines for netball courts and hockey fields – games we never played.

For the boys it was always football, football and football. The girls played quieter games like 'peever' (a form of hopscotch) or 'baws'. The latter involved bouncing a ball under one leg so it ricocheted off a wall, and then catching it again. Girls would sometimes tuck their skirts into their knickers to play (giving the boys a glimpse and a thrill).

I used to get myself ready for school, setting out my uniform and tying ribbons in my hair. During the winter I wore a liberty bodice under all my layers of clothing. This was like a double-breasted vest with ribbons that were pulled through and secured with buttons. I loved these bodices when I was young; they were cosy and comfortable. Later I grew to hate them because they were so damn unattractive.

I walked down three flights of stairs and into Garfield Street, ready for the blast of icy wind. Across the road was a local shop, which sold milk, butter and groceries. The guy that owned it was a rip-off merchant, according to Dad. 'He thinks he's better than the rest of us.'

A few doors down the street, I cut through a close and emerged on to a large block of spare ground where tenements had been torn down. It was littered with rubble and weeds. This was where local boys played soccer.

The school was on the next corner, less than five minutes away. Living so close I usually went home for lunch at midday and then went back to school until 3.30.

I loved being independent, but I realise now that it exacerbated my mother's neediness. She was always looking for praise and asking me if I loved her. This wasn't just about reassurance. She wanted me to love her *more* than anyone else . . . particularly my father.

As happens to most kids, people were always commenting on who I most resembled.

'Ah think she looks like Eddie,' they'd say.

'Nah, Ah think she looks like her mammy. Who d'ye want to look like, Marie, yi mammy or yi daddy?'

'Ma daddy,' I'd say.

This drove my mother crazy. I knew it would. That's how I reacted to her neediness.

Billy was more likely to say the right thing. He constantly

sought her approval, silently saying, 'Look at me. Look at me.' But my mother's eyes were focused on me. I was like the sun and she couldn't see Billy for the glare.

All the real dramas of my childhood seemed to happen in Garfield Street. Maybe that's because I was older and so the memories are stronger.

A lot them were fuelled by alcohol and resentment. My father began drinking before the bars opened – either swigging from a half bottle of whisky or slipping into his favourite bar. He was so adept at his job that he could slice his quota of animals in a fraction of the time it took other offal dressers. This gave him ample opportunity to drink and conduct business.

Mac's Bar on the Gallowgate was my father's 'office'. This was where he negotiated deals, tallied money and did his accounts. The landlord, James Parkes, was a great mate, who would pass on messages and let Dad leave envelopes of cash and bundles of meat behind the bar.

Billy reckons 'oor Daddy' made five or ten times more money stealing from his employer than he did from his weekly wage. He was supplying contraband meat to two butchers – one in Melbourne Street and the other on the Gallowgate. My mother even accused him of having an affair with a woman in one of the shops because Dad spent so much time there. Maybe he was.

To oil the wheels of free enterprise, various inspectors and foremen at the Corporation had to be 'looked after'. When Billy was old enough he was sent on errands, doing a circuit of certain pubs to pick up and drop off envelopes. He visited Dad's boss, Big Arthur, at 8.00 p.m. every Friday, handing him his 'share' and receiving five bob as a reward.

Big Arthur was a wonderful bloke and Eddie loved him. So did my mother. I suspect she appreciated the fact that he allowed her to live in the lifestyle to which she had become accustomed.

Despite having all this extra cash, my parents had to be careful about their spending habits. Dad couldn't go buying a house or a fancy car – people would suspect. Instead he bought things which weren't so openly extravagant, like a television, new clothes and records. On weekends he'd take my mother to the theatre, boxing bouts and dinner dances. Invariably she wore a new dress or shoes.

In all the years he worked for the Corporation, my father was only caught the once. He was fired, but Big Arthur managed to get him his job back. They never managed to catch him again. He was too canny.

At one point a security guard working on the main gate in Melbourne Street made it his mission to catch Eddie Lawrie in the act. He organised his rosters so they both worked the same shifts. He was there when Dad arrived every morning and he stayed until Dad left. And each time he saw him he said, 'Hey, Lawrie, yah cunt. Ah know you're at it. Ah'm gonna get yi!'

Initially, Dad found ways of getting around the 'blockade'. He even organised to hurl carcasses over the wall to people waiting on the other side. Wise to this, the security guard organised to patrol the fences.

After a month of this, Dad's clients began to grow agitated. They even threatened to look elsewhere for their supplies. These were not men to be trifled with.

The Melbourne Street entrance had great iron gates through which trucks would rumble in and out. The guards were stationed in the gatehouse, which had large glass windows. They could see everyone coming and going.

Unwilling to admit defeat, my daddy arranged for two of the blood boys (apprentices who emptied and washed the trolleys) to fill a couple of trolleys with boiling water. They pushed them, steaming, towards the front gate, while Dad followed behind pushing another cart loaded with meat.

The guards watched the boys approaching, scratching their heads. They couldn't see my father. As the boys reached the gate-house they suddenly up-ended the trolleys, pouring boiling water against the wall. Steam billowed up and instantly the glass windows misted over completely. The trolleys were then propped against the gatehouse doors, stopping them from opening. Eddie went dancing past the gates, pushing his trolley, singing, 'Ah, yi big dopey bastard, yer'll not catch me.'

The guard knew it was Eddie Lawrie, but he couldn't prove it. By the time he got outside, the meat was long gone.

'A man takes his own chances and makes his own choices,' my father would say, when describing his business philosophy. He was definitely not a Socialist. He championed free enterprise and saw himself as a self-made man and entrepreneur . . . a true Conservative.

It drove him mad when he saw people with large numbers of kids living off welfare. Once he started on the subject you couldn't shut him up.

For all his obvious skill and brazen cheek, I find it remarkable to think that my father lacked confidence. He was only really chatty when he was drunk. I don't know why. Perhaps it had something to do with the way he was belittled and humiliated by his own father.

With a few drinks under his belt, my dad became gregarious and charming – telling jokes and flirting. If he could have stopped at one or two drinks, alcohol would have served him well, but he couldn't do that.

One of his favourite jokes was about a bloke running to catch a bus. He had a half bottle of whisky in his back pocket, and as he lunged for the pole, he missed and tumbled backwards. Hearing the sound of breaking glass, he cried, 'Oh, no!' He reached back and felt the wetness of his trousers, praying, 'Please, let it be blood. Please, let it be blood.'

This story could easily have applied to my father, which is probably why it tickled him so much.

The pubs were shut by the time he finished work at 2.00 p.m., but he often managed to get himself locked in. I remember getting home from school and being sent looking for him. I'd knock on the bolted door of the bar and tell him that Mum wanted him home.

Although drunk, he never stumbled or fell. Instead, he walked with single-minded control, as though all his energy was focused on holding himself together. The only way you could tell was by looking at his eyes, which narrowed into slits.

When he came home by himself, Mum would have me looking out the window, watching for him.

'Is he coming? Is he coming?'

'Aye.'

'Quick. Run doon the sterrs and see if his eyes are chinky,' she'd say.

I'd dash down and meet him as he reached the close. 'Hello, Daddy,' I'd say, spinning on my heels. Then I'd sprint up again. 'Aye, Mammy, they're chinky,' I'd tell her.

He'd try his best to appear sober as I cooked the food he had brought home. Having eaten very slowly, he'd wander into the bedroom and fall asleep wearing his vest and blood-speckled trousers.

Mum would look at him in disgust. She hated him like this, but happily took advantage of the situation. She would sneak into the room and steal money from his trousers. I doubt if he had any idea how much he was carrying.

The real fights took place at the weekends, triggered by jealousy or money and fuelled by alcohol. Mum and Dad would often have been out together, but she would come home early. She knew Dad would be drunk when he arrived. She should have left him alone. But instead of waiting until he sobered up or slept it off she would launch into him. Insults rattled off the windows and abuse shook the photographs in their frames.

There were probably deeper issues at work, which I was too young to appreciate, but I couldn't understand why she goaded and provoked him. It was like watching someone pick at an open sore.

Some nights, before Dad arrived home, she would run into our room and push a chest of drawers in front of the door as a barricade. When he arrived she would start goading him through the door. She damned his 'bastard son' and the 'whore' he'd made pregnant.

'Ye'r a fuckin' whoremaster,' she screamed.

'Shut yer mouth, yi witch,' he slurred.

'Don't tell me to fuckin' shut ma mouth! Who's gonna make me? You and whose army?'

'Just be quiet, woman. Let me sleep.'

She always found the most cruel, shaming and hurtful way possible to attack. She accused him of having no self-control. He was like a dog on heat. He didn't deserve to have a family.

Billy and I begged her to stop. We clung to her arms, trying to pull her back as she yelled through the closed door. In tears Billy reached up and tried to cover her mouth with his hands. 'Please, Mammy, don't say any more. Just be quiet.'

But she couldn't help herself. All the bile and vitriol she had gathered over a lifetime of disappointment came pouring out. From the far side of the door my dad would roar in frustration, wanting to silence her. He just wanted to sleep.

When he finally snapped he forced open the door, sending the chest of drawers crashing to the floor. Billy and I huddled in our beds.

They hit each other, but my father was able to hit harder. He was drunk. He didn't know his own strength.

'Wait till my son grows up,' Mum screamed. 'He'll murder you for doing what you're doing to me.'

'You fucking leave Billy out of this.'

Even when cut and bleeding, my mother kept goading him. I don't know what she wanted to prove. Maybe she was looking for attention. Or maybe she wanted to be punished. Some people would rather be beaten and abused than ignored, particularly when they are lonely and hurting.

There were nights when the fights would wake me, but I was always ready to be woken. I slept with my muscles taut and my teeth clenched. My heart would fly into my mouth. Blinking into the darkness, I'd look across towards Billy. I didn't want him to cry. We'd huddle together, flinching as the fists landed. Neither of us wanted to believe our parents could hate each other so much.

Sometimes when it was over, Mum would fall asleep next to me. By the time she woke, Dad would have left for work and the house would be quiet. A fire burned in the grate. She'd examine her face in the mirror, gently touching the bruises and the black eyes.

Mornings were a time of barefaced lies and outrageous excuses. 'Silly me, Ah stepped on a brush,' she'd tell the neighbours.

This was totally unnecessary, of course. Tenement walls were thin and gossip travelled quicker than a contagious disease. I used to see the looks people gave us. My cheeks burned with shame, but I didn't look away. I looked them straight in the eye. That's what you do in Glasgow: you don't show any weakness.

My embarrassment was nothing compared to my father's sense of guilt. Mum knew this and played the martyr, making him feel even worse.

He tried to apologise and make amends, but she wouldn't let him forget. My mother had a lot of venom in her, eating away from the inside.

I don't know if they loved each other. Once, perhaps. I think Dad was always crazy about her, but she drove him to despair.

We weren't the only family with these problems. A lot of men drank too much and fought with their wives. Poverty, unemployment and broken dreams needed a safety valve. By morning when the hangovers had gone, life returned to normal. For all their faults, these were good people.

# 2

# 'She's a Rare Wee Chanter'

The radiogram took pride of place in our front room. It was huge, with wood veneer panels and cloth-covered speakers. The hinged top could be propped open and records could be stored in a well in the centre.

The 78s were blacker than coal. They were carefully lifted out of their sleeves and Dad would balance them on his forefinger as he gently rubbed a cloth around the grooves. He puffed out his cheeks and blew away any specks of dust. It was like watching a magic trick.

Some kids like hearing the same story read to them over and over again. I was the same way with songs. When I could barely walk, I would sit with my ear pressed against a speaker, feeling it vibrate. 'Play it again,' I'd say. 'Play it again.'

By the third time I knew the song. I could mimic perfectly the inflections and emotion, despite having no idea what the words meant.

My Da McDonald (my grandfather) would cry when he heard me singing a sad ballad. 'How can a wee lassie sing like that? How can she be so sad?'

Dad would buy all the latest records. He loved the crooners like Perry Como and Frank Sinatra as well as the likes of Mario Lanza. He had a marvellous voice and I loved hearing him sing. As babies, whenever we were fractious, he would wrap us tightly in a big tartan rug and 'shoogle' us gently up and down as he sang. By pressing an ear to his cheek, the reverberations of his voice would go right through me.

On the first Saturday in June 1953, every lamp-post, doorway and windowsill in Soho Street was decorated with bunting and streamers. Trestle tables were set up in the middle of the road, laden with food and drink. There were similar street parties all over the country to mark the Coronation of Queen Elizabeth.

The celebrations carried on past my bedtime, but I stayed at the window in the twilight, with my chin resting on my hands. People started to sing and dance. My father, who was more than a little drunk, spied me at the window. 'Gi' us a song, Marie, hen,' he called out.

I started singing 'In a Golden Coach', a song that had been written for the Coronation. It had been a No. 1 hit for the Billy Cotton Band.

> *In a Golden Coach*
> *There's a heart of gold*
> *That belongs to you and me . . .*

People stopped and looked up. 'You coulda heard a pin drop,' my dad would say later. 'Ah don't think any of them had heard such a rerr wee chanter.'

That was my first public appearance, although Mum would always tell people I could sing before I could walk. I had music all around me and it seeped into my soul. Whenever we had people over, long after I should have been in bed, I would open the door just a crack and peer out. If I waited long enough I knew somebody would notice me.

'What are ye doing up, Marie?' they'd say. 'Are ye going to sing us a song?'

Standing in my nightdress in the centre of the room, I'd put on impromptu concerts and wouldn't stop until Mum and Dad pushed me through the door and into bed.

In Glasgow everybody seemed to sing, and many of them better than me. When I say that, I have two particular people in mind. Rita Veitch and her brother Chic lived over the road from us in Soho Street. I don't know what happened to Mr Veitch, but they had an uncle, wee Johnny, who worked at the meat market with Dad. They were friends for decades.

Rita was a real rough diamond, but my mother loved her. She was about six years older than me and almost a teenager, which meant that she and Mum could talk about clothes and hairstyles. I think Mum enjoyed the company.

I realise now that Rita and Chic were not as well off as we were. They lived on the ground floor in a place that was even smaller than ours. And they didn't have the money for the nice clothes or special treats that we sometimes enjoyed.

Rita was the most fantastic singer. She had a big, big voice, almost like a man's, even at the age of eleven. She could sing anything, straight from the heart.

I often wondered why Rita didn't make a career out of singing. She certainly had the ability. I realise now that talent is only one small part of the formula. Rita was a big girl, with a lazy eye, and often wore a plaster eye patch. By comparison, I was small and neat, with big eyes. People used to say I was cute and confident.

Whenever it was too wet or cold to play outside, we kids would organise 'sterr parties' (stair parties). We'd get dressed up and borrow some make-up. And our mums would give us treats for the party, like a packet of biscuits or a bag of sweets to be divided up between us.

The stairwell was like a huge echo chamber, with the most wonderful acoustics. We'd sing songs that floated up the stairs into every 'hoose', where mothers could listen and be reassured their children were safe and happy.

Rita and I did most of the singing, but Chic also had a wonderful voice. He used to love dressing up in his mother's clothes and would insist on playing the 'Mammy' when we ate our party food.

Songs were just as important to the grown-ups. Everyone had a favourite song or routine that was dusted off and performed at parties. People didn't need a piano or a guitar accompaniment: voices were their instruments.

I loved it when my family sang together. Bitterness and rancour would be forgotten. Laughter filled the air. The feigned reluctance gave way to wonderful songs that had people tapping their feet and calling for encores.

Mum used to think she had the best voice, but we'd tease her, 'Nah, you're rubbish, Mammy. Ma daddy's the best.'

We often sang as a family, doing comic songs with all the actions and facial expressions. Things like:

> *I went to school with Maggie . . . Maggie Murphy.*
> *And Maggie Murphy went to school with me . . .*
> *Oh I tried to get the best of Maggie Murphy,*
> *But Maggie Murphy got the best of me.*

This would be the start of a medley of songs, which would have everyone laughing or singing along.

Billy was always a bit shy about performing. 'I wanna sing, I wanna sing,' he'd say. 'But yi have tae shut yer eyes. You cannae look at me.' He would do his song either hiding behind a curtain or with the entire audience turned away from him, laughing hysterically.

During the summer holidays we often rented a small two-bedroom apartment in Rothesay Bay on the Isle of Bute. It was about an hour by train from Glasgow and then another hour on a ferry across the Firth of Clyde.

Dad had to work during the week and would join us on weekends. He also took a holiday during the first two weeks of July when most of the factories and shops in Glasgow shut down during the Glasgow Fair. Thousands of workers would migrate from the city, heading for the seaside. Many had put money in a fund each week – just as they did for Christmas – to pay for their annual trip.

Sometimes we took Rita and Chic with us because their mother couldn't afford a holiday. I think Mum appreciated having Rita to keep her company while Dad was away.

I have a photograph taken on the Rothesay seafront: Mum is carrying Billy in her arms and holding my hand. I must be about three years old.

Mum loved Shirley Temple, and because of my father's curly hair I think she imagined I'd be a little Shirley Temple look-alike. Instead I had perfectly straight hair. I didn't sound like Shirley Temple either. Dad said I had a voice like a coalman – one of those men with blackened hands and face, who drove a horse and cart through the streets, singing out, 'Coooooooaaaal!'

Rothesay had a Punch & Judy man who put on shows from a small wooden booth near the pier. After each show he'd ask the children if anyone wanted to come up and give everyone a song. Mum nudged me forward. I looked around and edged towards the front. I could hear kids giggling.

I sang 'Lavender Blue':

*Lavender's blue, dilly dilly*

*Lavender's green,*
*When I am queen, dilly dilly*
*You'll be my king . . .*

I didn't notice the reaction I created; I simply loved to sing. But the Punch & Judy man recognised that people were fascinated. He invited me to come back the next day, and the day after.

One day Mum decided to take us on a little rowing boat out into the bay. Chic and Rita came too. Billy was just a baby. None of us knew how to row but we had great fun splashing and flailing with the oars.

I finally looked up and said, 'Will yi look at that then.' I pointed to the shore. Rothesay looked like a smudge on the horizon.

Mum tried to look unconcerned, but I knew she was worried. None of us had life jackets and nobody knew how long we'd been gone.

'Let's go back now,' she said nervously. We turned the rowboat and tried to row. Unfortunately, the current and tide kept pushing us further and further from shore. We were hopeless at rowing and couldn't make any headway.

It was late afternoon and growing cooler. We were hungry and tired. Nobody knew where we were. I kept asking when we were going back. Mum told me to be quiet. Billy started crying and that set me off.

Suddenly, this huge American warship appeared out of nowhere, filling the horizon. There were American naval bases in the Firth and I had often seen frigates and destroyers in the distance. Now we could see American sailors on the deck.

Mum and Rita started waving like crazy, wildly shaking their arms and yelling for help. The sailors began waving back and whistling, totally oblivious to our plight.

'We're not waving, we're drowning,' screamed Mum, growing hysterical.

The warship was moving away and would soon be out of sight. Something had to be done. Rita leapt to her feet, rocking unsteadily. Mum grabbed her around the waist. Rita put two fingers in her mouth and let loose a whistle that almost shattered my eardrums. It was so piercing that every head on the warship snapped around. The ship changed course and a tender boat was lowered into the water. Within a few minutes it was alongside us. We were towed back to Rothesay Bay, cold, hungry and exhausted. Rita's whistle had saved us.

The following year Dad took us to Blackpool for our summer odyssey. All my relatives came, including my grandparents. It was a horribly long bus ride. The men got drunk and sang and the bus pulled into pubs along the way so they could stock up on supplies.

Talent competitions were part of the fabric of a summer holiday. The one on Blackpool pier was huge. More than 2,000 people would sit in the sun watching contestants tell jokes, sing songs or play instruments. There would be a heat every day and then on Friday a final featuring all of the winners.

As well as the adult competition, the organisers had a similar event for children. Again my mother took me up, licking her handkerchief and wiping the ice cream stains from around my mouth.

The next youngest contestant was more than twice my age. We all stood in a line and were handed numbers. I was given '13', but I couldn't read numbers past ten. I hadn't started school.

When my number was called, I didn't step forward. I didn't realise. The girl next to me poked me in the ribs. The audience laughed and I was embarrassed. I also thought, 'Bloody cheek. What are they laughing at?'

The master of ceremonies wore a loud checked jacket and had slicked-down hair. He kept pulling faces and telling jokes. I walked to the front of the stage in my sticky-out frock. He made a big fuss of lowering the microphone. It was still too high for me, so he arranged to get me a chair to stand on.

He kept talking to me in a singsong voice, treating me like I was lost.

'Well now, little girl, and what's your name?'

'Marie,' I said, trying to sound grown-up.

'Marie what?'

'Marie Lawrie.'

My accent was unmistakable. 'Do you come from Scotland, Marie?' he asked.

'No. Ah come from Glasgow.'

The crowd roared with laughter. I remember frowning. Why are they laughing at me?

'Well, what are you going to sing for us, today?' he asked, pinching my cheeks.

I gave him a look, which told him, 'Just leave it!' I think he got the message. He took a step back and pulled a face. The crowd laughed.

I think they all expected me to sing 'Baa Baa Black Sheep,' but instead I launched into 'The Wheel of Fortune' by Kay Starr. I did the most exact imitation possible, grinding my hips and growling out the words. 'The whee-ull of for-chun . . . goh-ohs spinn-ing a-ah-rownd . . .' The crowd went crazy.

I won the contest and was given prize money of two pounds ten shillings. I gave the money to Mum. What use did I have for it?

*

Over the next few years I sang in a lot of competitions. I don't remember any of the other competitors, except for one girl who was about six years older than me, who had the most beautiful, soulful voice. I always thought she was a better singer, but I had youth on my side.

Of course, I couldn't rely on such things for ever. There is an annual tradition in Scotland for schoolchildren to enter Burns competitions. These start with every class being given a poem to recite. The best students from each school go on to a bigger competition, covering the whole district. Those good enough are then invited to a final covering the entire west of Scotland.

In the 1950s these recitals were big public events run by prestigious Burns clubs. They coincided with annual dinners, and the cream of Glasgow society was always invited.

I won my first competition at the age of five. I stood on the stage of the Bridgeton Town Hall, dressed in my school uniform, with my hair in ribbons. In a big, booming voice I recited a poem that I had spent hours practising in front of the mirror.

Having been successful, I entered every year and continued to do well. When Billy was old enough I encouraged him to do the same, even though he was shy. We rehearsed together and I had him copy me action for action – every nuance, scowl and facial expression.

We both made it all the way through to the final that year, reciting a poem called 'Willie Wassel'. It was about a weaver who was married to the ugliest woman in the district.

Billy looked amazing in his kilt, white shirt, tartan bow tie and black patent leather shoes with large buckles. I slicked down his hair with milk and gave him a Marcel wave so that he looked like a proper little gentleman. Although nervous, he performed brilliantly.

The master of ceremonies called us all on stage and the audience gave us a big round of applause. I was quietly confident, having been here before. You can guess what happened next. Billy was named the winner and I tried not to look shocked.

According to Mum and Dad, our performances had been identical, but I guess Billy was three years younger. I no longer had youth on *my* side.

*

When I was about eight years old, Alec Crichton, a friend of my parents, took me to a record store in Glasgow which had a recording booth. Alec had been a merchant seaman and I thought he was handsome and charming.

The booth was very small, with a chair and a microphone.

'What am Ah supposed to do?'

'Just sing,' he said.

'And this is gonna make me a record?'

'That's right.'

I didn't have any musical accompaniment. I sang 'Garden of Eden' and 'All in the Game'. Afterwards Alec gave me the record as a keepsake. It had a plain white sleeve.

'When ye grow up nobody is gonna believe a wee lassie could sing like you do. Now you've got the proof.'

Soon after my next birthday, my mother's cousin, Wullie Wilson, came to her with a business proposition. A local band leader, Billy McPhee, was looking for a singer for his Sunday concerts.

The thirty-piece Caledonian Accordion Band were Orange order favourites and played the sort of rousing, patriotic fare that had people stomping their feet and marching up and down the aisles.

'I cannae see why they need a singer,' I said, as Wullie tugged at my hand, walking me to the bus stop. I was wearing a Stuart kilt and a fuzzy-wuzzy jumper, with a white ribbon in my hair.

'Ye cannae expect the band to play non-stop,' he said. 'They want someone to sing when they have a wee break.'

The truth was that Billy McPhee had a younger brother who was a drummer. Ian had been pestering Billy for months about wanting to play pop or rock 'n' roll songs. All he needed was a singer: 'a rare chanter to keep the crowd happy'.

The audition was at the Bridgeton Town Hall – the venue in which the Burns poetry recital had been held. The band were all assembled, sitting on chairs with accordions between their knees.

Billy McPhee wore a colourful waistcoat and had a bow-legged walk. He looked at me dubiously. I could see him thinking, This wee lassie is barely out of nappies.

Uncle Wullie nudged me forwards. 'Sing for the man.'

'What d'ye want me to sing?'

'Just sing anything.'

'What key do yi sing in?' asked Billy.

I looked at him as though he was daft. Why did I need a key to sing? Keys were for opening doors. 'Ah don't need music anyway. Ah can sing without it.'

I launched into 'The Great Pretender', which had been a big hit for The Platters. Billy waved his arms, signalling for the band to catch up with me.

Afterwards, he didn't say very much. He and Wullie were deep in discussion, while I waited on the front steps, scuffing the toes of my best sandals. Eventually they came out and Billy patted me on the head.

'I want yi to learn a couple of songs by next weekend,' he said. 'Let me know what they are. Ah'd like to gi' the band some advance warnin'.'

The following Sunday I made my professional debut. At 6.30 p.m. the hall was packed with 1,000 people. Most of them were Orange lodge members and their families.

The Caledonian Accordion Band played for an hour before taking a break. Billy McPhee bounced on stage to introduce me. He was the ultimate showman, chatting to people in the audience and cracking jokes.

'Aye, it's a fine thing to see so many smilin' faces,' he said. 'Ah can see Mrs Jamieson is here tonight but Ah cannae see your husband. Oh, there he is – hiding behind her skirts. Willie McAlister, is that yi down the back? Pubs aren't open, Willie, there's no point slipping out. And is that another wee'un, Mrs Doherty? How many is that then? Yi'll hiv a football team soon . . .'

Having got everybody into a good mood, he made my introduction. 'Well, we've got a rare treat for ye tonight, ladies and gentlemen. Someone very special t' sing for you. She's one of oor own – a wee lassie with a big voice. Put yer hands together and give her a big welcome – MARIE LAWRIE!'

Billy picked up his accordion and Ian gave me a drum roll. I sang 'A Tear Fell' – a big hit for Teresa Brewer – and 'Only You' by The Platters. Once I started, all my anxiety disappeared. Singing could do that for me – transport me to another place.

When I finished, the crowd yelled for an encore. I hadn't planned another song. Billy nodded and I sang 'Roll a Silver Dollar'. I left them wanting more, which Billy said I should always do.

In the second half of the show the accordion band cranked up the tempo. Being a Sunday it was illegal to play sectarian songs, or to wear blatant sectarian clothes like bowler hats and orange sashes. These laws were designed to stop any religious or racial trouble on the Sabbath. Billy got around this by ending the show with a medley of American songs that just happened to have the same rousing tunes as the Orange order favourites 'The Sash My Father Wore' and 'The Old Orange Flute'.

People were dancing in the aisles, clapping hands and stamping their feet. They danced out into the night, already planning to come back next week. The concerts were a sell-out, with Billy charging five bob at the door. He probably made a fortune.

He gave me thirty bob a week and I used the money to buy a new frock. I had my own dressmaker – a woman who made clothes for the local dancing school and amateur theatrical productions. I also bought records so I could learn whatever songs were in the charts – mainly things by Connie Francis, Neil Sedaka and Brenda Lee.

I didn't set out to imitate – I just sang the way I heard it on the record. I had never been trained to sing, or taught how to read music. When I tried to learn the piano, my teacher slapped me for playing by ear. I didn't go back again.

Mum was pregnant again and her hormones were all over the place. She and Dad were still fighting. One night she threatened to give herself a miscarriage by jumping off the settee.

Mercifully, she did nothing of the sort and Edwina was born at Duke Street Hospital in September 1959. She looked a lot like Billy, with blonde, curly hair. Even as a baby she had a tremendous light in her eyes – a real energy that signalled what sort of personality she would have.

I was virtually running the house by then. Mum stayed in bed with Edwina, while I got Billy ready for school. I think she would happily have sent him off to school with his shirt or jumper turned inside out, to hide the dirt or conceal the fact that it hadn't been ironed. I hated that. I wouldn't let him leave unless he looked his best.

I don't know if Mum hated housework, but I do think she was depressed. Everything in her life seemed to disappoint her, except her children.

Every Friday at lunchtime Dad would give her the house-keeping money for the week. After school she would send either Billy or myself to 'get the rations', which she called food shopping. On Saturday morning she went to have her hair done and then dropped into Marks & Spencer to buy herself a little treat. By the time she arrived back, the 'hoose' would be spotless. I would give Billy a bedroom to do, but was never satisfied so I always cleaned it again. Everything had to be perfect.

Mum would bring home sweeties for us. I would dole them out, using the old trick of, 'One for you, Billy, and one for me. Another one for you, which is two – so I better take two for me . . .' It took him years to work out why I always had twice as many as he did.

'You've been here before,' Mum would say, which meant I had an old soul. Another favourite was, 'I don't know who's the mother in this house, you or me.'

When Mum and Dad went out on a Saturday night I would backcomb Mum's hair and put hairspray on it. Then I would check her outfit and help her with her make-up. We were like best friends. She would tell me things that mothers don't usually talk about with their children – treating me like a confidante. When she bad-mouthed my father I tried to defend him, or at least keep the peace.

I had already learned how to avoid him when he was drunk. I also knew how to manipulate him when I wanted something. That's what I begged Mum to do – stay out of his way and let him sleep it off. He wasn't a violent man by nature.

He only once threatened to raise a fist to me. 'Ah'm no' yer wife,' I snapped at him, giving him the eye. 'You try that wi' me and Ah'll send ye straight to jail.' He stopped in his tracks.

If anything, I was far more likely to fight with Mum than with my father. The two of us were a volatile mixture and neither would back down in an argument. Mum could never make me cry, no matter how hard she tried. This riled her even more. She would drag me around by the hair, banging my head against the wall, but I refused to give in to her. Billy would be chasing after us, saying, 'Don't bother with her, Mum. I love you more. I love you more.' She didn't hear him.

When she finally gave up, I'd say, 'Do you feel better now?' It was the sort of thing I'd hear her say to Dad after he hit her. Like mother, like daughter.

# 3

# *Kiss, Catch or Torture*

My first crush was on a boy who lived near my Auntie Nellie. His name was Scot and I used to sneak glances at him in the playground. Later I fell for Bobby Carroll, who went to Campbellfield Street School at the same time I was there.

He was smaller than me, but very cute, with blond hair and grazed knees. Bobby's brothers were equally good-looking and I fancied each of them at some point – starting with the youngest.

When I moved to Thompson Street School, a boy called Michael Heron took a shine to me. He was completely different to Bobby. To begin with he was tough, rough and very scary. He used to run after me, punching my arms and pulling my hair. Any more Neanderthal and he would have banged me over the head with a club and dragged me off to his cave.

One day he pushed me too far. 'Do that again and Ah'll wallop ye,' I said.

He laughed.

'You think Ah'm jokin', don't ye?' I hit him on the side of the head. He came back at me, but I kept flailing my arms. I was so angry that I totally lost control. It was the most terrifying experience.

Word soon got around that Marie Lawrie wasn't to be messed with. When Billy started school, people would say, 'Don't hit him, that's Marie Lawrie's wee brother.'

Romances were very odd in those days. If a boy chased you, he liked you, but nothing was ever said. Nobody asked you to 'go steady' or swapped keepsakes or made pacts. Boyfriends and girl-friends didn't even hang out together. Everything happened within groups.

My first serious infatuation was with Bobby Ure (a cousin of Midge Ure of Ultravox fame), who was in my class at Thompson Street School. Bobby used a proper handkerchief instead of having a snail-trail of snot up his sleeve like most of the other boys. Things like that impress a girl. He was also the best fighter in the school and captain of the school football team. Being 'liked' by him was a big status symbol.

During games he would always try to catch me, rather than any other girl. Although he would then pull my jumper or my hair, it wasn't designed to hurt. It was more a romantic form of rough play.

As we all grew older, the games began to change. At parties we played 'Spin the Bottle' and 'Kiss, Catch or Torture'. The torture normally took the form of a Chinese burn or a tug of the hair.

Snogging was called 'winching' and a pretty lassie was a 'stoter'. If a boy was 'winching a wee stoter', he was in luck.

Once a week I would take a sheet off the bed and put all the other soiled linen and dirty clothes inside. I'd tie up the corners to make a big bag and put this into an old pram. This was wheeled down to the 'steamy' – a big industrial wash-house where people from the tenements did their laundry.

Bobby Ure lived just near the steamy. I was always mortified that he might see me pushing the pram like some old washer-woman. I used to put my head down and push as fast as I could, hoping I didn't knock anybody over.

The steamy was the sort of place that gave small children nightmares. It looked like one of the underground scenes from the film *Metropolis*. Steam billowed from large cauldrons and the machines hissed, gurgled and spluttered. Water sluiced down drains on the concrete floors and women screeched over the noise.

Sheets were washed in the cauldrons, but the rest of the clothes were scrubbed on washboards. Women dressed in aprons and boots hovered like witches over the metal tubs, scrubbing their husband's overalls. Cigarettes dangled from their lips and they had rollers in their hair covered by scarves tied at their foreheads. Steam was the enemy. It could turn a hairstyle into a lank, tired mess.

I looked upon the women at the steamy as old crones, who cackled and griped. They were always complaining about their husbands and gossiping behind each other's backs. One of the biggest insults of the day was to say, 'Your ma's knickers are the talk of the steamy.'

Many of the women had no teeth – a legacy of Glaswegians' love of sugar and a legion of local dentists who encouraged people to have all their teeth pulled out rather than take better care of them.

False teeth were uncomfortable and only worn at meal times or for going out. Without them a thirty-year-old woman looked sunken-cheeked and twice her age.

I didn't want to go to school after Edwina was born. Caring for a baby was much more attractive than algebra and logarithms. Very few of my teachers inspired me to learn. Most of them terrified me. They were old-school, fire-and-brimstone types, who walked between the rows of desks with a leather strap in one hand and a book in the other.

Some seemed to hate children. There was no acceptance that each child had different strengths and weaknesses. Instead we were plonked on a conveyor belt and mass-produced like widgets in a factory. Anyone who didn't conform had to be beaten into shape.

Even though I was considered precocious and strong-willed, I couldn't buck a system this entrenched. At the same time, I didn't bow to it. I simply lost interest in learning. I had already worked out what I was going to be. I would become a hairdresser and sing in a band on weekends. I'd get married and have lots of children. We'd live in a house in a nice part of Glasgow, with an inside toilet and its own washing machine, so I wouldn't have to go to the steamy.

By the time I reached the age of twelve, school had become a chore rather than a mark of independence. At best I was an average student, although I didn't try very hard. It wasn't a matter of discipline. I didn't mind following orders or sticking to a regime. It was more a case of my life at home not supporting going to school. I rarely had a full night's sleep. Even when Mum and Dad weren't fighting, I lay awake waiting for them to start.

This sense of fear and relentless tension didn't just belong to me. It was something that Glasgow seemed to instil in people. If somebody brushed against you in the playground you immediately spun around, with fists raised, ready to fight. It was a survival mechanism – an instinctive response to your environment.

My father used to say, 'If anyone starts anythin' wi' ye, make sure ye get in first. Hit them wi' everythin' yer've got and make sure they don't get up. If they do – run like fuck! It means they're tougher than you are.' This advice applied to girls as well as boys.

The streets where we lived were in between the areas controlled by the Tongs and the Monks – two of the city's notorious gangs. I knew the gangs existed but I chose to ignore them. It was more a male thing, although the Shamrocks had a lot of pretty girls in their gang.

Billy became involved when he was about ten, but he never became firmly entrenched. One guy called Whitey, who lived around the corner from us, was with the Tongs and also the Mary Hill Fleet. Billy played football with him and he was at school with me.

Whitey was only small but very tough. He normally carried a weapon, either a knife, an iron bar or an axe.

One Sunday evening Mum and Dad wanted ice cream. They sent Billy out to the shops, but on his way back he was beaten up by two guys from one of the gangs. They slapped him about and warned him he could expect worse.

Billy was in his smart suit with his wee tie. He came back with blood on his face and with his clothes creased and dishevelled. I saw him before Mum and Dad did.

'What's happened to ye?'

He wouldn't tell me.

'C'mon, Billy, tell me who did this t'ye?'

He shook his head. 'Tell me! Was it Whitey? Did he do this? It was him, wasn't it?' I was already halfway down the stairs. Billy was yelling after me, 'No, no, no.' I wouldn't listen. He tried to catch up with me. My blood was up. At that very moment Whitey happened to walk around the corner. I grabbed him by the throat and pushed him up against a wall. 'If you did this Ah'll have you,' I said.

Billy arrived. His face went white. 'It wisnae him, Marie,' he stammered. 'Let 'im go . . . please.'

Whitey had an odd grin on his face. If I had known how tough he was, I might have thought twice about taking him on, but they were *all* tough in those days. I also knew that Whitey had a soft spot for me.

'Here's what Ah want,' I told him. 'You go wi' Billy and find out who did this. Make sure they never touch him again. Is that clear?'

Whitey nodded.

Billy's attackers were two leaders of the Shamrocks, Burnie and Lightbody. Whitey took Billy down to Whitevale Street and told him to wait. A little while later he brought Burnie and Lightbody along.

'Ah'll hold 'em doon, while you kick fuck oot a them.'

'Ah cannae do that,' said Billy. 'They'll kill me.'

'Don't you worry about them,' said Whitey. 'They won't be touching anybody.'

On the streets of Glasgow, this is how problems were sorted out. I didn't look at Whitey and see a tough, axe-wielding psychopath. He was just somebody I grew up with. He was my pal. I really liked him.

There were always feuds and vendettas being played out around me. When we lived in Soho Street a family from a neighbouring tenement took against my father and mother. There were four brothers in the family and one of them had a big wife with dyed black hair.

She seemed to hate the fact that my mother always had new clothes and my dad wore nice shirts and suits. As a couple, they were too young, had too much style and spent too much money.

Coming home from work one day, as Dad turned up the close he was attacked by two men. One of them sliced open his face with a razor. Although drunk, Dad managed to stumble up the stairs and get away from them.

He recognised one of his attackers as a hired thug who came from a different part of Glasgow. He also realised he had seen him earlier in the day, obviously following him.

Dad 'marked his card' and bided his time for retribution. He waited months and then picked his moment. He and wee Johnny Veitch planned an ambush, staking out a 'hoose' while their 'mark' was at a football game. To fortify themselves, they drank two half bottles of whisky.

'Get doon! Get doon! We don't want him seeing us,' slurred Dad, when he spied him coming.

'OK, OK,' whispered Johnny.

They were hiding in the close. As the guy walked around the corner Dad jumped him from behind, wrestling him to the ground and holding him down.

'Hit 'im, Johnny! Hit 'im!'

Johnny was dancing from foot to foot, holding a broken bottle. 'Where? Where?'

'Just fuckin hit 'im, ye cunt! Come on.'

Johnny kept hesitating. The guy was screaming and cursing. Dad was struggling to hold him down. 'For Christ's sake, just hit the fucker!'

Johnny finally went whack. He missed the target and cut my dad from one side of his hand to the other. It left a huge scar which he carried for the rest of his life – along with all the others he earned at work when the knife slipped.

Still holding the guy down, Dad demanded to know who had hired him. It was the neighbouring family.

'How much were ye paid?'

'Thirty bob and a bottle of wine.'

'Yer fucking jokin'?'

'Nah.'

Dad missed two weeks' work while the stitches healed. I don't know how he took his revenge on the family, but he must have done something. My dad was no fool. In Glasgow you didn't turn the other cheek, unless you wanted that one sliced open as well.

I don't know what happened to a lot of these people. Many gang members and thugs finished up in jail, convicted of serious crimes. They were living proof of what can happen if you live in an environment full of unresolved anger, bitterness and tension. Unfortunately, the end result is often violence.

I had an escape route. I couldn't see it yet, but my voice was going to save my life.

*

Having become popular at the Sunday evening concerts, Billy McPhee put my name on the posters. He also gave me longer on stage, which meant learning more songs. For my encore I always sang 'Calvary', an old hymn which the crowd loved.

Occasionally we performed out of town, as far away as Fife, which meant not getting home until late. Mum didn't seem to mind. I think she envied me.

She was always searching for something that would take her out of the humdrum of her life, even just for a few hours. That's why she loved the cinema. She would never go and see an English film. They were too silly and slapstick, she said. American movies were polished and sophisticated. It was like a promised land . . . a place she dreamed about.

We always went to the cinema before 6.00 p.m. because the fruit shops were still open. She would rush to the greengrocer on the corner and buy exactly six oranges. Then she would sit in the cinema, peeling the oranges with her fingers and popping segments into her mouth.

She also preferred American music and this obviously influenced me. I grew up listening to the crooners and great soul singers. I studied their photographs on record sleeves and thought how incredibly elegant and cool they looked.

One Sunday night after the concert a man approached my mother. He was the manager of a young band in which his son, Billy Adamson, was the drummer.

'You have a very talented daughter, Mrs Lawrie.'

'Aye, she's great.'

'Ah was just wondering if she had ever considered singing wi' a proper band, doing pop songs?'

'What would she want t'dae that for?'

My ears had pricked up. 'Listen to what the man has to say, Mammy,' I said, tugging at her sleeve.

She folded her arms and let him say his piece. The band was called The Bellrocks and was made up of four young guys, aged seventeen and eighteen, who had been together for a few months.

Mr Adamson had heard about me and had come to see the concert. He commented on what a well-presented young girl I was, who clearly came from a good family. My mother preened herself.

A few days later he came around to the house and met my dad. They seemed to get on well as he answered their questions.

'Why don't you let Marie meet the boys,' he said. 'She can listen to them play and then decide.'

Mum and Dad agreed and I went along to a small youth hall in Cranhill where The Bellrocks were rehearsing.

It wasn't an audition. They wanted *me*, which was very flattering. One of the first songs they played was 'Stupid Cupid', which had been a big hit for Connie Francis in 1958. After a few bars I joined in.

> *Stupid Cupid, you're a real mean guy*
> *I'd like to clip your wings so you can't fly*
> *I'm in love and it's a crying shame*
> *And I know that you're the one to blame*
> *Hey hey set me free*
> *Stupid Cupid stop picking on me.*

It was great. They were doing modern songs and were young and keen. They had plans to play the hippest clubs in Glasgow.

The following Sunday I broke the news to Billy McPhee that I was leaving. He offered me more money to stay but my mind was made up. I had spent three years with the accordion band and it was time to move on.

Within a month The Bellrocks were doing regular Saturday-night gigs at places like Stirling Public Halls and the Barrowland Ballroom on the Gallowgate, one of Glasgow's most famous dancehalls.

Located at the top of a long set of stairs, it had a bouncer on the door who kept watch for drunks and anyone carrying a weapon. It didn't serve alcohol, but most of the guys would down a few pints of scrumpy across the road and get their girlfriends to hide half bottles of whisky in their handbags.

The kids were always immaculately dressed. The girls wore cardigans, sweaters or blouses, over straight, tight-fitting dresses or skirts, with seamed stockings and high-heel shoes. The bigger the hairdo the better, lacquered to the consistency of concrete.

The guys, meanwhile, sported 'moonie' cuts, a shaggy look with the fringe swept across the forehead. They wore made-to-measure suits and shirts with button-down collars. The jackets were two- and three-button mohair, known as bum-freezers because they were cut to just above the cheeks. They were worn with a thin tie and a matching handkerchief in the breast pocket. Trousers tapered down to a 13- or 14-inch width at the bottom, and shoes were always spotlessly polished, with saddle-stitching around the edges. In Glasgow, even if you couldn't afford to eat, you always wore the right clothes.

The Barrowland had a large dance floor waxed to a brilliant sheen. The stage was at the far end, raised several feet above the floor. The boys would all be against one wall and the girls against the other. It was a vast distance to cross, with all your pals watching, to ask a lassie to dance. Would she turn you down? Would she say yes? The patter would go a bit like this.

'Are ye dancin'?'

'Are ye askin'?'

'Aye, I'm askin'.'

'Aye, well, I'm dancin'.'

Sometimes The Bellrocks played the US airbases, such as Abbotsinch, about thirty miles from Glasgow. We travelled in a battered van, or sometimes a big, yellow American convertible owned by one of the guys. I had to ask permission from Mum because it meant getting home late.

The Americans used to call me Scotland's Brenda Lee, because I sang a lot of her songs, which suited my voice. Word seemed to spread and more and more people would come to see us. At the same time I was discovering hundreds of wonderful new songs that never made the charts – rhythm and blues numbers and soul classics, mainly American.

I was mad about Ray Charles and bought everything I could find of his. I also loved The Drifters ('Under the Boardwalk'); Sam Cooke ('You Send Me'); and Solomon Burke ('Cry to Me').

Most of the band had proper jobs through the week, working as apprentices or studying. I was still at school, so the money from the gigs was basically pocket money for me. I was the best-dressed girl in the playground – able to buy expensive pixie shoes instead of having to wear big, clumping shoes like the other girls. I also had my dresses made for me and my hair done at the best hairdressers' in Glasgow.

My mother was obsessed with clothes and hairstyles. She also loved markets, second-hand stalls and sales, and always managed to source great fabrics through wholesalers or off the back of a lorry. These were delivered to tailors and dressmakers, with precise instructions about what she wanted. She would send me on errands to drop off parcels of material or pick up the finished outfits.

When I finished primary school the top 25 per cent of kids were sent to Whitehill Secondary School while the rest went to Onslow. I wanted to go to Whitehill because all my friends were going there. I also liked the uniform – dark blue pleated skirt, crisp white blouse and blue blazer.

Although my grades didn't warrant it, my teachers recommended that I should go to Whitehill. Apparently I had done well on the IQ tests and was guilty of not working hard enough.

The expectation that this would be different at a new school was sadly misplaced. I didn't want to spend all my time struggling to keep up with my classmates. I also hadn't banked upon having a headmistress like Mrs Hutchinson, who had serious issues with me.

She was a typically stern, authoritarian educator, who I doubt had ever married or had children. Right from the beginning she marked me out as a rebel. Although I wasn't disrespectful or insolent, I was outspoken and opinionated. I also had what Mum and Dad referred to as 'a look that'll get yi murdered'.

Having become something of a local celebrity, with my name in the newspapers and on posters, I enjoyed quite a bit of status at school. I wore shorter skirts and had bigger hair . . . none of which impressed Mrs Hutchinson.

My hair was mousy and fair, which I thought was quite boring. One fateful day, soon after my thirteenth birthday, I decided to get a rinse. I wanted something to make my tresses look a little red in the right light.

I went through the process and sat beneath the dryer, flicking through magazines. When they finally lifted it clear I gazed at the mirror in shock. I had carrot red hair that looked like a beacon.

It wasn't going to wash out and there was no way of hiding it. As I climbed the stairs at home, I knew I had to face the music.

Mum went mad, of course. 'Oh my God, wait till yer daddy sees ye. He'll go mental. He'll blame me.'

'Well, you let me go,' I said, trying to deflect the responsibility.

'Don't you go blamin' me. Look at the state of yi!'

She wasn't wrong about Dad. He blew his top and then glared at her accusingly. 'She's thirteen years of age, woman. What were ye thinking?'

After a lot of shouting and swearing he calmed down. There was nothing he could do. The red would have to grow out over time . . . (About thirty years, as it turned out.)

On Monday I had to face school. The teachers were shocked. At first I tried to brazen it out, but I couldn't hide my shame. At the full school assembly, Mrs Hutchinson called me out in front of everyone. She made a point of walking round me, staring at my hair.

'Ye think this is going to make the boys like you more?' she sneered.

Everyone laughed. I was mortified.

'Ye think this makes ye look pretty?'

'No, Miss.'

She took a comb out of a jar full of disinfectant and, instead of shaking it dry, she thrust it into my lacquered hair. She did it time and again, destroying my styling. I had tears in my eyes. I had never been so humiliated.

Mum and Dad went up to the school to complain, but it was already over for me. By mutual agreement I transferred to Onslow Drive School, just along the road. Academically it was a step down, but that didn't matter. I didn't want to be at school any more.

Occasionally, The Bellrocks had a guest sax player, who also played for another band, The Gleneagles. They had a regular Sunday-evening gig at a jive club called the Lindella in the centre of town. It was up a narrow set of stairs that opened into a large loft, with a low ceiling and polished wooden floor.

The Lindella was a happening club, where young people came to learn how to jive. On a Sunday night they had 'live' music and the kids showed off their best moves.

I sang with The Gleneagles a few times and it seemed completely natural for me to join up with them. My mother met the band, and also Betty and Alec Houston who owned the Lindella.

At one point Betty's sister had been my mum's best friend, which seemed to satisfy her that I was in safe hands.

Most of the band were in their late teens or early twenties. Jimmy Dewar, who played rhythm guitar, had a brilliant voice and later went on to join Stone the Crows and the Robin Trower Band. Ross Nelson, the lead guitarist, was very tall, with big, dark, soulful eyes. Dave Mullen, the drummer, had a wicked sense of humour, and Tommy Tierney, on bass, had one of those thick Glaswegian accents that is all growl and phlegm.

The Bellrocks had been a part-time band, whereas The Gleneagles were a bit more sophisticated and grown-up. They wore matching tartan jackets that made them look professional and played cutting edge songs that were coming out of Europe and America.

Soon I was singing things like, 'It's Gonna Work Out Fine', an Ike and Tina Turner song; 'Working in a Coal Mine' by Lee Dorsey; and 'Mockingbird' by Charlie and Inez Foxx.

We did a lot of the same venues as The Bellrocks, including the American airbases, but drew a hipper crowd. People would queue to get in to see us. I didn't mind having distinctive hair any more. It was like a trademark.

A young guy called Alec Bell turned up at the Lindella one night and asked if there were any vacancies in the band. I fell for him immediately. He was very handsome and well-dressed, with dark hair and big eyes.

Trying to appear really cool, I convinced the rest of the band to let him audition. I don't know what I would have done if they had said no. We hired him as a singer, mostly out of deference to me, although he did have a very good voice.

Alec became my first official boyfriend. He was three years older and came from a nice middle-class area of Glasgow. It certainly wasn't the sort of house you'd walk into and hear the mother and father fighting and swearing at each other.

Our relationship was very innocent. Alec would take me home

after gigs. We'd catch the tram or bus and be able to 'winch' up the back, as long as there was nobody on board who knew my mother.

I had a strict curfew – I had to be home by 10.30 p.m. This was OK for gigs in Glasgow, but a nightmare if we went out of town. When we played the American airbases, for instance, I might not get home until one in the morning.

Dad would go mad if he discovered I'd missed a curfew. Thankfully, it was mostly noise and hot air rather than violence.

Mum was more indulgent. One night I begged her to let me go to a club in the city with the rest of the band. Alex Harvey, a local singer, had been in Hamburg performing in cellar clubs, just like The Beatles had done. Now he was back and there was a real buzz of anticipation.

It was 1962 and the pop boom had just started. The Beatles had released 'Love Me Do', their first hit. The MerseyBeat sound had been coined and music and fashion would never be the same.

The influence of America was also becoming stronger. An amazing mix of sounds and styles had come together – elements of jazz, hillbilly, rhythm and blues and gospel. These were adapted, bastardised and electrified to create new forms of popular music.

Bill Haley and Jerry Lee Lewis launched rock 'n' roll, but soon we were listening to Buddy Holly, Roy Orbison, Elvis Presley and Bobby Darin.

Like Liverpool, Glasgow was a major port, and this meant it enjoyed a constant influx of foreign ships and sailors. The Americans brought records with them. We were hearing these new songs well before the rest of the country – blues, soul, country and western. We were hungry for it.

In the dark belly of a basement club, I sat waiting for Alex Harvey to emerge. The rest of the boys were drinking cokes mixed with aspirin, but they were very protective of me. Alex

came on stage dressed in skin-tight black leather. He looked emaciated, with black hair and pale skin, just like The Beatles had
looked when they returned from Hamburg.

Then he started to sing. 'Weeeeeeeeeeeeell, you know you make
me wanna shout!'

Oh my God! The place went wild. He sang with a female
range – high and with so much energy. There was a real anger
there, a 'fuck you' sound; the sound of youth. It was amazing!

Who knows what Alex was on? What did it matter? It was an
absolute revelation for me. No other music had ever resonated
with me in quite the same way. I was in awe. I knew I had to do
that song.

I crept home from the club, up the stairs and into bed. I
thought I'd got away with it, but Dad knew. There were lots of
growls from him for the next week or so, but he eventually for-
gave me.

In the meantime, I set about learning 'Shout'. I discovered it
had been a hit for The Isley Brothers in America. I practised it
with the boys and we performed it at the Lindella one Sunday
night. It became a real favourite among the jivers.

One night a young television director called David Bell came
along to the club and saw us play. He was working on a TV show
in Glasgow called *Roundup*, which was a mixture of light entertainment and pop music news.

One of the segments was very much like *Juke Box Jury* – a
successful show on the BBC. A panel reviewed the new pop singles being released that week, trying to spot possible hit records.
*Roundup* used teenagers on the panel and David asked me if I'd
take part.

There were three of us reviewing the records. One of the
teenagers was John Reid, who later went on to become Elton
John's manager and have a long career in the music industry.

David Bell had similar success, becoming Head of Light Entertainment at London Weekend Television and the producer of the Stanley Baxter shows.

The idea of appearing on TV was particularly exciting. Nobody I knew had ever done that before. Television was relatively new and I could still remember our first television set – a 12-inch screen encased in a wooden box in the big room.

The first time we saw commercial television was at my Auntie Annie's in Comelypark Street. Billy and I lay on the floor, with our chins in our hands, learning every jingle.

The fact that I could sing and was a bit of a schoolyard celebrity wasn't always a good thing. One particular gang of girls, whether through jealousy or spite, decided to make my life a misery. They chased me home from school and threatened to beat me up. One day they cornered me in a close and took turns holding me down as each punched me. I was frightened they would mark my face. Maybe I wouldn't be able to sing.

From then on I tried even harder to avoid school. I began pleading with Mum to let me stay home. She forced me out the door each morning, but I stood in the street, calling out to her, begging her not to make me go. 'I'll be good. Please. Don't make me . . . please . . .'

I used to see her watching me from the upstairs window. I'd walk a few paces and turn, pleading with her again. More often than not she'd relent. I was her best friend. She knew I wasn't born for the classroom. She also liked my company.

# 4

# 'Why is Wee Marie Not at School?'

The boys were packing up after a gig at the Lindella while I chatted to some of the regulars. A moon-faced man with glasses hovered nearby, waiting for me. I had noticed him once or twice before in the club and knew he was a friend of Betty and Alec Houston.

'You should have a manager,' he said, making it sound more like a question than a statement.

Richard Stern was a Jewish businessman who lived in Newton Mearns, an affluent area of Glasgow. I'm not exactly sure how he made his money, but he wasn't the sort of person to miss an opportunity.

He arranged to see Mum and Dad and filled their heads with stories of my untold promise and the benefits of good management. I don't think Richard had any particular experience, but he treated the music industry as simply another business.

A contract was drawn up and signed. Richard became my manager, along with Alec Houston. The two of them spent hours discussing my future, although nothing concrete ever emerged.

One night Richard invited a young Londoner along to the

Lindella. Tony Gordon was visiting Glasgow to explore the possibility of opening a new nightclub, based on an idea that had come from France – the discotheque. He eventually opened Le Phonograph in Glasgow and an identical club in Manchester.

Although only in his early twenties, Tony had the confidence and charm of someone much older. He was handsome, beautifully dressed and well spoken. Straightaway I could tell he was a mover and shaker. I could almost see his mind working, looking for angles and working out deals.

He saw something in me that night. He said it was an indefinable quality that set me apart and could make me a star. People had been telling me things like that since I was a little girl, but this time it was different.

The first time Tony met my parents he came running up the stairs at Garfield Street two at a time. He wore a dogtooth black-and-white-checked jacket, a little, black button-down shirt with mother of pearl buttons, grey slacks and Gucci loafers. He was small, dapper and very cool.

Mum and Dad liked him immediately. They too recognised that Tony had far more worldly sophistication than locals like Richard Stern and Alec Houston. He said that I needed a recording contract and began investigating the best way to get one. Knowing the value of publicity, he called various journalists and began singing my praises. One of them was Gordon Reed, the showbiz writer for the *Scottish Daily Express*.

The timing was perfect. The *Express* had been running a campaign to unearth Scottish talent to rival the likes of The Beatles, The Shadows and Gerry and the Pacemakers, who were dominating the pop charts.

Scotland boasted just as much talent, declared the *Express*, as it launched a national competition with regional heats and a final. It then challenged the English record companies to 'come north and *not* sign someone'.

Unfortunately, the record company executives who made the journey were decidedly unimpressed by what they heard. There was nobody they wanted to sign.

It all looked very embarrassing for the *Express*, until Tony Gordon called and told them about an unknown teenager called Marie Lawrie who was singing at the Lindella every Sunday night. Without ever having heard me, Gordon Reed dragged the visiting Columbia/EMI rep down to the club.

I sang that night totally unaware that there was anything at stake. It wasn't until afterwards, when Tony dropped me home, that I realised what had happened.

He sat in the front room, sipping a cup of tea and talking to Mum and Dad. Mum was pregnant again and Dad was on his best behaviour.

'Get to bed, Marie,' Mum said. 'Yi've got school tomorrow.'

I listened at the door, only catching snippets of the conversation. Tony was telling them about EMI. I heard words like 'London' and 'audition'.

'She cannae go on her own. She's only fourteen,' said Mum.

'The boys from the band will go with her.'

'And what about school?' asked Dad.

'It's only for a day or two. Then she'll be home again.'

My heart was in my mouth. I turned away from the door and lay on my bed. Above me on the walls were posters of The Beatles, or more precisely Paul McCartney and John Lennon. I was madly in love with both of them.

I wanted to pinch myself. How could this possibly be true?


I had never been to London. The furthest south I had been was Welwyn Garden City, which was north of the city, to visit relations. England had always seemed like a foreign country. I read about it in magazines and saw it on TV, but it still wasn't Scotland.

We left early on a Sunday morning, piling our bags and instruments in the back of a beaten-up Thames van. Alec Houston came with us, driving his Jaguar. I don't think Alec wanted to let me out of his sight. I rode in the Jaguar while the boys shared the driving of the van. We stopped for lunch at a motorway café. I hadn't slept for days because I was so excited. Exhaustion finally caught up with me and I fell asleep until we reached the outskirts of London.

It was a dark, grey, wet afternoon. The traffic crawled and we edged through North London. Alec took me to Tony Gordon's parents' flat in St John's Wood, where I could get changed, wash my face and put on a little bit of make-up.

Our first appointment was with Ron Richards at Columbia/EMI. We met at a studio in West Hampstead.

'What are you going to sing?' he asked.

We had already planned to do 'Shout' as our first song and then '24 Hours from Tulsa'. I wanted to sing a ballad and not just something fast and loud, to show my versatility.

I had to wrestle with the microphone to get it down to my height. 'OK, when you're ready,' said Ron.

Despite my nerves, I thought it was a pretty good audition. I glanced at the boys and smiled hopefully. Ron Richards pursed his lips and paced the floor. I was trying to read his mind.

'I want you to go and see Peter Sullivan at Decca,' he said.

'Why?'

'Because I don't think you're right for us.'

My heart sank. After all the build-up and the newspaper stories, I had visions of going back to Glasgow empty-handed.

We drove to another studio around the corner and met Peter Sullivan, a slim, reed-like figure, with sharp features and blond hair. He wore a beautifully cut suit and starched white shirt and tie. His long fingers held a cigarette and smoke curled from his lips.

'Just relax,' he said, looking amused when he caught sight of me. I was a bundle of nerves.

Peter sat outside the studio with his feet resting on the console. I launched into 'Shout' and immediately the technicians signalled me to stop. My voice had broken the ribbon on the microphone. They looked at each other as though nobody had ever done that before.

'Maybe you should stand a little further away from the mike,' suggested Peter.

I nodded and took a step back. Then I started again. 'Weeeeeeeeeeell, you know you make me wanna shout . . .'

I sang both songs and then glanced up at Peter, hoping he wouldn't keep us in suspense. The guys fidgeted with guitars and drumsticks. I could feel myself rocking from one foot to the other.

Peter put out his cigarette and swung out of his chair. 'Let me talk to a few people and I'll come back to you,' he said, giving nothing away.

We drove back to Glasgow that evening still unsure if we had a recording contract. I kept thinking how ironic it would be if Decca signed us. They had turned down The Beatles, who had been signed by Columbia/EMI. Maybe the complete opposite was going to happen to me.

The management issue now became more important. Decca made it quite clear that it wasn't happy negotiating with Richard Stern and Alec Houston. I don't know if this was a case of personal chemistry or if they regarded them as not being experienced enough. At the same time I had Gordon Reed and the *Daily Express* trumpeting the fact that they had 'discovered' me.

Poor Mum and Dad were caught in the middle. Contracts were being thrust in front of them and people were giving them conflicting advice. They took a long time to decide what to do.

Tony Gordon had been instrumental in getting me to Decca and had done everything he had always promised. He had no desire to manage me, but he was quite happy to negotiate with Decca on my behalf. He quickly reached an agreement with Richard Stern and Alec Houston which saw them relinquish any control.

Tony looked over the Decca contract, which was fairly standard except for one very important detail. The record company wanted me, but not the rest of the band.

'You've got to be joking,' I said, angrily.

'They want to use session musicians,' explained Tony. 'They say the boys aren't good enough.'

'Forget it! Tell them to get lost!' I was horrified. How could I possibly abandon the band? We had been together for nearly two years. Alec Bell was my boyfriend!

This wasn't just about loyalty. I didn't want to be alone. I was barely fourteen. What were they thinking?

I held my ground. It was all or nothing. Decca blinked first.

I expected my life to change suddenly, but nothing happened. It was months before I went to London to record. In the meantime, The Gleneagles continued doing gigs and the *Scottish Daily Express* kept writing about us.

In all the years I had been singing for people I had never imagined fame or stardom. I didn't dream of hit records, TV appearances or singing at the Carnegie Hall. And even when the ink was drying on my recording contract, a part of me still wouldn't believe it was actually going to happen. To be safe, I always took the attitude of wait and see.

Glasgow isn't the sort of place that lets you get too highfalutin. People are more than ready to knock you down a peg. That's why my feet stayed firmly on the ground.

The only thing that transported me was the music. On stage I felt alive and totally in control. I could escape from the humdrum and mundane. I could forget about my problems at school and my parents' nightly fights. Time stood still. Nobody could touch me. This was my *real* home.

Although Tony had negotiated my recording contract, he still had no desire to manage me. It seems ironic now, considering he went on to successfully manage Boy George, among others.

In 1963 he wanted to concentrate on opening discotheques with his brother-in-law, Gerry Massey. He also believed, given my age, that it was more appropriate for a woman to manage me.

Tony's sister Marian had been a promising opera singer, trained by Dino Borgioli, head of the Cambridge Theatre Opera Company. At the age of seventeen she had been offered a place at the Vienna State Opera Company, but had fallen in love with Gerry Massey and chosen marriage instead.

She had become the perfect trophy wife, with three small children, several staff, a butler and a beautiful house in Holland Park. She spent her days shopping, lunching and having her hair done at Vidal Sassoon.

Despite this enviable lifestyle, Marian was bored. She needed a project and Tony decided that it should be me.

I didn't meet Marian until I came down to London for our first recording session. We drove down in the van again and had to keep swapping seats because it was so cold. Anybody sitting in the front had to shed clothes because the fan heater was blasting out, but none of this heat reached the back, where Alec and I huddled beneath a blanket. Not surprisingly, I came down with a shocking cold.

The Beatles were dominating the charts and I knew that several people had recorded their songs. In the back of my mind I was hoping that Decca might let me do the same.

'We want you to sing "Shout",' Peter Sullivan told me.

'What? That old song!'

Although I loved 'Shout', I had been singing it for nearly two years. I wanted to do something new and fresh.

With a runny nose and a head full of cold, I went into the studio for our first recording session. I looked awful. My hair was in rollers under a fur beret and I wore a baggy cardigan to keep warm.

The whole process was remarkably simple. We did several takes of 'Shout' and I listened to them being played back. Peter wanted to recreate the sort of energy I had when performing live.

As we listened to the recordings a striking woman arrived in the studio. She swanned through the door wearing a three-quarter-length, anthracite-grey Persian lamb coat, with a huge chinchilla collar, a pencil-straight skirt and high-heel Chanel court shoes. She looked every inch a film star and was unquestionably the most glamorous creature I had ever laid eyes on in real life.

Marian took one look at my puffy eyes, runny nose and pale skin. 'What on earth are you doing to this poor girl?' she declared. 'She should be home in bed.'

'I'm OK,' I said, feeling embarrassed.

'Nonsense! You should be resting. We have to look after you.'

After finishing recording she hustled me out of the studio and into the front seat of her car. I had never smelled leather seats. She drove me to John Bell & Croyden, a pharmacist off Wigmore Street, where she bought me cough medicines and decongestants.

Every time Marian opened her mouth she had the clearest enunciation, with perfectly rounded vowels and clipped consonants. This could have made her seem cool and distant, but instead she was incredibly warm and tactile.

She was fascinated by me, asking me questions about my family and how long I'd been singing and what sort of music I liked. It was as though I came from another world. I kept sneaking glances at her perfectly groomed, shiny black hair, large eyes, painted red lips and strong nose. She was like a rare exotic creature, who had grace and style and wit. I wanted to learn from her. Better still, I wanted to *be* her.

Marian flew to Glasgow to meet my family and reassure them I was in good hands. She admitted right from the start that she knew nothing about the music business. She was on a steep learning curve just as I was. We would learn together.

In Glasgow you learn not to trust strangers, but I trusted Marian. We were complete opposites, but the attraction worked both ways. I think she admired my honesty and courage. I was in awe of her sophistication and elegance.

A few weeks later I came back to London to have photographs taken for the record sleeve. I went to Marian's home in Ilchester Place, one of the most desirable addresses in London. A butler answered the door and called me 'Miss', which nobody had ever done before.

Tony and Marian were determined to find me a new name. Marie McDonald McLaughlin Lawrie just didn't do it for them. For days they tossed ideas around, trying to think of something bright and catchy, which captured the spirit of my youth.

Tony was sitting at the piano, while Marian paced up and down. Finally, in exasperation she said, 'Well, all I know is that she's a real lulu of a kid.'

They looked at each other. Both had the same thought. It was short, cute and sounded American.

I wrinkled my nose when they told me. I repeated it several times in my head, as if trying it on for size.

'You could be Lulu and the Luvvers,' said Tony.

'What will the boys say?'

'They'll just have to like it.'

It was a bit daft as names go, but so what? Considering we had The Animals, The Beatles and The Rolling Stones, silly names seemed to be the way to go.

Decca still had to decide on a release date for 'Shout', but struck a problem. By Scottish law I wasn't supposed to leave school until I turned fifteen and had finished my leaving certificate. I couldn't promote the song if I was stuck in a classroom.

Decca decided to wait, and I eventually left school six weeks after my fifteenth birthday, at Christmas 1963. I never did finish my leaving certificate. Six months later a school inspector knocked on Mum and Dad's door.

'We want to know why Marie hasn't been at school,' they said.

Mum laughed. 'Do ye nae read the papers or watch TV?' she asked. 'She's a pop star.'

Marian learned very quickly the importance of marketing and promotion. Her first masterstroke was to team up with Tommy Sanderson, a hustling agent who had an office off Tin Pan Alley. Through Tommy she met Leslie Perrin, the doyen of British press agents.

Leslie was a middle-aged, hard bitten, former Fleet Street hack, who chain-smoked and drank like a fish. He was also a fairy god-father to dozens of bands and recording artists because of his ability to hose down scandal and make problems disappear. People listened when he spoke – particularly newspaper editors.

Putting his mind to my record launch, he blinked through a cloud of cigarette smoke and announced, 'We need a big party. Lots of booze and sandwiches.' Cigarette ash dotted his sleeve. 'These guys have seen it all. It's not easy to impress them. They've got to think *they* discovered her.'

In early April 1964 he arranged to take over an Italian restaurant in Fleet Street and invite dozens of Fleet Street's finest. When I arrived it was already four deep at the bar and the air was thick with smoke. They weren't all showbiz journalists. Leslie had issued an open invitation and the lure of free booze had brought out the news reporters, feature writers and columnists. Some had no idea what the launch was about and didn't care as long as the drinks kept flowing. At the same time they all respected Leslie as being one of their own.

I was introduced to various people, most of whom smiled and nodded, having seen it all before. Then someone said, 'Why don't you sing for us?'

I looked at Marian, who shrugged. A chair was found and I stood in the midst of the throng.

'Weeeeeeeeeeeeell, you know you make me wanna shout!'

With that one line I had them. Leslie had known this all along. By the time I finished I had dozens of journalists asking me questions and jotting down notes. Judith Symonds, a Fleet Street legend, had a drink in one hand, a notebook in the other and a cigarette hanging out of her mouth. She scribbled furiously as I told her about singing before I could walk.

The photographers took me outside and had me leaning on lamp-posts and hanging from the back of a double-decker bus. The most famous picture – which has haunted me for years – is a shot of me cupping my hands and shouting.

'LULU MAKES YOU WANNA SHOUT' said the headlines the next day. I made the news pages of almost every paper – not bad for an unknown.

The single was released on 15 April 1964. One critic described me as a 'teen sensation with a gravelly voice'. Another said I was '62 inches tall, with cedar red hair and her own in-built amplification system'.

People were amazed when they discovered my age. Some thought I sounded black, which I took to be a huge compliment.

Everything now rested on the chart position. The most influential music show on TV was *Ready, Steady, Go!*, shown every Friday at eight minutes past six. Its slogan was 'The Weekend Starts Here'.

Billy and I were always glued to the screen. On Fridays Mum

and Dad usually went to the pictures or to a dance. Billy and I would get to have fish and chips for our tea, despite Dad complaining, 'Ye never know what they're bloody feedin' ye.'

It was always a race to push Mum and Dad out the door and get the fish and chips in before the show started. On this occasion Billy volunteered to get the tea (he liked sneaking chips on his way home), while I warmed up the TV, put the salt and vinegar out and buttered the bread.

He still wasn't back when Keith Fordyce and Cathy McGowan introduced the show. Paul McCartney and John Lennon were special guests. Wow! They were both irresistible.

Cathy McGowan chatted to them about the week's new releases.

'Well, my favourite is a song called "Shout",' said John. 'It's by a girl called Lulu.'

My jaw dropped to my ankles. I ran to the window, thrust it open and leaned out. Billy was hurrying down the street, carrying the fish and chips while stuffing them in his mouth.

He jumped a foot in the air when I started screaming. 'Billy! Billy! They picked me! They picked me!'

He came tearing up the stairs, two at a time. I was kneeling down in front of the TV, unable to get any words out. I had never been so excited in my entire life. They had picked me!

# 5

# 'Don't be Ridiculous! Ah'm Covered in Spots'

'Shout' entered the charts four weeks later. Lulu and the Luvvers were suddenly in big demand. There were radio and TV appearances, magazine interviews, photo shoots and concerts. Occasionally we flew or took trains, but mostly it was hundreds of bum-numbing miles in the back of the Thames van. My first time on a plane was from the wee airport in Glasgow on a flight to London. Nobody in my family had ever left terra firma.

We appeared on TV shows like *Thank Your Lucky Stars*, *Juke Box Jury* and *Ready, Steady, Go!*, as well as performing on local radio and TV shows in England, Ireland and Wales. There were dozens of TV companies in the sixties and we did them all – Granada, Yorkshire, Lothian, Grampian, Ulster, Harlech and Scottish TV. First came the interview and then I'd either sing or mime 'Shout'.

Bigger stars wouldn't bother with many of these stations, but we took the decision not to leave any stone unturned. This was what you had to do if you wanted to reach the widest possible audience. Records had to be promoted. Only Led

Zeppelin managed to get away without doing any, but that was much later on.

As well as having a manager, I also had an agent, Dick Katz, who was responsible for booking our live performances and helping negotiate our appearances on TV and radio.

There had been no advance for the deal with Decca. We had to pay our own way by doing gigs. With a hit record we could now earn £100 a gig, instead of £30. Even when split between the six of us it seemed like a fortune. Soon we were able to upgrade to a new Commer van, with decent heating, as well as new amps, drums, a PA system and our own driver, Chris Cooke.

Marian often came with us – still wearing her cashmere sweaters, stilettos, and with her Vidal Sassoon flick-up hairdo. She would look totally bemused as she listened to six Glaswegians chatting to each other and was unable to comprehend a single word. I think she was quite relieved when we hired Chris. 'At least he speaks English,' she said.

After filming *Ready, Steady, Go!*, the producer, Vicky Wickham, and a whole gang of people invited me to San Lorenzo, a restaurant in Knightsbridge. It was very posh and I tried hard to look as though I belonged.

As we sat down I glanced around the restaurant and saw a familiar face. Bobby Darin! I couldn't believe it. Here was one of my all-time favourite singers and he was less than twenty feet away. American stars were people you read about, but I never expected to actually see one.

'Oh, my God, that's Bobby Darin over there!' I whispered, looking gobsmacked. They all turned. 'Don't look! Don't look! He might see you staring.'

They all laughed at me.

'I can't believe it,' I whispered, telling them all about how much I loved his voice. I even quietly sang them some of the songs.

At that moment the owners of the restaurant, Mara and

Lorenzo, came to the table and I was introduced to them. 'This little girl is Lulu,' said Vicky. 'Today was her very first time on *Ready, Steady, Go!* She has a big hit record.'

Mara, a striking-looking woman with a thick Italian accent, began to mother me. 'Ah, she's just a bambino. Beautiful Lulu. Are you eating properly? You are so small.'

As we chatted, the others hatched a plan. Twenty minutes later, as our main courses arrived, Bobby Darin appeared at my side.

'Are you Lulu?' he said. My heart stopped. 'You were just on *Ready, Steady, Go!* You were fabulous.'

My eyes widened and I blushed. Everybody at the table was laughing. I didn't know whether to be embarrassed or flattered. The main thing I wanted to do was run to the phone and call Mum.

'Yi'll no' believe who I just met. Bobby Darin.'

I hadn't even thought what might happen if the song was successful. Yes, I knew I would spend time travelling and performing, but I didn't envisage having to leave home or move away from Scotland. I expected to commute.

We had another baby in the house, Gordon. I wanted to look after him, just as I had done for Billy and Edwina. The thought of having to leave them all was too painful to even think about. Who would iron their clothes and polish their shoes? Who would keep them safe when Mum and Dad were fighting?

On my first few trips to London I had stayed in a small hotel in Cromwell Road, which was clean and neat. The Luvvers were put up in a bed and breakfast around the corner. Each trip lasted a couple of days and then we drove back to Glasgow in the van.

Although I didn't realise it at the time, I was leaving home bit by bit. It was never a case of packing my bags and saying goodbye to Billy, Edwina and wee Gordon.

Whenever I was away I tried to call home at six each evening. It became a standing joke in 'oor hoose', as Mum started watching the clock. She wanted to know everything – where I'd been, who I'd met . . . We could talk for hours.

'Remember, Mrs Lawrie, that's a phone you have in your hand, not a bone,' Dad would tease her. 'It's never away from your mouth.'

Some nights we chatted for so long that the rest of the family had finished eating, cleared the table, washed the dishes and were watching TV by the time we finished. Mum would relay all my news to them, never leaving out a detail. According to Billy it felt as though they were taking the journey with me.

The next night I would be on the phone again. Neither of us wanted to hang up. We were both lonely, but in different ways. I was fine while we were busy, doing interviews and playing. But once we finished for the day and I went back to my hotel, I was on my own.

I was used to living in a crowded two-room tenement and falling asleep listening to Billy's breathing. Now I had a room to myself. I lay on my hotel bed, crying myself to sleep, desperately wanting to be home.

Marian could see how unhappy I was. She couldn't expect a girl of my age to get a flat with someone or live by herself. Something had to be done.

She took me to meet her parents, Janey and Alf Gordon, who I'd met when I first came down to London for the audition. They had a large apartment in St John's Wood, which is where Tony, Marian and their sister Felice had grown up.

Janey was in the kitchen making sandwiches for the Luvvers. I took over from her. 'I do this at home,' I said, determined to be helpful. I think that really impressed her.

Marian's plan was for me to move in with Janey and Alf, who would look after me. Mum and Dad flew down to London, bringing Billy, Gordon and Edwina. They met with the Gordons and satisfied themselves that I was in good hands.

Meanwhile, the Luvvers moved into a flat in Leinster Gardens, Queensway. I used to drop around and sometimes do their washing or style their hair. Mainly I bossed them around and acted like a mother hen.

The image of the band was very clean cut, and the boys wore matching jackets, ironed shirts and trousers. Sometimes I was aggressive with them, particularly if they got something wrong on stage. I would even dare to push and shove them, which mortified Marian. 'You can't go around hitting people,' she told me.

'They don't mind.'

'Well, one day they might.'

I was harder on myself than anybody else. If a performance had gone badly, I would sit in the dressing room almost in tears out of utter frustration. Nobody dared talk to me.

I don't think Marian had any idea of how big a job it would be to manage the band. Apart from the constant requests for interviews and appearances, we had sacks of fan mail arriving every day and foreign rights deals to negotiate. Decisions also had to be made about new songs.

As the front person for the band, I had to do most of the interviews. My broad Glaswegian accent might have sounded quite cute, but it was hard to understand. I had to change the way I spoke, softening certain vowels and finishing each word – the Glasgow accent is full of half words and slang.

My favourite 'Glaswegian' story was told to me by Tommy Docherty when he was coaching Manchester United. He took over the team during a rebuilding phase and signed a lot of Scottish players. Some of their accents were so broad that even he had trouble understanding them.

This applied to one player in particular, Tam Forsythe, a Scottish international, who had the sort of accent that pretty much announced, 'Ah'm from Glasgow and Ah'm proud of it.'

After one particular game, Tam was trying to explain to his team-mates why he had failed to control a ball that had come to him.

'It wasnae ma fawt,' he protested. 'Big eat the breed blootered it up ra park; it skited aff mah shed an went fur a shy.'

Translated into something approximating English, he'd said, 'Big eat the breed' (a big, well-fed centre forward type) 'blootered it up ra park' (kicked the ball hard up-field); 'it skited off mah shed' (it glanced off my hair parting) 'an went fur a shy' (and went for a throw-in).

Who says Scotland isn't another country?

One of my first TV appearances was on *Juke Box Jury*. The compère, David Jacobs, a well-known DJ, identified a small but very important problem with my teeth. I had a big gold filling in my upper teeth, almost right in the centre. On black and white TV it looked like a large, black hole.

David Jacobs didn't mince words. He took Marian aside and told her, 'The first thing you have to do is fix her teeth.' And he gave her his own dentist's name.

A few days later I was introduced to Fison Clarke, a miracle worker with invisible fillings and dental cement. He gave me a white crown that matched my other teeth perfectly and replaced all my other gold fillings. It looked fantastic.

'Shout' stayed in the charts for thirteen weeks. With the record sales and gigs, I was earning more money than I had ever seen in my life. Marian's husband, Gerry, insisted that everything be very business-like and fair. In particular he wanted me to have a good accountant.

There are so many horror stories of artists being ripped off by unscrupulous accountants, managers, promoters and financial advisers that I regard myself as being so lucky. I was surrounded by good people, like Marian, Leslie Perrin, Dick Katz and Peter Sullivan.

My weeks were planned down to the last minute. Sometimes I had to be up at six in the morning and be singing by nine. This was after not getting home until late. There were no weekends off, but I didn't care.

I was so caught up in the whirlwind that I didn't realise a revolution was going on and I was part of it. London was the centre of the world. Whether it was music, fashion, art, film, photography or design, the rest of the world was taking its lead from London.

The streets were full of bright colours, short skirts, jackets without lapels, tight trousers, psychedelic swirls, platform shoes, Cuban-heeled boots and big hair. Pop music and rock 'n' roll dominated the airwaves.

One of my first big concerts took me back to Glasgow in early June 1964. Billed as 'The Big Beat Show', I headlined ahead of Dave Berry and the Cruisers and a band called The High Numbers, later to become The Who.

After the gig I invited The High Numbers back to Garfield Street to meet my parents. We all piled into their van along with their manager, Andrew Loog Oldham.

I thought Roger Daltrey was really cute, but it was Keith Moon who had a crush on me. He was only a year older than me and was really sweet and attentive. For years afterwards he would always call me up and make a point of coming to see me.

All of us crowded into the front room. Billy had to go down to the shops to get extra cans of lager and a half bottle of whisky. I don't know what Dad made of it all – he didn't say much. Billy was beside himself. Within a year The Who had a hit single with 'My Generation' and were one of the hottest bands in the country.

A month later I met The Rolling Stones, who were also managed by Andrew Loog Oldham and had signed with Decca. We did a gig together at the Queen's Hall in Leeds. Hanging around backstage, trying to appear grown-up, I waited for someone to introduce us. Mick Jagger sauntered over. 'Alloe Loolooo,' he drawled, curling back his lips and taking it all in. He missed nothing. He seemed such a dark, dangerous piece of work, who intimidated and fascinated me in equal measure. I'm sure this was exactly the impression that Mick wanted to create.

Andrew Loog Oldham was already manufacturing their bad-boy image and trying to create a rivalry with The Beatles. Sometimes it verged on pantomime, but the Stones certainly had a harder edge and appealed more to brooding university students than screaming teenagers.

Andrew wanted the Stones to write a song for me. Mick Jagger and Keith Richards came up with 'Surprise, Surprise'. They wanted me to sound like I did on 'Shout', but you could never repeat a song like that. Jimmy Page played guitar on the recording, which Decca released in early 1965. Although it made the charts, it didn't reach the heights.

For years in Glasgow I had considered all English singers to be rubbish. Only black American stuff was cool. All that changed with The Beatles. I met them at their second annual 'Christmas Show' at the Hammersmith Odeon in London. The Yardbirds were the opening act and I watched Eric Clapton play guitar for the first time. What an awesome talent.

The Odeon could take 3,000 people, but there seemed to be twice that many. Most were screaming girls, all of them my age, desperate for a glimpse of John, Paul, George and Ringo.

I felt like I was one of them, except I had the privilege of standing backstage, watching the band from the wings. Near the end of the show, after three encores and a standing ovation, the boys started running back and forth off the stage and on again. The girls were going crazy.

I was standing watching this when a breathless Paul McCartney dashed off. He turned on the run and caught sight of me. 'Oh, it's Lulu!' he exclaimed in that wonderful accent. Then he was gone again.

Oh, my God, he knows who I am! I could have died and gone to heaven.

When the encores were over, they invited me back to their dressing room. This was huge! These were my idols. It might sound silly, but I will never forget the thrill of watching Paul McCartney wet his hair under a tap and push it back with his fingers. My heart was pounding.

Perched on the edge of a chair, trying to look relaxed, I couldn't think of anything to say. I think they recognised my nervousness and were really sweet. They were so cool and so smart. More importantly, they had a way of writing songs that blew me away. I could never imagine being able to write something like 'Can't Buy Me Love' or 'Paperback Writer'.

I wasn't in the same league as The Beatles, but then again, who was? It was just nice to know them. From then on we began to meet up a lot. I would do radio shows where they got to choose the guests, and later we began going to the same clubs and parties.

Paul had a girlfriend – the actress Jane Asher – and John was already married to Cynthia, who became one of my closest friends. When Paul bought a house in St John's Wood, he was just around the corner from me. Occasionally, when he took Martha, his Old English sheepdog, for a walk, he would drop in to see me at the Gordons' flat.

I had a little Yorkshire Terrier called Dog, who was like a toy poodle compared to Martha. One afternoon, as Paul sat in the kitchen having a cup of tea, Dog decided that Martha was a mountain worth conquering. He tried every means possible to copulate with her. I was mortified, but Paul couldn't stop laughing. It might have been different if I'd been a country girl, but the sight of animals at it always made me turn the other way.

*

Janey and Alf Gordon had become like grandparents to me. Whenever I came in from a gig or a party I would sit on the edge of their bed and tell them everything that had happened. I'd sing them songs I'd heard and tell them who I'd met. I think it gave them a whole new lease of life having a teenager around the house again.

For the first time in my life I had a room of my own. The flat had a lovely bathroom with hot water. The Gordons even had a car, which was a real luxury.

It was a different world, but I was never daunted. One night Marian and Gerry took me to a restaurant called the White Elephant in Curzon Street. Marian's sister Felice and her husband Norman Bognor, who was a writer, came too. The food was French and the décor very sophisticated, with lots of white linen and polished silver.

I didn't have a clue what any of the dishes were. Rather than admit this, I simply repeated what Norman had ordered.

When the snails arrived I looked at them and tried not to appear surprised. Everybody was watching me, waiting for my reaction.

'They look like whelks,' I declared, and I tucked in. They all agreed and laughed. Thankfully, they were delicious.

In situations like this I didn't feel over-awed or anxious. When I didn't know which knife or fork to use I simply waited for somebody else to start first. Right from the outset I decided there was no running away from challenges, big or small. Even when I cried myself to sleep at night, desperately missing Mum and Dad, I never once considered going back.

It broke my mother's heart when I finally left home. She wanted to come with me – to escape from Glasgow and hitch up for the ride.

Years later, when I had the money, I offered to bring her to London to live with me, but she said no. The chance had been lost.

This didn't stop her living through me. She wanted to hear every detail of what I'd been doing – about the shops and the bright lights and the famous people I was meeting. She wanted to dream my dreams even if she couldn't live them.

My leaving home affected her deeply. She didn't have what you would call a classic nervous breakdown, but she certainly suffered terribly from depression and loneliness. Nowadays, people would recognise the symptoms and help her, but back then she suffered alone.

It wasn't just my leaving that hurt her. As I became more famous, I no longer belonged to her but to the world at large. Even worse, another woman had stepped into her shoes.

In the beginning she had been very positive about Marian, but as she saw me leaving home bit by bit she grew jealous of her. A worldly, rich woman was taking me away. She was teaching me how to be a lady; taking me to the best hairdressers and fashion houses; being my confidante and guide.

Although she was never mean about Marian to my face, she constantly questioned her decisions and tried to drive a wedge between us. I would argue with her, telling her she was wrong. I hated seeing her like that. I loved her.

I still phoned every evening, but there was a part of her I couldn't reach – a part that I hated. It was her whining, clinging neediness. She had become a victim.

The worst moment came when Mum phoned a Scottish journalist and bad-mouthed Marian, making ridiculous claims about her having virtually kidnapped me. Thankfully, Leslie Perrin managed to get the article 'spiked'. Stories were easier to hush up in those days.

Another incident could have been even more damaging. Mum and Dad were fighting and Billy and Edwina were trying to keep them apart. Typically, Dad was drunk and Mum was goading him. Edwina tried to hold Dad back, but he accidentally pushed her.

She tumbled from the bed and fell awkwardly. Her head hit the floor and she was knocked unconscious. The fighting stopped instantly. They rushed her to the hospital where she eventually came to. Dad was beside himself with worry.

The press got hold of the story and interviewed the neighbours. They learned about the drunken fights and violence. My family's worst trait and best-kept secret was about to be splashed all over the papers.

Leslie Perrin came to the rescue again and quashed the story. I don't know how he did it. Perhaps he promised them something better.

Although I was prepared for my life to change, I don't think any of my family realised how their lives would suddenly be put under the local spotlight. Mum couldn't go out shopping unless she put on her best clothes. If she dared go out in rollers and a scarf, she would hear people saying, 'There goes Lulu's mother.'

At other times she'd say, 'When I meet somebody I have to answer twenty questions. Everyone wants to know if you've changed and why we're living in the same place instead of with you.'

When I did manage to get home it was pandemonium. Neighbours would see the taxi pull up in Garfield Street and word would spread. Soon there were dozens of people on the footpath waiting to catch a glimpse of me. I was expected to visit all my relatives and meet their friends. After the mandatory cup of tea and piece of cake, I would find another crowd waiting outside.

It was great seeing Billy and Edwina again. Gordon barely knew me, which made me sad. I felt terribly guilty about abandoning them. Billy, in particular, had a tough time. Not everyone in Glasgow was proud of what I'd achieved. Some were jealous. Billy, like my Dad, would leap to my defence, threatening to deck anyone who bad-mouthed me.

Dad was much more relaxed than Mum about my celebrity. He used to laugh when his mates called him 'Mr Lulu' and was filled with pride.

I missed them all terribly. My parents did a lot of things wrong in raising their children, but they also managed to do a few things right. Somewhere in my childhood I was encouraged and given choices.

In Glasgow there weren't many ways to climb clear of the crumbling tenements and bleak housing estates. Football, boxing and music were among them. I was lucky enough to have a 'ticket'.

It wasn't a case of running and not looking back. I couldn't do that. I was constantly looking over my shoulder, remembering my roots. I loved Glasgow for all its problems – the fights and flaws. I loved my family for the same reason.

Although we were still getting plenty of work, it had been a year since 'Shout' came out. Lulu and the Luvvers were in danger of being labelled one-hit wonders.

Our second single, 'Can't Hear You No More', failed to make an impact and our third, 'Here Comes the Night', caused barely a ripple. It was produced by Bert Burns, a legendary R&B writer/producer, who had come to England from America to work with Decca.

Bert did the same song with a young Irishman, Van Morrison, which annoyed me a lot, but I have to admit that Van's version was better. It was his breakthrough song.

Jimmy Page was working in the studio with us and came in one day with a tiny box that he plugged into his guitar.

'A friend of mine has been working on this,' he said, hitting a chord. The guitar almost farted. Everybody went 'Wow!'

The 'fuzz box' distorted the chords, creating a metallic, drawling 'Wah-wah' sound.

Jimmy kept playing and Bert started singing a Rufus and Carla Thomas song:

*You told me that you love me. Say that your love was true.*
*How in the world could you love me baby, lovin' my best friend too.*
*It ain't no good.*
*It ain't no good.*
*Woooaaah it ain't no gooood.*

It was amazing. Nowadays, effects like this are easy to create, but in 1965 it was a huge breakthrough. I don't think any of us realised the impact that Jimmy and his little silver 'fuzz box' would have. Within five years half the teenage boys in the country wanted electric guitars for Christmas.

Still searching for our second hit record, the Luvvers performed at the British Song Festival in Brighton in 1965. The song 'Leave a Little Love' had been written especially for me. The format was a little like *Pop Idol*, with people calling in to vote for the best performance. We finished second to Kenny Lynch, but there was controversy over whether all the votes had been counted. People complained of not being able to get through. I guess nothing changes.

'Leave a Little Love' was released in June 1965 and went to No. 8. It stayed in the Top 40 for eleven weeks. I finally began to feel as though we belonged.

We were doing gigs up and down the country, working with some of the hottest bands of the day. I was operating on pure adrenalin and takeaways. I didn't treat myself particularly well. Usually we'd arrive at a venue starving and duck into the nearest curry house to fill up. Then I'd get dressed in the toilets and go straight on stage. Then it was back in the van for the drive home. We'd stop into a motorway café in the early hours of the morning. A lot of times we'd see another van parked up – maybe

Herman's Hermits, or The Who, or The Hollies. It was bacon, egg and chips all round.

Tommy Sanderson also worked as an agent for The Hollies and put a package together to take us all to Poland. Very few western bands had ever performed behind the Iron Curtain.

Although I had been to Paris and Germany on promotional tours, Poland was an entirely different story. It looked like the end of the world. For twelve days we travelled all over the country on rattling, slow-moving trains. Out of every window I seemed to see crumbling cities, blackened by soot and haunted by the legacy of the war.

I had never seen such poverty, not even in the worst streets of Glasgow. There was nothing to buy in the shops and people queued to buy food. I spent all my money on phoning home.

At the age of seventeen I wasn't politically aware, but I realised how lucky I was to live in Britain. Glasgow had its problems, but at least there weren't soldiers on every street corner and people weren't frightened to look each other in the face.

I spent a lot of time hanging out with The Hollies. Graham Nash kept taking photographs of everything until the police threatened to seize his camera.

Although foreign pop groups were a rarity in Poland, western music had still managed to make it through – smuggled across borders and swapped between teenagers. We were like 'gods' who had descended from another planet – me with my short skirts and the boys in their fancy suits.

Thousands of teenagers came to our shows, and you could see them almost sitting on their hands, desperate to wave them in the air, or get up and dance. But every time someone defied the rules they were forced back into their seats or dragged outside by the police. Some were beaten with nightsticks.

Occasionally, a group of kids were brave enough to unfurl a

banner declaring, 'Welcome Lulu'. Within seconds it was seized and they were beaten. I watched them being carried backstage with terrified looks on their faces.

Despite this sort of intimidation, the audiences gave us so much positive feedback that we were determined to give them the best show we could. They roared for more and we were happy to keep playing encores until the authorities cut the power and silenced the music.

Back in the UK I toured with The Beach Boys, who had a huge hit with 'Good Vibrations' at the same time as 'Leave a Little Love' was at No. 8. Brian Wilson didn't make the tour, but I got to know Mike, Bruce, Carl, Dennis and Al Jardine.

Marian once asked me who in the world I most wanted to work with as a producer. I told her Brian Wilson. I thought he was a genius in the recording studio.

I loved all things American and The Beach Boys were no different. We had great fun on the road and I happily listened to their harmonies every night.

Sadly I split with the Luvvers soon afterwards. Our first album had been successful, with two hit singles, but session musicians had been used on some of the later recordings. Although nothing had been said, I knew the boys were unhappy about this.

There were other rumblings. Right from the beginning it was obvious that I was the focus of the band. Photographers were always taking pictures of me and I was the one being asked the questions at interviews.

Jimmy Dewar was the first to leave in 1965. The others soon followed, slowly gravitating back to Glasgow. I tried to hold us together, but Decca had wanted this all along and did nothing to help me.

I felt particularly bad about Alec Bell, my first serious boyfriend. Mum and Dad adored him and his parents were very fond of me. If we had stayed in Scotland we probably would have married by the time I was seventeen. I wrote a letter to his parents saying how sorry I was that it hadn't worked out. I kept in touch with them for years – long after Alec had married and started a family.

I wasn't nervous about going solo. I had good people around me. It also helped my confidence when I was voted Britain's most promising newcomer and top girl singer.

Newspapers and magazines had made me a pin-up girl. There was a constant stream of stories asking what clothes I liked to wear? Who did my hair? Did I have a boyfriend?

From the first time I saw my photograph in a magazine I became conscious of how I looked. By 'conscious', I mean highly critical. Although I didn't regard myself as being overweight, I didn't think I was thin enough. My face was too round. I wasn't tall enough. I had this cheerful, well-fed look.

Marian was always telling me how pretty and cute I looked, but like every other girl in the world, I wanted to be more like the fashion models, with long, blonde hair, no tits and great long legs that went on forever. Twiggy was adorable but too thin. My ideal body belonged to someone like Patti Boyd or Britt Ekland who were both stunning.

Initially, Marian had a big say about what I wore on stage. We were always discussing the right outfits, but I appreciated suggestions rather than instructions. I was very strong-minded. Mini-skirts were OK, but I drew the line at some of her other suggestions. At one point I went to a gig and I didn't have the right colour bra. These days it doesn't matter because bras are often on show, but back then I wanted everything to be just perfect.

'You'll look fine without a bra,' said Marian. 'Nobody is going to notice.'

'Are you mad? No bra? I can't do that!' She might just as easily have suggested I go naked.

I didn't have a liberated bone in my body. My mother had never undressed in front of me or walked about naked. The female body was something to be covered up and wrapped in layers. Underwear was like extra protection – from what I don't know.

My new body consciousness didn't quite fit in with my junk-food lifestyle – spending long hours on the road, staying up late and sleeping in. Later, thanks to Julie Driscoll, a stunning singer, I discovered the macrobiotic diet. It was all about eating things like wheatgerm, natural yoghurt, carrot juice and honey. Julie lost heaps of weight, but I could only manage a week on and a week off.

In the midst of a mini-crisis over pimples, Marian arrived with an invitation for me to appear in a TV commercial.

'They want you to advertise Lux soap,' she said.

I was mortified. 'Don't be ridiculous! Look at me, Ah'm *covered* in spots.'

I had grown up seeing famous film stars and screen beauties advertise Lux soap – women like Natalie Wood and Grace Kelly. How on earth could I compete with them? People were going to laugh at me.

In her best Jewish voice, Marian said, 'What? You think those film stars look good every morning? They have a whole box of tricks.'

She was right. I learned some important lessons about beauty when I filmed the commercial. I discovered what can be done with the right make-up, the right camera angles and the right lighting.

It also reinforced something my mother had always told me when I complained about having a round face.

'One day, sweetheart, you're going to be grateful. You're never going to look old with a face like yours.'

# 6

# *From Crayons to Perfume*

Growing up in Glasgow, it never occurred to me that we didn't own the roof we were sleeping under. Ownership wasn't an option. People rented. Every month the landlord came knocking on the door and people retrieved the monthly payment from the jar behind the bread bin or the old flour tin on top of the fridge. Houses were something you inherited. They weren't within reach of the working poor.

That's why it was such a big thing when I bought Mum and Dad an apartment in Meadowpark Street, not far from where they lived. It had a bathroom, a laundry and two bedrooms.

At roughly the same time I bought my own townhouse in London. I had lived with the Gordons since I was fifteen and it was time to move out. Alf had died a few years earlier and Janey was on her own. I asked her to come with me.

The house in Priory Terrace, St John's Wood, had belonged to Marian's sister Felice and her husband Norman. They were moving back to America. It was very new, modern and clean, with three bedrooms and three bathrooms. My neighbours included a well-known fashion photographer, as well as John Paul Jones, the bass player for Led Zeppelin.

My other major purchase was a big saloon car – an Austin Princess Vanden Plas. My road manager, Chris Cooke, gave me lessons, but I still managed to fail my driving test twice in London. I took it a third time in Glasgow. 'Those bloody southerners won't pass me,' I told the instructor.

'Well, don't you worry, Marie,' he said. 'We'll soon fix that!'

Sure enough, I came back with a licence.

Soon afterwards I bought an oyster pink Mini Cooper automatic, with a big sunroof. It had an eight-track tape player that took up most of the dashboard. I loved zipping around town with Aretha Franklin blaring out of the speakers and Dog sitting up in the passenger seat.

I laugh when I see photographs of myself back then. I was always wearing things like a plum suede short suit with matching cap and boots. Everything had to co-ordinate in the sixties. Hemlines had risen above the knee and were inching ever upwards. The mini-skirt became the mini-dress and hung straight on to the hips. False eyelashes were all the rage.

My favourite designers were Mary Quant, Ossie Clark and Barbara Hulanicki. They were household names, and so were the models who wore their clothes – girls like Twiggy, Jean Shrimpton and Patti Boyd.

I was seventeen years old and hanging out with the coolest, hippest crowd. Cynthia Lennon, Maureen Starkey and Patti Boyd were my girlfriends. We met up at gigs or went to the same clubs – places like Scotch, Revolution, Ad-Lib and the Speakeasy. Some nights we'd jump into John Lennon's big Phantom V Rolls-Royce, which he'd painted paisley, and cruise from club to club, sitting on each other's laps. There was no question of me being under-age. We were musicians, actors, models, singers, photographers and rock stars hanging out together.

Owners like Johnny Gold always put celebrities in one corner and roped it off. The crowds mingled on the far side, looking at us like exhibits at Madame Tussauds.

We dined at restaurants like Mr Chow's, San Lorenzo, La Gavroche and Aretusa. We bought clothes from Biba, Quorum, Cannibal, Cordoba of Bond Street, John Stephen in Carnaby Street and Granny Takes a Trip. The latter sold psychedelic shirts, shiny velvet jackets and platform shoes covered in stars.

I was at the Bag o' Nails the night that Paul McCartney met Linda Eastman in May 1967. Afterwards we piled into Paul's Mini Cooper and went back to his place.

It was a wonderful time to be young, single and successful. The world was like one big candy store. Even so I had to work hard to make it possible. The following is a typical week from my diary in January 1966:

WEDNESDAY 19TH
*12.00* – photo shoot.
*2.30* – rehearsals.
*4.00* – interview with *NME* [*New Musical Express*].
*5.00* – photos.
Went to the pictures to see *The Collector* and then to Scotch until 5.00 a.m.

THURSDAY 20TH
*10.00* – rehearsals
*Arthur Haynes Show* with The Seekers. Athol [Guy] took me home and came in for coffee at Marian's.

FRIDAY 21ST
*Morecambe & Wise Show*. Received flowers from Athol. Photo in *NME* with Gerry Marsden. Went shopping with Cynthia.

SATURDAY 22ND
Went to Paris for the day with Angela. Bought pink boots
and a few other things.
*Juke Box Jury*.


SUNDAY 23RD
Not too well. Had swollen eyes. Stayed in all morning.
*3.00* – interview for *TV World*.
Dad's birthday.


MONDAY 24TH
*10.15* – flight to Newcastle. Tyne Tees TV.
Performed at Dolce Vita. I'm here until Saturday and then
to Bradford and Doncaster.


Marian was my number one fan and believed that nothing was
beyond me. She wanted me to star in films and wasn't thinking in
terms of pop star movies like *A Hard Day's Night*. She believed
I could cross over and become a serious actress doing proper
dramatic roles.

Although flattering, the notion didn't turn my head. I was naturally very cautious. What did I know about acting?

Marian's sister Felice worked for John Heyman, a well-known
casting agent. Word reached them that James Clavell was looking
for teenagers to be in a new movie.

Clavell was a famous author, scriptwriter and director, but I
certainly didn't recognise him when he turned up backstage after
one of my concerts. He was tall with combed-back hair and had a
pipe resting in the palm of his hand.

'You'll have to change the colour of your hair if you want to be
in my film,' he said bluntly.

I replied in kind. 'If you want me in your film then you'll take
me the way I am.'

Everything about my attitude said, 'I don't give a toss,' which is exactly what impressed him. He was looking for youngsters who had a bit of attitude.

We sat in the dressing room and James Clavell told me about *To Sir With Love*. It was about a black schoolteacher played by Sidney Poitier, who is sent to a rough school in the east end of London. The students try to break him, thinking him soft, until he slowly gains their respect.

'These kids think they're tough,' he said. 'They think they know what it's like to be looked down upon. But they know nothing compared to a black man. He's going to teach them how to survive.'

It all sounded a bit serious. Why did they want me?

Eleven days after I signed the contract, in April 1966, filming began. The press loved the idea of a pop star being involved. On our first day on location in the east end, I was mobbed by local children, chanting, 'We want Lulu!'

All the kids in the cast were from drama school except me. They were slightly in awe of me because I was a pop star who hung out with The Beatles and The Rolling Stones. At the same time, I envied how comfortable they seemed in front of the camera and how their lines sounded so natural.

I had met Suzy Kendall before. She was married to Dudley Moore. Christian Roberts was incredibly tall and handsome – a younger version of Charlton Heston. Adrienne Posta became my best pal. She was funny and talented, although deeply insecure. We used to squeal with laughter as we talked about clothes, make-up and boys.

The cast was together for about a week before the cameras started rolling. I couldn't understand why it was taking so long. Only later did I realise that James Clavell had done this for a reason. He wanted to create a chemistry between us. Friendships would form and natural leaders emerge, just as they do in a real classroom.

Although nobody had asked me to change my accent, I spent a lot of time listening because I wanted to sound like a cockney. I was supposed to be cheeky, high-spirited Barbara Pegg, who was a bit mouthy and loud. No problem.

My speaking role was very small at first, but it grew with each day of filming. James Clavell was like a benign headmaster, who knew the benefit of allowing actors to explore their roles. He often departed from his own script and encouraged us to improvise.

'OK, listen up,' he'd say, as he explained the purpose of the scene. 'I'm going to put the camera on you and I want you to react. Think of what Barbara Pegg would say.'

In one scene Sidney Poitier was chatting to a female teacher in the corridor and all the kids were watching them through the door.

'Who's she bleedin' think she is?' I said, obviously jealous. James loved the idea that Barbara had a crush on her teacher and would mouth off about it. He kept it in the film.

I was completely in awe of Sidney Poitier. It had been a huge year for him, having already made *Guess Who's Coming to Dinner* and *In the Heat of the Night*. He was tall and very handsome, but at the same time rather distant and stand-offish. He kept to himself rather than mixed with the rest of the cast. He had an acting coach, which I thought was quite strange given his reputation and track record.

I was fascinated by his finicky ways. He was very careful about his diet and looked at British fry-ups as though someone was trying to poison him. He preferred to sit in a quiet corner and very methodically break his orange into strips, eating it piece by piece.

I sat next to him one day and tried to be cute and chirpy. 'How's it going, Sidney?'

'Fine, thank you.'

'How's your wife?' I asked, sure I'd read somewhere that he was married to the actress and singer Diahann Carroll.

'Excuse me?'

'Diahann Carroll? How is she?'

He looked at me very coolly and arched an eyebrow. 'I have never been married to Miss Carroll!' End of the conversation.

It turned out that Diahann Carroll had been his lover for nearly six years while both were married to *other* people. Sidney had divorced his real wife only a year earlier – after fifteen years of marriage and four children. Oops!

With hindsight I can see why Sidney maintained his distance. It was very difficult for a black man in the sixties – even a famous one. I remember an incident when Petula Clark and Harry Belafonte were singing on a TV show and she touched his hand. They had to stop the filming and do a retake because the sponsors wouldn't let the show go out with a white woman touching a black man's hand.

One of the clauses negotiated in my contract was to sing the film's title song. I imagined getting something wonderful written by Carol King or Burt Bacharach and Hal David. Sadly, I discovered otherwise.

Screengems were publishing all the music for Columbia Pictures and kept coming up with truly awful songs. As we neared the end of filming, I began to panic. What if nothing decent turned up? What if they *made* me do a terrible song?

'How much power do I have?' I asked Marian. 'Can I tell them no?'

'Not indefinitely. Eventually they'll find someone else to do it.'

Marian had started managing one or two other people, among them a young singer, songwriter and comedian called Mark London. He was a Canadian who had moved to London, hoping to get his big break. Mark was lovely and I would often sit at the piano with him at Marian's house, listening to his stories and funny songs.

'You write me a song,' I suggested to him. 'You know the kind of thing I like.'

'Nah, they'll never use it,' he drawled.

'How do you know? Please . . . write me something. I know it'll be better than anything they come up with.'

I begged and begged until finally he agreed. Within half an hour he had come up with a wonderful melody. He phoned the lyricist Don Black, who was then better known for managing the singer Matt Monro. Don had the lyric ready the following day and I sang the song for the producers of the film.

I knew it was fabulous and wanted them to agree. In the end they nodded and took my word for it. They didn't really care about the music as long as Screengems got the publishing rights to the song.

Having gone solo I'd also changed record labels, signing with EMI. My new producer Mickie Most was a South African, who had started his career as a rock 'n' roll singer and then moved to the other side of the microphone. His first big break was discovering The Animals and he repeated this success with Donovan and Herman's Hermits. Later he went on to create his own label, RAK, and record hits with the likes of Suzi Quatro, Hot Chocolate, Mud and Smokie.

Mickie had an amazing sense of what made a successful pop song. Unfortunately, he had a real blind spot regarding 'To Sir With Love'. I just couldn't get him inspired. I kept telling him, 'Big film. Huge Hollywood star. Brilliant song . . . etc . . . etc . . .'

Mickie shrugged.

'*Sidney Poitier*! He's huge.'

'Yeah, yeah, yeah.'

I turned up at the studio to record the song expecting to see at least a dozen violinists. Mickie had hired four piddling strings.

'This is supposed to be a stirring song,' I said. 'It's the big finale of the film. Can't we have some more?'

Again he shrugged. 'Nah, that's enough.'

We argued but I couldn't sway him. Mickie regarded the entire film project as a nuisance that was keeping me away from important work. He also had a reputation for recording on the cheap and had made a fortune doing it.

He had so little belief in 'To Sir With Love' that he put it on the B-side of my next single. For the A-side he preferred 'The Boat That I Row', a Neil Diamond song.

*To Sir With Love* premiered in America in June 1967 – a year after we finished filming. Just before the opening, James Clavell organised a private screening for the cast.

I was quite nervous as I sat in the darkness waiting for the opening credits. Nothing had quite prepared me for what followed. I was fifteen feet high and filled the screen. I was pale, fat, ugly and spotty. Worse still I couldn't act. It was a disaster . . . a joke. Everybody was going to laugh at me.

I couldn't watch any more. I ran to a phone box and called Marian. In a flood of tears I told her my career was ruined. 'How could I have done this? It's terrible! A joke!'

She tried to calm me down. 'Surely it can't be that bad.'

'You haven't seen it! You just wait!'

Judgement came soon enough and took me completely by surprise. In America *To Sir With Love* was an instant hit. Columbia Pictures sent me a telegram saying that never before had a film made so much in so short a time. Box-office records had been broken right across the continent.

The song 'To Sir With Love' had been released in June, but didn't enter the US charts until eleven weeks later. By October it was the US No. 1 and stayed there for five weeks, becoming the biggest selling song of 1967, with sales of over two million copies.

Effectively it was 'selling' the film – something that few songs had ever done before.

Judy Geeson and Christian Roberts, the young leads in *To Sir With Love*, had been taken over to America to do promotion. Everywhere they went they heard the same question: 'Who is this Lulu? Where is she?'

A wee baby with a very big name – Marie McDonald McLaughlin Lawrie.

Mammy and Daddy, Eddie and Betty Lawrie, on their wedding day.

All of fourteen, and off to school. But not for much longer . . .

Holidaying in Rothesay Bay with Mum and Billy.

I just wanna shout! Lulu and the Luvvers are born, 1964.

From popstar to screen goddess . . . not quite! James Clavell cast me as a cheeky schoolgirl in *To Sir With Love*.

With the very handsome, tall Sidney Poitier.

On tour with Roy Orbison and The Walker
Brothers, in 1967.

Roy only had two facial expressions,
and both were the same.

Scott Walker captured my heart . . .
and thousands of others.

A very public engagement to Maurice Gibb, in October 1968 . . .

. . . and an even more public wedding, in February 1969. More than 3,000 fans turned up.

A month into married life.

My second TV series for the BBC. Jimi Hendrix made history, for all the wrong reasons.

All of twenty-one, and already a show-biz veteran.

An ageless girl plays an ageless boy. My first major stage role, in 1972.

Single again, and looking for a new challenge . . . Step forward David Bowie.

Has there ever been an odder couple?

My Chicago-gangster look, for the launch of 'The Man Who Sold the World'.

Finally Columbia sent me a telegram. It said simply, 'America wants Lulu. Please send soonest.'

The publicity machine at Columbia cranked into gear and I was flown first class to New York, arriving on a wet Sunday afternoon. I looked out the window to see a limousine waiting on the tarmac. Most of the back seat was taken up by flowers.

A dozen photographers took pictures of me stepping off the plane. Marian and I were whisked to a suite of rooms at the Drake Hotel to freshen up. The thrill of being in America was much bigger than when I arrived in London for the first time. Here was a place that had always been writ large in my imagination, and even more so in my mother's fantasies. I had grown up idolising American stars, listening to American music and watching American films.

From the hotel I was taken to the TV studios to appear on the *Ed Sullivan Show*.

'She's only here for one day,' said Ed. 'She has the number one . . . a fabulous song . . . it's Lulu.'

I sang, I bowed, I thanked them and I said goodbye. Within twenty-four hours I was back on a plane to London. I had commitments that I couldn't break.

Over the next few weeks the clamour from the Americans grew even louder and couldn't be ignored. I was soon back there – this time for two weeks.

I appeared on *The Tonight Show*, hosted by Johnny Carson, and *The Joe Bishop Show*. Joey, a member of the legendary 'Rat Pack', introduced me to the audience as 'a little English girl'.

I interrupted. 'Excuse me. Let me set ye straight. Ah'm not English. Ah'm Scottish.' The audience laughed and thought it was cute. They wanted me to speak 'more Scottish'.

After the show Joey took me home to meet his family – or more precisely his son, who was about my age.

I appeared on *The David Frost Show* on the same evening as The

Kinks, Peter Sellers and Sir Laurence Olivier. I didn't feel over-whelmed. At that moment in time, people wanted to see *me*. I couldn't walk down the street without being recognised, stopped or whistled at. Taxi drivers would lean out their windows and yell, 'Hey! Look! It's that kid from that film with Sidney Poitier.' It would set up a chain reaction and other drivers would join in. 'Yeah, it's Lulu! Hey Lulu! How ya doin'?'

There were queues at every box office to see the film. Columbia kept saying to me, 'Do you know the reaction you're getting? It's about you.'

'Of course not.'

'It's true. They go mad for you every time you appear on screen.'

'Yes, they're all laughing at me.'

Finally a publicist convinced me to see the film again. She took me to a cinema on Times Square and snuck me in after the lights had gone down.

I sat at the back, ready to cringe, but as soon as my name came up on screen the whole place erupted into cheers. From then on, whenever I appeared, they would laugh and applaud. They thought I was a great comedy actress.

People just seemed to be delighted with me. I made them smile. I think some of them appreciated the fact that it was really *me* singing in the film, and not some actress who had had her voice dubbed, which was quite common.

I loved America. Everything seemed to be bigger, newer and brighter. I was walking on the ground where all my favourite American bands and singers had walked. I was appearing on the same TV shows. Joey Bishop was friends with Frank Sinatra!

I loved the way people talked, the twenty-four-hour radio sta-tions, the music, the fashions and the food. The hotels were unbelievably plush, with double beds so big I felt marooned in the middle of them. I discovered coffee, real hamburgers, fruit platters with cottage cheese, iced water with meals, different telephone rings and stretch limousines. New York had the biggest, shiniest apples I had ever seen and strawberries the size of oranges. Everything was exotic because it was different.

Mum wanted to know every detail. I was living her dream.

Having become America's favourite sweetheart, I was under enormous pressure to stay. My US agent Sandy Gallen was a young, very bright operator, who became a huge figure in Los Angeles. Big offers were being bandied around, including a five-year contract worth at least a million dollars to host my own TV show.

Marian said no on my behalf. I had already done a TV series for the BBC and another was in the offing. Why did I need America?

Marian had her own interests in mind as well as mine. She was married with three young children. She didn't want to uproot. Equally, she knew how homesick I had been when I first left Glasgow. How much harder would it be if I lived on the other side of the Atlantic?

Despite Mickie Most's lack of enthusiasm, 'To Sir With Love' still managed to chart well in Britain. It may well have been a No. 1 if it had been the A-side single. We'll never know. 'The Boat That I Row' reached No. 6, which Mickie can at least take credit for.

The movie premiered at the Astoria in London on 7 September 1967. There was no red carpet or lavish party afterwards. The overall reaction in Britain was lukewarm. I don't think British audiences really wanted to see another English film with kids talking in cockney accents.

It was about the only place in the world where it wasn't a big hit. I had fan mail from as far away as the Philippines, South America and the Middle East. I still get letters.

I don't think anybody – except perhaps James Clavell and Sidney – realised how important *To Sir With Love* would become.

A lot of black actors have since called it a breakthrough film which could never have been made in America in 1966.

Here was the story of a black schoolteacher in a white classroom, having a romance with a white teacher and being the subject of a white teenage girl's crush. The outcry would have been deafening.

Having my own television show seemed to be a natural progression for me. Marian saw it as a way of extending my career. I know that sounds bizarre considering I was only eighteen, but I understood her reasoning.

The struggle to find the right songs and to stay in the charts is very hit and miss. Musical tastes change. Artists come and go. Marian saw television as a way of counteracting this. It put me in people's living rooms and let me showcase new material.

Even more importantly, TV offered a comfort zone. Instead of rattling around the country in draughty old vans and living on takeaways, I had my own dressing room with my name on the door, with a hairstylist and make-up girl. I had a musical director, an orchestra and a set designer. It's very easy to be seduced by these things.

My first TV series was *Three of a Kind*, starring Ray Fell and Mike Yarwood, two enormously talented comics. The format was mainly comedy sketches and I often played the straight woman (quite literally).

Mike Yarwood had worked with Danny La Rue for years at his cabaret club in Soho and was brilliant at camping it up. He was so good I kept telling him, 'You realise you're supposed to be acting?'

He and Ray were both straight, but loved talking in 'Polari' – a gay slang used by homosexuals to protect themselves in an era where this could mean arrest or being beaten up. It was a collection of different phrases and rhyming slang. 'Vada the lallies on her' meant 'Look at the legs on him'.

Although I enjoyed working on the show, I wasn't entirely comfortable doing comedy. There are some people (Tommy Cooper was one of them) who could read a shopping list and have me crying with laughter. This is a real gift. I hadn't been blessed in the same way. The producer/director John Ammonds from the BBC encouraged me to do more comedy, but I much preferred to sing.

My first solo TV series was broadcast in May 1968. *Lulu's Back in Town* was very modest, by which I mean low budget. Each show was only thirty minutes long. I had to squeeze in four or five guests in that time. Rolf Harris was among the first. I sang 'Can't Take my Eyes Off You' and 'Thoroughly Modern Millie'.

I rehearsed for five days, recorded on the sixth and then had a day off.

The world at large may have treated me like a star, but the BBC didn't believe in pampering or mollycoddling celebrities. The rehearsals were like going to school and having a stern headmaster reprimand me for not having learnt my lines. I might not have had a formal education, but the BBC is where I learnt my trade-craft.

Working to camera came naturally and I became quite good at 'following the light' (when a camera is filming it displays a red light). I played up to the cameras and sometimes had to stop myself from being too aware that they were there.

There were no autocues or cue cards. The BBC viewed them as being some awful American invention. Instead I had to learn the introductions by heart. During later series, when I had fourteen weeks of shows to do, with dozens of new songs and scripts to learn, I used to beg them to let me use cue cards.

'We don't *do* that at the BBC,' was the response.

The shows were filmed in advance, but directors like John Ammonds wanted to create the same energy and edginess of a 'live' performance. This meant that rehearsals were vital. You could never just walk on and wing it.

One of the first things Eric Morecambe ever told me was, 'You have to rehearse, rehearse and rehearse and when you're finished you rehearse again.' Do it properly and things will look spontaneous, even though they have been planned and practised down to the last detail.

If we filmed on a Sunday I would arrive on the previous Tuesday morning and go through the script. Normally I had four or five songs to learn, plus a couple of dance routines and one or two comedy sketches, as well as the links.

The guest stars arrived to rehearse on Wednesday. The Americans were always a little surprised to have no cue cards, but were very respectful. I think they viewed the BBC as a venerable institution.

I was conscious of how young I was. Most of my guests were older and I tried hard to seem as worldly and experienced as they were. When things went badly, I had nowhere to hide. There were times I wanted to run home to my mum, but I had to carry on. This was the role I had taken.

A lot of people were trying to make pop stars into something they weren't in those years – partly to try to cash in on their popularity.

*To Sir With Love* had been perfect for me, but it didn't mean I was a great actress who could play lots of different roles. I realised my limitations, although I don't know if Marian always did.

'A producer wants to meet you,' she said one day. 'He's an Arab film mogul.'

'What's the role?'

'He wants you to play Nefertiti.'

I laughed. 'Ah can't play Nefertiti. She was an Egyptian queen.'

The idea was ridiculous. How could a wee Scottish lass with red hair, pale skin and a button nose play a legendary Egyptian beauty, with dusky skin and a long nose?

'You can play Nefertiti,' I suggested to Marian. 'I'll be your hand maiden.'

She chided me for being so negative. 'It might not be this project, but it could be the next one.'

We arrived at the Dorchester and were shown to an amazing suite overlooking Hyde Park. A few minutes later the film mogul appeared. He was in his early forties, with slightly greying hair, and he spoke in a very polished English accent.

He motioned around him. 'Do you like this place?'

'It's very nice.'

'Come. Let me show you the rest of it.'

I followed him into the next room and spied a mirrored ceiling and a ten-foot-wide bed, covered in a mink rug. I looked around nervously. Marian was standing in the doorway. 'Just be polite,' she whispered.

After the guided tour he insisted we sit down. 'What can I get you, Lulu?'

'I'm fine, thank you.'

'No, I insist. What will you drink?'

'Nothing, really.' Cyanide would be nice, I thought to myself.

'Perhaps something to eat. I have my own chef. He can fix you something.'

'No thank you.'

He was so unctuous and eager to please, I felt uncomfortable. All my instincts told me not to trust him. He began talking about the film – a love story set in ancient Egypt.

Nefertiti! Me! You've got to be kidding, I thought. Maybe I could play some rough diamond or urchin, but not a celebrated beauty. He kept talking and I began eating from a bowl of nuts on the coffee table. I had never had pistachios before. I didn't realise how many I'd eaten until I had a small pile of shells in front of me.

'You like them?'

I nodded.

'I'll get you some more.'

'No, I'm fine.'

He had already disappeared. He emerged from a cupboard with two huge sacks of pistachio nuts – enough to last me a year. He insisted I take them, despite my refusals.

'My tailor is coming. He is making me some leather outfits . . . jackets and trousers. Let me buy you something. You would look good in leather.'

'I don't wear leather.'

He didn't seem to hear me. 'He can measure you now. He is very quick. Perhaps a leather mini-skirt . . .'

'No. Really.'

Marian was trying to hide her amusement. He went on and on about these clothes until I felt like screaming. He only relented when I told him maybe another time.

I wanted to get out of there, but Marian insisted we stay. He then suggested taking me to dinner. I looked at Marian, desperate for a way out. She took me to one side.

'Ah'm no goin' anywhere wi' him,' I said.

'It's just a dinner. He's a very important film financier,' she whispered. 'You go, you have a meal, you say goodbye – what can be the harm in that?'

Reluctantly, I agreed. The following evening he collected me in his chauffeur-driven Rolls-Royce and took me to Annabel's. He was very charming and the food was lovely, but halfway through the meal he reached across the table and clasped my hand.

'I think you are so talented and so beautiful,' he said, staring into my eyes.

Uh, oh, here it comes, I thought. He kept going on about my beauty and poise, treating me like some goddess. I might have been sexually naïve, but I knew where this was going. I also knew exactly how I looked in the mornings!

I made an excuse about powdering my nose and called Marian

from the far side of the bar. 'I'm getting out of here. I'm not going back to the table.'

'No, you can't do that,' she said, fearing a scene. 'Everybody knows you. Go back and tell him very politely that you want to go home. Tell him you have a boyfriend . . . that you're in love. That'll do it.'

'Then what?'

'You thank him for the meal and leave.'

Taking a deep breath, I followed her instructions. But rather than blurt out this new piece of information, I tried to weave it into the conversation. I told him I had to go home because my boyfriend was due to call from America. I thought he took the news quite well and we ended the evening with a very diplomatic kiss on each cheek.

Unfortunately, he didn't quite get the message. He phoned me the next day . . . and the day after . . . and the day after. He kept sending me flowers and asking me out. He wanted to know when I was coming to be fitted for my leather clothes.

It became a running joke, but also quite embarrassing. Whenever he phoned he'd say, 'It's your superman.' Cringe!

I finally couldn't take any more. I asked a male friend to speak to him on the phone and I think it might have frightened him off. The film never happened, of course. I doubt if it was ever more than a vague idea anyway.

# 7

# *Sex, Drugs and Cleaning Ashtrays*

The sexual revolution had arrived in Glasgow by the time I left, but I must have been working that weekend.

When I left home I knew almost nothing about boys or sex. Mum didn't sit me down and give me 'the lecture'. She didn't have to. Without ever saying a word, she had sent out thousands of little signals. In essence, sex was something that men enjoyed and women endured. Although not exactly dirty, nor was it something good girls did – not unless they were married.

I had grown up watching romantic movies and musicals. The formula seemed pretty clear to me: boy meets girl, they fight, they make up, they get married and live happily ever after. I liked this idea. That's what I wanted to do.

The mechanics of sex terrified me. I knew so little about it. Kissing was fun – I could do that all night – but I certainly had no desire to 'go all the way' or 'get off at Paisley' as the locals described coitus interruptus.

It seems bizarre when I look back on it. I had the keys to

London at the height of the swinging sixties and I didn't know what to do with them.

Part of the problem came down to perception. When people saw me performing, swinging my hips and batting my eyelids, they thought I was a hot little number. The photographer David Bailey told me he thought I was 'a hot potato'. Tom Jones said I was 'a real firecracker'.

It simply wasn't true. I was terrified. If I fancied someone, my insides turned to water. I could barely stay in the same room, let alone talk to them. Billy didn't inherit any of these inhibitions. I discovered later that he had sex at the age of twelve, when he slept with one of my friends. He was totally liberated.

I might have been shy, but it didn't stop me defending my honour. One night at a party in London a young guy tried to kiss me and put his hand up my skirt. I told him I wasn't interested. He kept pushing and touched me again. I walloped him with my handbag. Then I ran after him and hit him again. I was shaking with rage.

When I told some of my girlfriends they were horrified. 'What were you doing? He could have hurt you,' they said.

'He wouldn't have lived to tell the tale.'

The first person to bruise my heart was Scott Walker, a thin, frail-looking boy with a rich, lustrous voice. His real name was Scott Engel and he was one-third of The Walker Brothers, who were huge in the UK.

I toured with them in 1967, along with Roy Orbison. These were Americans! Wow! Roy had jet-black hair, coiffed high at the front, and a face that was so pale he looked anaemic. He only had about two facial expressions and both of those were almost identical. He barely moved a muscle on stage. I doubt if he even blinked, although it wasn't possible to tell because he always wore black sunglasses. I thought he looked quite scary, but he was a lovely man and a brilliant songwriter.

The Walker Brothers were all the same age, though not related. A club owner in Hollywood had told them they all looked alike and said it would be a good idea for a name. Gary Leeds was from California, John Maus from New York and Scott from Ohio. Strangely, they had far more success in the UK and Europe than in America, with nine songs reaching the Top 30. The best known were 'The Sun Ain't Gonna Shine' and 'My Ship is Coming In'.

I toured with them for six weeks and it was like an ecstatic torture. I went to bed dreaming about Scott each night, listening to dozens of young girls calling his name from outside the hotel. At the concerts they swooned and became hysterical, reaching their arms up towards him. I watched from the side of the stage, thinking, 'Please pick me. Please pick me.'

He had the most incredible voice. Mainly he sang sad songs, which seemed to reflect his personality – highly strung and vulnerable. Just my type. I pictured him as one of those tortured beatnik poets in a black polo neck sweater, sitting alone in a coffee house, smoking filterless cigarettes and studying a book on existentialism.

On a very innocent level I could talk to my mother about boys. She was the first to say, 'Oh, aye, he's gorgeous,' if she saw a good-looking man.

I told her I was in love with Scott and how much it hurt inside.

'Whit dae you know about love?' she said, scornfully. 'You're just a wee 'un.'

She carved me up like one of the carcasses at the meat market. A few quick flicks of the wrist and my heart had been cut out. She didn't mean to be cruel, but I don't think she realised how fragile teenage confidence can be. With me it was always 'love', and my heart would break so completely I couldn't imagine it ever being repaired.

I thought I was hiding my feelings, but Scott realised I had a crush on him. I looked all calf-eyed at him and would get flustered when talking to him. All he did was pat me on the head and treat me like a little sister. I don't think he fancied me, but we became friendly in a detached kind of way.

I met Tom Jones when I first arrived in London. He too had signed with Decca and Peter Sullivan was his producer. Arriving at the studio one day, I looked into the booth and saw someone who seemed quite a bit older than me, with dark, curly hair. He was singing 'It's Not Unusual'. What a voice!

'Who is that?' I asked Peter.

'Tom Jones.'

What a ridiculous name, I thought. Why would you call yourself after a book? I didn't realise it was his real name.

Having seen me sing and dance, Tom was convinced I had to 'fool around', not just a little, but a lot. I think he was disappointed to discover he was wrong. Even at that age he oozed sex appeal and had no trouble finding girls. His raw sexuality was quite intimidating . . . at least to me.

For a while I had a very innocent romance with Peter Noone of Herman's Hermits. They were the first British band to be huge in America, with a string of number one hits.

Peter was lovely and seemed to be mad about me. We were about the same age and made a cute-looking couple. He used to call me every day from America when The Hermits were touring. We chatted for hours and often I had to hang up, or I would have fallen asleep with the phone in my hand. It was very flattering, but I knew it wasn't love.

Being sexually liberated was a big part of sixties, but I didn't feel as though I was missing out. Even so, I wish I'd been less terrified of men. All my girlfriends seemed to know what they were doing. They didn't seem shy or nervous. They didn't get tongue-tied or clumsy. I was younger, but it still didn't seem fair.

I first met Eric Clapton when we did a gig together at the

Marquee in Wardour Street, London, in 1964. He was a young mod with The Yardbirds, wearing a button-down shirt with a tiny collar. He was very friendly and asked me out, but I wasn't interested. It wasn't until later, when he joined Cream, that I thought he was dead sexy. By then my hormones were raging.

I made the mistake of telling this to Paul McCartney. He never let me forget it. For years afterwards he would bring it up in conversation. 'How's Eric?'

'Oh, God, you're not still on about him.'

One Sunday I organised a party at the Gordons' apartment and invited loads of people, including The Beatles, The Who, The Animals, Cat Stevens and Cream. The main motive was to see Eric, of course, but I tried not to make it obvious.

At some point I found myself talking to him outside, where he'd gone to have a smoke. He put his arm around my shoulders and sighed. 'What am I going to do with you, Lulu?'

'What do you mean?'

'You're not ready to do what I'd want to do.'

I nearly died of embarrassment. How did he know I was a virgin? Was it that obvious? I'd been trying so hard to pretend that I was worldly and cool.

When men discover a girl hasn't been with anybody else, they react in one of three ways. They either want to take you home to meet their mother before marrying you; or they want to plant their flag where no-one else has been; or they pat you on the head like a little sister and become all protective and brotherly. Eric did the latter. He was very sweet and let me down gently, even if it was the last thing I wanted.

Unfortunately, for my love life, he set the standard. I seemed to be drawn to guys like him, who wanted to protect and look after me. I had a dozen 'big brothers' looking after my interests – ready to scare off any undesirable suitors who wanted to have their evil way with me.

Around that time David Bailey took a photograph of me that appeared in a magazine with the caption 'The Virgin Queen of Pop'. Again I was horrified. How could he possibly have known? I hadn't announced my virginity or preached chastity. I thought I'd done a good job keeping it hidden. Obviously not.

The girls I hung out with were all liberated, confident, sexy and experienced. I wanted to be the same – or at least appear to be. In magazines and newspapers I was portrayed as this sexy young pop star, who wore great clothes and dated handsome guys. I was the epitome of the 'swinging chick', whereas in reality I felt like the last remaining virgin in London.

I realise now that there were thousands of girls just like me. Some felt pressured into having sex and doing things they didn't really want to do. Others pretended to be 'liberated' and tried desperately hard not to be found out.

'Sexual liberation', of course, had nothing to do with saying yes to every guy. It was about freedom of choice. Girls could choose whether to have sex early or late; married or unmarried; the time; the place; the position. They could also say no. I know that now, but in 1967 I thought I was the oddest kid on the block. There is a loneliness that comes with that.

In June 1967 The Monkees arrived in England and were met by thousands of screaming fans at Heathrow Airport. They performed at a series of concerts at Wembley Arena and I was on the same bill.

I first met them backstage during rehearsals. Peter Tork, Mike Nesmith and Micky Dolenz were lovely, but for some reason I was almost determined not to like Davy Jones. I pictured him as being smug and conceited. When he barely said a word to me it only reinforced this view. Later I discovered that he was actually quite shy.

Davy and I had a lot in common. He came from Manchester

and had a very similar sort of childhood to mine. His father had worked for British Rail and he grew up in a flat with no bathroom or hot water. He was very close to his family and missed them enormously now that he lived in America.

The Monkees were the stars of a TV series that spoofed the British music invasion of the US. It followed the adventures of a young pop group, who looked very much like The Beatles and who were always getting into strife and almost missing concerts.

The band's first album had sold over three million copies and made them huge stars. Nobody seemed to mind that they were a manufactured band. Even The Beatles embraced them, despite the obvious attempts at parody.

The moment I knew I'd be singing at the Wembley concerts Edwina began driving me crazy. She pleaded with me to introduce her to Davy. I laughed at her breathless enthusiasm and knew exactly how it felt to have a schoolgirl crush.

Davy brought his father and sisters down from Manchester to see the show. Beforehand he knocked on my dressing-room door, apologised and asked if I minded signing autographs for them.

'On one condition. You have to meet my little sister and be very sweet to her.'

We made a deal and each kept our promise. I saw more of Davy from then on. A lot of guys didn't know how to take me, or understand where I was coming from until they heard me sing. It was as though my personality shone through on stage and projected who and what I was. Davy told me as much.

Brian Epstein, who was managing The Beatles, had organised The Monkees' tour. After their last concert, he arranged a huge party at his country house in Sussex. I knew loads of people there, including The Beatles, Manfred Mann, Eric Clapton, Dusty Springfield, The Who, Patti Boyd, Jane Asher and Samantha Juste.

There were drugs everywhere and everyone seemed to be totally out of it. I remember having a conversation with Ringo Starr, who was deep and philosophical. 'If you think it's a bus, it's a bus,' he said. 'If you want it to be a lamp, it's a lamp.' He was clearly stoned and it terrified me because I didn't know what to say. I kept nodding knowledgeably, while looking over his shoulder for some form of escape. I didn't want to say the wrong thing, but more importantly, I didn't want to seem different to everyone else because I wasn't taking drugs.

Later, sitting around a table with loads of cool people, I noticed a joint being passed around. We were all laughing and chatting, but I could feel a smile frozen on my face. What am I going to do when it gets to me? Will anyone notice if I pass it on? Will I still look cool? What if someone says something? What if they insist I try it?

The joint was getting closer and closer. It was torture. I was terrified of smoking it and equally scared of being found out. I desperately wanted to be part of the gang.

What made me so afraid? Once or twice in my life I had lost control – usually when I was really angry. It is a frightening thing to lose touch with reason. That's what I feared might happen if I took drugs. I had also heard the stories of people throwing themselves from windows or locking themselves in cupboards during bad LSD trips. Don't go there, I told myself.

In truth, I didn't need a chemical high. I was getting a big enough rush out of life. Perhaps if I'd been a songwriter it would have been different. Some of my friends swore that LSD was a brilliant creative spark. Others took drugs to push back their boundaries, but I wanted to stay within mine.

I was also very lucky to have Marian and the other people who took care of me. If I had been looked after by a younger management team, I'm sure there would have been more drugs around and more opportunity for me to experiment. I could have found myself

on tour, a long way from home, overworked, depressed or homesick. Someone might have said, 'Here, just take this pill and you'll
feel much better,' and who knows, maybe I would have said yes.

The joint eventually reached me and I casually passed it on. I
didn't think anyone noticed. Who was I kidding?

Certainly not Kenny Everett. In those days he was a popular
DJ, hysterically funny and Liverpool-bred. He was mad about
John Lennon and followed him everywhere. In his autobiography,
years later, Kenny described the same party. He made fun of the
fact that I was the one cleaning ashtrays and making tea while
everyone else was stoned.


The summer of 1967 proved to be a turning point in the sixties. It
marked the height of the general hysteria and moral outrage over
drugs, whipped up by newspapers and politicians. The police were
given new powers and began raiding nightclubs and the homes of
rock stars.

The most notorious raid was on Keith Richards' house in
Sussex during a country weekend, when his guests included Mick
Jagger, Marianne Faithfull, George Harrison and his wife Patti
Boyd.

Keith was given a one-year prison sentence, despite being a
first offender and not being found in possession. Mick was given
three months for having four amphetamine tablets, which could be
bought over the counter legally in Italy.

There were protests outside the court and people were arrested.
It wasn't just young people who criticised the harshness of the
sentences. *The Times* ran an editorial headed: 'Who Breaks a
Butterfly on a Wheel?'

At the same time letters signed by prominent people like scien-
tists, lawyers, doctors and showbusiness figures were published in
newspapers calling for the law to be changed. Possessing cannabis
should either be legalised or punishable by a small fine, they argued.

Paul McCartney was among those who signed a letter. He also admitted on TV to having tried LSD and suggested that people should perhaps try it before condemning it. I had no idea of this when a journalist confronted me outside a studio and asked, 'Do you agree with Paul McCartney that everyone should try LSD?'

Of course Paul had said no such thing, but I didn't know that. I told the journalist, 'People talk about love as if you have to be on drugs before you can be part of it. In fact love is far older than pop music . . . it goes right back to Jesus and before that. I'm a believer in love. I don't need drugs to find it.'

A government minister picked up the comment and mentioned it in the House of Commons. I was held up as being a paragon of virtue. It was splashed all over the newspapers and portrayed as some sort of pop music feud between myself and Paul McCartney.

This upset me. I felt as though I was being used. My words had been twisted for political reasons when I had no desire to become involved in the debate. It marginalised me in many eyes. I wasn't 'cool' any more because I had spoken out against drug use.

I talked it over with Marian and we decided that it didn't really matter. If as a result one kid chose not to experiment with LSD and it saved him from a bad trip then it was worth it. Drugs didn't make me who I was. I didn't need them to feel good or be creative. I chose not to go there.

At the same time, I never preached or commented upon how any of my peers lived. I didn't think less of them, or choose not to be around them any more. I loved them for who they were and I hoped they felt the same about me. Paul didn't make an issue out of it. He has never said a word to me about it.

On 31 July 1967 Keith had his conviction quashed on appeal and Mick's prison sentence was reduced to a conditional discharge.

A month later, Brian Epstein was found dead from an overdose of tranquillisers at his house in Belgravia. Whether it was

accidental or deliberate was never established. I was in London
when I heard the news. The shock was enormous. The godfather
of this musical revolution was gone and it meant the end of an era.

Although many people knew that Brian suffered from depression, the thought that he may have committed suicide cast a
cloud over all of us. It also seemed to be the catalyst for so
many other sad moments. The Beatles seemed to age overnight
and drift apart. Cynthia and John broke up. There were arguments
over who was to blame. The sheer, unadulterated joy of the
sixties had been spoiled. It was never the same after that. We all
had to grow up.

My best friend, Joanne Nuefield, was Brian's secretary. She
worked in the house with him and was broken-hearted. She knew
what pain he must have been in. He was only thirty-two.

After that there seemed to be a procession of others who suc-
cumbed. Jimi Hendrix died on 18 September 1970 from an
overdose of sleeping pills. Janis Joplin went a month later. In
1974 Mama Cass died of a drug-induced heart attack at a London
flat owned by singer Harry Nilsson. Ironically, Keith Moon died
in exactly the same flat four years later when he accidentally over-
dosed on medication to combat his alcoholism. John Bonham was
found dead after a drinking binge at Jimmy Page's house in
1980 . . . Each death brought a little darkness into the world.

I will be for ever grateful that nobody ever forced me to take
anything, or slipped me something, which is how The Beatles
first experienced LSD. A lot of people around me were very protective. Most came from a similar working-class background in
cities like Liverpool, Manchester and Birmingham. We were all in
it together, looking after each other.

The music industry was much smaller then. There were a limited number of radio stations, TV shows, magazines and venues.
That's why bands were always bumping into each other and hanging out together.

Nowadays it doesn't happen in the same way. Artists keep to themselves and hide behind the dark windows of limousines. They travel with huge entourages, which include stylists, hairdressers, bodyguards, fitness instructors, yoga teachers, agents, personal assistants and their favourite photographer.

Bands don't bump into each other any more. If they do you can almost guarantee that it's been arranged and even scripted. It will be a photo opportunity rather than a good night out.

# 8

# *Making a Monkee Out of Me*

The Bee Gees had emerged from Australia with a unique sound and amazing harmonies. Their first single, 'New York Mining Disaster', was in the charts at the same time as I had a hit with 'The Boat That I Row'. We were invited to appear on *Top of the Pops* in the same week.

There were five members of the group – three Gibb brothers, Barry, Robin and Maurice, as well as Colin Petersen on drums and Vince Melouney on lead guitar. I first saw them in the BBC canteen and thought they all looked rather flash. Then I watched them rehearsing and was amazed at the harmonies they could produce.

My friend Joanne Nuffield called me up a few days later. She had been at their manager Robert Stigwood's office and overheard them chatting.

'Maurice Gibb fancies you,' she said excitedly.

'How do you know that?'

'Because I heard him say it.'

'Well, he didn't say a word to me.'

'He's not likely to tell *you*. He's probably shy.'

A month later I was in the south of France with Mickie and Chris Most. Mickie had brought his boat and was trying to teach me how to water-ski, without much success. His idea of lessons involved me bobbing up and down in the water holding a rope, whereupon he gunned the engine and sent me aquaplaning across the bay on my face. I must have swallowed half the Mediterranean.

Later, as we walked along the foreshore, we bumped into the Bee Gees who were staying on Robert Stigwood's boat. Maurice and I chatted happily and he talked about us getting together in London. We didn't make any definite plans, but he phoned a week later and invited me out to the Saville Theatre. Pink Floyd were playing.

I called him 'Mo' and I thought he was cute. We talked about music and mutual friends. We started seeing more of each other but were both so busy that it was difficult to find the time. Often we had to make do with talking on the phone.

By the end of 1967 the press had picked up on the romance. The Bee Gees were still relatively unknown and Mo wasn't referred to by name in the first story. He was 'the Bee Gees' bass guitarist'. I don't know who leaked the story, but I suspect it probably came from Robert Stigwood's office.

All the brothers seemed to vie for Stigwood's attention – Mo and Robin especially. Barry was eighteen months older and more secure. He was the major creative force behind the band when it came to songwriting and singing. Robin had the most unique voice and Mo was the strongest musically, capable of picking up almost any instrument.

The Bee Gees were playing in Glasgow and I rang Billy and suggested he go and see them. 'Tell them you're my brother.'

'Ah'm not doin' that.'

'Go on. At least give Mo a call.'

Billy was only sixteen and quite awestruck by the people I was mixing with. Finding the courage, he called and Mo immediately put him at ease. 'Hey, we're doing Dundee tomorrow. Do you want to come along?'

Billy was bowled over. He spent the next day travelling with the band and hanging out with them backstage. Barry's new girlfriend, Linda Gray, even kissed him on the cheek. His mates at school were going to be green with envy.

Although I liked Mo a lot, I didn't really take our romance very seriously. He was a year younger than me and, if it seems possible, even less sophisticated. I told him I wanted to cool it for a while, but he still kept in touch. He told his friends that whatever happened he was going to marry me.

On 13 January 1968 I saw Davy Jones again. I was doing a week at Caesar's Palace in Luton when he decided to surprise me.

'I thought you were back in America.'

'I missed you.'

'Rubbish.'

He clutched his chest and pretended to be mortally wounded. Then he gave me a cheeky smile and asked me out.

After the show we went to Ronnie Scotts in the West End and listened to jazz until the early hours. Then he came back to the flat. I was due to fly to America in four weeks to perform at the Coconut Grove in Los Angeles.

'I'll show you around when you arrive,' he said. 'And I can find you an apartment near the beach. You don't want to stay in a hotel.'

I thought he was very sweet and I quite fancied him. It didn't make any difference to me that Davy was quite small, although I remember my mother saying to me, 'Don't marry a wee man, Marie. They all have Napoleon complexes.'

For the next month Davy and I became pen pals. His letters

were full of stories, poems and pressed flowers. He also sent me an album with a particular song he thought I should record. As much as he loved Hollywood, I think Davy secretly missed England and was quite lonely. Once or twice he phoned me, getting the time difference all wrong and waking me up.

I was still talking to Mo on the phone most days. He came to see me at Caesar's in Luton before flying to Germany with the Bee Gees. Tom Jones was there on the same night. He was due to open in Las Vegas at about the same time as I opened in LA.

A few days later Robert Stigwood was quoted in the press saying I was madly in love with Maurice and had pictures of him plastered all over my walls. I called him and raged down the phone.

'How dare you use me like that. I'm not stupid. I know what you're doing . . .' I slammed down the phone.

Poor Mo got the worst of it. He was trying to calm me down, but I wasn't willing to listen. What chance did we have of a proper relationship if people tried to manipulate us?

On 12 February I opened a new show at the Talk of the Town in London. Mum and Dad came to the opening night and sat alongside Cynthia Lennon, Patti Boyd, Sandie Shaw, Engelbert Humperdinck, David Hemmings and Mo. Two days later I was voted Top Girl Singer and Top TV Personality at the Disc and Music Echo Awards. Mum and Dad had dinner with me afterwards and told me how much they liked Mo.

I wrote in my diary that night: 'What am I going to do? I seem to be caught. Every time Mo goes I feel like crying. But then I get a call from Davy, or one of his letters, and I start looking forward to seeing him.'

For two weeks I did shows at the Talk of the Town. Mo was in the audience every night. The day after I finished I flew to LA. I had meant to send a telegram to Davy saying when I was arriving, but didn't have time. Instead a stewardess on the plane managed to forward a message. I was a little disappointed when he wasn't at the airport to meet me. He called my hotel.

'Welcome to California. How's it going?'

'It's hot.'

'Yes. That's true.'

'And the band is too bad for words.'

My first rehearsal had been a disaster. For shows at home I normally had my own musicians, but for this gig I was told I had to use their's. I had two days to rehearse. When I complained to the management about the orchestra I received a blunt message: 'Do you know who they've worked with before? Sinatra, Ella, Sammy Davis . . . I don't think *they're* the problem.'

I fought back my anxiety and hoped for the best. Davy sent me two dozen roses and dropped by to wish me luck before the opening night. It didn't help. The show was a disaster. At one point, having introduced a number, the brass section and rhythm section of the orchestra played completely different songs.

I waved them to a halt. 'Let's start that one again,' I said, trying to laugh it off. 'Little bit of a language problem here. Must be my accent.'

The audience laughed with me, but I was mortified. My big night – with a star-studded guest list – had been ruined. I fled upstairs to my suite in tears. Marian couldn't console me. Mel Ferrer, the film director and actor husband of Audrey Hepburn, knocked on the door.

'I just wanted to say I thought you were brilliant,' he said.

'But the band . . .'

'Nobody noticed. We should do a movie together. How would you like to play Peter Pan?'

I laughed, unsure of whether to take him seriously.

Drying my eyes, I went downstairs for the first-night party. Photographers were falling over each other. Davy pulled me close and we had lots of pictures taken together. Then he grabbed my hand, saying, 'Let's get out of here.'

'Where to?'

'Anywhere.'

He took me to Arthur's, a trendy nightclub, with four of his friends. I didn't get back to my hotel until 3.00 a.m.

Marian let me sleep until midday and then came bounding into my suite clutching the reviews. *Variety* declared: 'Lulu's a Winner'. The *Hollywood Reporter* said I had a contagious, unaffected charm, and the *Los Angeles Times* called me 'Another amazing production of modern showbusiness' with a 'stage presence unusual in one so youthful'.

The season at the Coconut Grove was a sell-out. I did two shows a night and there was normally a sprinkling of celebrities in the audience, people like Michael Crawford, Georgie Fame and the singer/songwriter Lee Hazlewood.

After one show Tom Jones took me out for a drink and we bumped into George Hamilton. He looked like a Greek god, with a perfect tan and a chiselled jaw. He invited us back to his place but we managed to get lost trying to find it. Tom and I finished up having coffee and pancakes at 4.00 a.m. on Sunset Boulevard.

Davy was filming *The Monkees* and was busy during the day. He still managed to make at least one show a night. Afterwards, he took me out or we sat talking and necking passionately in my suite. Often he wouldn't leave until 4.30 a.m., and then only with a lot of coercion.

I wrote in my diary: 'He really didn't want to go. Part of me felt the same way. I kept thinking, "Oh, my God, what am I going to do?" I really think I'm falling. I just hope it doesn't hurt too much . . .'

I told him I didn't want to get hung-up or involved. He nodded his head and kissed me. A part of me was very flattered by his attention. His picture was in every teen magazine in America and girls went mad for him. Yet here he was pursuing me.

TUESDAY MARCH 12TH

Davy came at 1.15 – as arranged. He took me to the studio and I watched them filming. I stayed all afternoon and we had fish & chips. We decided to go to Mike Nesmith's house but got lost on the way. We were stuck on the freeway for two-and-a-half hours and finished up arguing. Saw a side of Davy I didn't like – bad tempered and surly.

We gave up and went back to my hotel . . . We began necking and talking and talking and necking. At 2.00 a.m. I decided he should go home. I really have fallen hard.

After the Coconut Grove I was due to fly to Miami to do a stint at the Narm Convention, where Jack Jones was also performing. Davy said he didn't want me to go. I didn't know what to do. Sometimes I thought I loved him, but at other times he wouldn't turn up as planned or would forget to phone.

When I went to Palm Springs for a short break, Davy said he'd fetch me on Sunday and bring me back to Los Angeles. Instead he went to Las Vegas to see the Sonny Liston fight. I flew back to LA and when I arrived at my hotel I turned on the TV. The Bee Gees were on the *Ed Sullivan Show*. I felt my heart lurch when I saw Mo. The British newspapers had been running stories about my romance with Davy. What must he think? Had I hurt him?

I flew to Chicago the following day and caught a connection to Miami. I called Davy from the Diplomat Hotel where I was working. He said he missed me. I almost believed him. Yet despite all the flowers and the long phone calls, I still sensed something was wrong. I heard whispers about another girl. He only once invited me to his house. He preferred to come to my suite or to take me out.

When I discovered the truth I was totally heartbroken. He

had a long-time girlfriend, Linda Haines, who, I found out later, was pregnant with his child. Maybe that's why he broke off contact so suddenly. Then again, maybe he was trying to have it both ways – a girl at home and another one away. If so, I wonder what he told Linda when she saw pictures of us together. Perhaps Davy said it was a publicity stunt.

I like to think that he loved me – but he obviously loved Linda too. Their baby daughter, Talia, was born in October 1968 and they married later that same month in Mexico.

Years later Davy wrote in his autobiography: 'In show business, or any other type of business that exposes you to the media, when you're seen out with a member of the opposite sex, the press immediately assumes that the next step is marriage . . . Ridiculous, really. I couldn't have – my girlfriend would have punched me out.'

Shame he didn't tell me that!

Nursing a few emotional bruises, I tried to put Davy Jones out of my mind. I had a new TV series to rehearse and a cabaret season in Manchester. After one of my shows I was taken to a local club to unwind. Sitting quietly in a corner I noticed a familiar face.

George Best was propped at the bar, surrounded by admirers, but he made his excuses and asked if he could sit down next to me.

I would never call myself an expert on football, but growing up in Glasgow equips a girl to know a little about the game and the men who play it. I knew, for instance, that George had a gift and was already being hailed as the greatest player of his generation.

That night he invited me to his next game. Manchester United was playing Everton at home. He sent a car to pick me up beforehand and I met him at the team's private bar afterwards. All the players were there. He drove me back to my hotel and I arranged to meet him after that night's show. We went to the Phonograph – Tony Gordon's club – and flirted like crazy. George tried to talk me into bed, but I managed to fight him off. Even so, I didn't get home until 6.30 a.m.

I thought George was gorgeous, but he talked a lot of claptrap – telling me how I should manage my career and take care of my money. I looked at him and thought, Why am I getting advice from a football player? It wasn't as if George was particularly famous for his money sense or clean living.

The press went crazy when the news leaked out. The champion footballer and the pop star made for great headlines. Yet despite the romance, it was never going to be serious. George couldn't belong to one girl. Both of us knew that.

From then on, whenever I worked in Manchester he would come to hear me sing and I'd watch him play. I once phoned him from Portugal when I heard he'd been injured. He told me he was in love with me and we should get married. I told him it was the painkillers doing the talking and he shouldn't be drinking.

On his seventeenth birthday in August 1968, Billy left Glasgow with dreams of being an actor. He planned to audition for RADA in the New Year and, in the meantime, hang out with me. He moved into my house in Priory Terrace.

I took him shopping to Mr Fish in Clifford Street, the trendiest men's clothing shop in the city. He got a wardrobe full of made-to-measure shirts, matching kipper ties, jackets and trousers. He was the best-dressed teenager in town.

I was still working with Mickie Most and releasing new singles. It meant doing promotional trips to Europe. Billy came with me to Scandinavia, Belgium, France and Germany. After six weeks of having the time of his life, I sat him down and said, 'OK, you've had your fun, what are you going to do?'

He shrugged. 'Get a job, I suppose.'

'Good idea.'

Although he would have been quite happy tagging along, I think Billy was lonely when the 'carnival' stopped moving and he was left in the flat by himself. I spoke to a few friends in the music industry, including Don Black, who had helped write 'To Sir With Love'.

Don had become a director of NEMS Enterprises, working alongside his brother Cyril. They interviewed Billy and took him on as an office boy. A few months later the company expanded, launching its own record label.

Billy had impressed them and they offered him a job as a record plugger. 'Cyril here is going to take you around the radio stations and introduce you to the producers. He'll show you how plugging works,' said Don.

Billy was nervous, but he agreed to try. He turned out to be a complete natural. People liked him. Many of them had already met him through me, but he quickly stepped out of my shadow. He was soon headhunted by RCA and started working with people who went on to become huge songwriters and producers. The music industry was moving at an incredible pace and you had people barely out of their teens heading up A&R departments with huge budgets.

Billy never did audition for RADA. He had found his niche.

My private life was being played out in newspapers and magazines, but I didn't think this was unusual. I didn't know any different. People would say to me, 'How do you cope with all the publicity and attention?'

I answered, 'What choice do I have?'

In truth, I loved the attention. There is a romance about being constantly photographed and wearing nice clothes. I was young and impressionable . . . one of the chosen few.

In those days the paparazzi didn't hang around outside clubs and restaurants waiting to snap you leaving at five in the morning. Thank goodness! They would have gone crazy if they'd seen George Best leaving my hotel room at 4.30 in the morning.

And being famous certainly had its advantages. Restaurants always found a table and I could get tickets for 'sold out' shows.

It didn't always work. I went on holiday to Portugal with Adrienne Posta, Billy and a few of the gang. We rented a lovely villa for the week. It seemed quite odd when we arrived because there was food in the refrigerator and someone had left clothes drying on the balcony.

We were tucked up in bed that night when the family arrived home. The villa had been double booked. We had to pack our things and move in the middle of the night with no idea of where to go.

Peter Grant, who was managing The Animals, had a villa next door. We finished up sleeping in his garage on fold-up camp beds. We spent a week with Peter because we couldn't find any other accommodation. The locals would come to the front of the villa and shout my name, hoping to get a glimpse of me.

It should have been a nightmare, but none of us really minded. Adrienne was so wonderfully funny that I exhausted myself laughing.

Back in England my friend Joanne Nuefield had become engaged to Colin Petersen, the Bee Gees' drummer. One Sunday they invited me out to a studio where I found Maurice sitting at a piano with a few friends. As soon as I saw him I realised how much I'd missed him. The chemistry was still there – only stronger.

'I started drinking when you left me,' Mo said.

'You never needed a reason to drink.'

He laughed. 'That's true.'

We started dating again and this time I think I was ready for a relationship. We also made more of an effort to find time for each other. I was busy rehearsing during the day and Maurice was recording an album. We went to clubs, watched movies and spent our weekends buying things for Mo's flat. I was still better known and sometimes his nose would be put a little out of joint when people asked for my autograph and then said, 'Yours too, Barry.'

There was something about Mo that I found completely irresistible. He was charming and eager to please in a shy sort of way. He had a great sense of humour and was easy to be around. His generosity seemed boundless. He was always picking up restaurant tabs and buying presents for people. He lavished gifts on me.

Of course, I was also attracted by his talent. He could pick up almost any instrument and write a song from thin air. He could harmonise with such ease. Music was like a glue that drew us together and held us there.

The media made a big deal about us. We were a golden couple – young, attractive and famous. There were daily stories written about us, speculating as to whether we'd get married. I felt as though the whole world was watching me.

By the end of October, only weeks after getting back together, Mo asked me to marry him. I said yes straight away but wanted a long engagement. I didn't think I had a choice. We were both so busy that I doubted whether we could find time for a wedding.

At the same time, I really wanted us to make it official. I had remained a virgin – despite all the obstacles, temptations and some marathon kissing sessions. The sixties were nearly over. I was nineteen, going on twenty. Talk about now or never.

I was filming a Christmas show for the BBC and rehearsing for a new thirteen-week series, *Happening for Lulu*, starting at the end of November. This time I had an hour-long show to fill each week. It meant rehearsing a couple of dance routines, as well as learning new songs, a few comedy skits and also the introductions.

Marian was very sweet when I told her about the engagement. Mum and Dad were thrilled. They loved Mo. He was successful and came from the same sort of background as me. Even more importantly, they saw that he was crazy about me.

Billy's reaction was completely the opposite. He sat at the kitchen table with his head in his hands, pleading with me to reconsider.

'He's too young for you, Lu. He doesn't have enough common sense. It isn't going to be equal – you're too strong for him.'

Billy had spent a lot of time with Mo and they had become good friends. He loved both of us, but believed passionately that we were making a mistake. The more he pushed, the more determined I became to ignore him.

'Don't tell me what to do,' I said angrily.

'This is the biggest mistake you'll ever make. It cannot work.'

'Yeah, well, people have been telling me what to do all my life. I make my own decisions.'

Barry Gibb was another who questioned the engagement. He was quoted in a newspaper as saying we shouldn't get married because we were too young.

I was shocked. 'How can your own brother say something like that to the newspapers?'

Mo shrugged and told me to ignore it. 'Just look at the ring on your finger and ask yourself if you're happy.'

He knew the answer. We'd chosen a beautiful ring from a jewellers in the Burlington Arcade. The main stone – a cabochon sapphire – had been set in an Edwardian pendant surrounded by diamonds.

'I'd like a ring like that,' I told the jeweller.

His eyes lit up. 'Madam, we can set that same sapphire in a ring for you.'

I finished up getting both – the ring and the necklace. It was unbelievably expensive, but neither of us cared. True love didn't come with a price tag.

*

We announced the engagement publicly on the first show of my new series at BBC Television Centre in Wood Lane. Mo and I sang a love song together. There were no points for subtlety!

Thankfully, it wasn't the most famous moment of the series. That honour belonged to Jimi Hendrix and his band. He created one of the most famous moments on television on Saturday 4 January 1969.

The show was almost over and everything had gone smoothly. Jimi was supposed to do a live version of 'Voodoo Chile'. Suddenly, halfway through the song, he stopped. On 'live' TV he announced, 'I'd like to stop playing this rubbish and dedicate a song to Cream, a great band who broke up today.' Then, totally off the cuff, he launched into an incredible version of 'Sunshine Of Your Love'.

This wouldn't have been a major problem, except for the fact that he didn't stop playing. Stanley Dorfman, the producer, tried to pull the plug but Jimi was having none of it. He uttered a four-letter word on prime-time Saturday night TV and then said, 'We're being put off the air.'

The show had over-run by one minute 46 seconds. The BBC was furious and banned Jimi from ever appearing again.

The other momentous (I use the word loosely) aspect of that series was the 'Song for Europe' contest. Bill Cotton, the Head of Light Entertainment, wanted me to sing the British entry.

'Why would I want to do that?' I thought the Eurovision was outdated, the voting too 'political', and many of the songs very ordinary.

Bill looked to Marian for support. She was all for the idea. 'Think of the viewing figures. It's a Saturday night, prime-time, with a huge audience right across Europe. You'll reach a whole new market . . .'

My instincts said no, but I listened to people who I thought were older and wiser.

Initially the BBC planned to hold a contest to select the British entry. Hundreds of songs were submitted and a shortlist of six decided upon. I was to sing each of them over six weeks of the show and the public would vote for their favourite.

I had the Johnny Harris orchestra backing me during the series. They were all top session musicians and a great bunch of guys. We started taking bets on which song we thought would win. We all knew it would finish up being the song we disliked the most. One was way out in front – 'Boom Bang-a-Bang'. It was a classic Eurovision song, with an oompah-pah beat and sugary lyrics.

> . . . *my heart goes boom bang-a-bang, boom bang-a-bang, when you*
>   *are near,*
> *boom bang-a-bang, boom bang-a-bang, loud in my ear,*
>   *pounding away, pounding away, won't you be mine?*
> *boom bang-a-bang bang all the time . . .*

Mark London and Don Black wrote another of the songs, but my favourite was by two newcomers, Elton John and Bernie Taupin. Sadly it finished up coming sixth in the voting. The winner, of course, was 'Boom Bang-a-Bang', which I've been trying to get out of my head ever since.

# 9

# 'We're Just Goin' For a Wee Walk'

Mo and I wanted a quiet wedding. We had some crazy idea that we could keep the whole thing secret, but we forgot about the massive media interest. On the morning of the wedding, 18 February 1969, our secret location was announced on the radio and mentioned on TV.

By early afternoon the roads were jammed for half a mile around St James's Church at Gerrard's Cross in Buckinghamshire. I arrived twenty minutes late, having detoured twice. So many people lined the roads that it felt like a royal procession.

When I finally reached the church there were 3,000 screaming fans outside. As the car door opened they surged forwards. I was surrounded by a dozen policemen who tried to force them back.

'You have to let me in, I'm getting married,' I begged.

They formed a scrum around me and we inched our way to the church steps. Although I tried to keep smiling, I was frightened and dazed. I kept telling people to calm down and please let me through. Dad held on to my hand, scared that I'd be swept away.

Having reached the steps, I turned and waved. There were

photographers perched in the branches of trees and standing on ladders. Outside broadcast vans were parked in the side lane.

All the Bee Gees were there, although Barry arrived late, which was unfortunate because he was the best man. We also invited Robert Stigwood, Mickie Most, Cynthia Lennon and some of our relatives – we wanted to keep it small. Marian's daughter Sharon, then fourteen, was the maid of honour. Our pages and brides-maids were Mo's baby brother Andy, and his niece Berri, as well as Edwina and Gordon. They looked adorable in wee kilts and velvet jackets.

I wore a mini-dress covered by a floor-length, mink-trimmed coat with a hood that looked like something out of *Dr Zhivago*. My boots were white and I carried a bouquet of snowdrops.

As I stood at the entrance, looking down the aisle, I glanced across at Dad. He had tears in his eyes. 'Noo, hen,' he said. 'We're just goin' for a wee walk.' He took my arm.

After the ceremony we stopped for photographs on the front steps, waving to the crowd. Then we were spirited away in Mo's white Silver Cloud Rolls-Royce, back to London for a reception. We took over La Gavroche near Sloane Square, one of the best restaurants in the city. There were more than fifty guests, includ-ing my Da McDonald and many of my aunts and uncles. Goodness knows what they made of it. Each bottle of champagne cost more than their weekly household budgets.

The wedding was featured on the Pathé Newsreel shown in cinemas around the world. A very posh voice announced, 'And this week in London, pop singer Lulu marries Maurice Gibb of The Bee Gees . . .'

The BBC gave me the day off, but I had to be back at rehearsals the next morning. We had to postpone our honeymoon until after the Eurovision Song Contest, five weeks away.

In the meantime, I moved into Mo's house in Kinnerton Street, Belgravia. It was a lovely mews cottage with hanging baskets and cobblestones outside. It was just the right size for the two of us, but way too small for our surrogate 'child' – a Pyrenean mountain dog called Aston.

I have no idea why Mo decided he needed a dog. Nor why he chose an animal that could dribble for England. Aston was huge. He took up the entire back seat of the car and every time he voided his bowels he buried the back garden. He peed everywhere and was too strong for me to take him for a walk.

Mo used to tell people how much I loved Aston, but it wasn't true. Although fully grown he was mentally a puppy. For one thing, he had no idea of his own size or strength. He would try to crawl under a table and lift the entire thing up. And if he wasn't drooling, he was shedding fur. Visitors would send us their dry cleaning bills.

Clearly we needed a bigger house. This had already been taken care of. Even before I married, Gerry Massey had convinced me to buy a seven-bedroom house in Highgate, not far from Hampstead Heath. It was now a 'work in progress', with walls being knocked out, pipes removed and wires rerouted. But as one problem was solved, others appeared. The move would just have to wait.

In late March I flew to Madrid, along with Mo, my mum and Mrs Barbara Gibb. Dad had stayed at home to look after Edwina and Gordon. He told the newspapers he'd be too nervous to be in Madrid for the contest. The truth was far more prosaic. He hated travelling, foreigners and having to remain sober. Instead he intended to sit quietly at home, watching the TV, and drinking as much as he wanted without my mother being around to berate him.

I had letters from all over the country wishing me luck, including one from my local minister in Glasgow who said his parishioners were all praying for me.

I had only just started to realise that I was on a hiding to nothing. Most of the other entrants were virtually unknown outside their own countries. They had nothing to lose and everything to gain. I was an internationally famous pop star and, consequently, the raging favourite. Anything less than outright victory would be seen as a failure.

The contest was held at the Teatro Real in Madrid. It began with images of Salvador Dalí's melting watch motif projected on to a white screen. Then the presenter, Lautita Valenzuela, greeted the sixteen nations of the 1969 Eurovision Song Contest.

I performed seventh – squeezed in between the Italian and Dutch performers. I wore a pink dress covered in red and white flowers. My backing singers, Sue and Sunny, wore dark blue. Afterwards the performers had to wait in a room as the votes were announced and counted. It was surreal. We were all trying not to make eye contact, or smiling nervously at each other.

I see shows today like *Pop Idol*, where young kids are voted off and then interviewed immediately afterwards. 'How does it feel?' they're asked. I want to scream at the television, 'How do you think it feels?' Shows like this are intrusive, abusive and horrible.

The Eurovision felt like a slow form of torture played out in front of an estimated audience of 250 million people. Mo told me afterwards that he had never seen me so nervous – not even on our wedding day. 'I could almost hear your heart beating.'

Early in the voting I was ahead, but then I slipped behind. With only Finland's votes still to be counted, Spain, Holland and France all had eighteen points and Britain had seventeen. The Finnish announcer calmly awarded four of his country's votes to Ireland and Italy – both lagging well behind and then gave me the single point I needed.

It took a few moments for the audience to realise what had happened. It was a tie – the first in Eurovision history. Four countries had finished with exactly eighteen points – Spain, Holland, France and Britain.

I felt nothing but relief. Imagine if three other countries had won. Technically, I would have finished fourth – a disaster, considering the burden of expectation I carried.

A few people in the audience called for a 'sing-off' or a recasting of votes, but all the joint winners were happy to let the result stand. None of us wanted to lose.

The winner was supposed to receive a gold cup from the sponsor – a Spanish sherry company – but they only had one cup. This meant there couldn't be a presentation, but none of us minded.

I flew back to the UK the next day. A scrum of reporters and photographers were waiting at Heathrow. 'I'm not disappointed that I didn't win outright. We were all worthy winners,' I told them. Asked about my immediate plans, I could only think about our two-week honeymoon. 'Then I'll take a month off and just be a housewife, nothing more.'

A day later we flew to the West Indies and then to Mexico's Acapulco Beach. Barry and his girlfriend Linda Gray came with us. It was incredibly hot. I had such pale skin that I couldn't spend all day lying beside the pool. They all went brown, while I turned a blotchy pink. I looked gorgeous – white skin, carrot-red hair and a pink nose!

We stayed at the Las Brisas Hotel in Acapulco, one of the most famous in the world. It had little pink haciendas, pink swimming pools and a pink-and-white-striped jeep. The place was full of celebrities and rich Americans. We spent a lot of time with Robert Culp and Bill Cosby, who were filming their TV series in Mexico.

Everybody seemed to be smoking Acapulco Gold, the strongest dope in the world. Mo, Barry and Linda were no exception. I finally decided, what the hell, I might as well try it. Taking a puff, I blinked through the smoke and wondered if anything was happening. Soon I became paranoid. I kept asking people, 'Did I just repeat myself? Am I making sense?'

After the fourth puff I curled up on the sofa and went straight to sleep. So that was it! Instead of getting high, I got sleepy.

I tried it only once more. Back in London after the honeymoon, Mo and I went round to Barry Gibb's penthouse in the city. Billy came with us. Apparently we smoked Acapulco Gold but I have no recollection of what happened next. By all accounts Billy and I finished up sitting on the floor of the lift, laughing uncontrollably, with Mo telling us to get up.

Of all the Eurovision winners that year, 'Boom Bang-a-Bang' became the biggest hit. In that sense Marian was right – it brought me a huge new audience across Europe. I was in demand to do concerts and TV specials, which meant being apart from Mo. I hated saying goodbye.

It felt nice to be married . . . comforting and secure. I called myself Mrs Gibb and ordered chequebooks in my married name. We talked about having children and wanted at least three or four.

I turned down a lot of offers because I didn't want to be separated from Mo. Tours of South America and Australia were out of the question. Even America seemed too far away. It was easier for me to cancel things. Mo was part of a group and had to consider the other Bee Gees.

I liked the fact that Billy and Mo were friends. They even decided to go into partnership, writing and producing hit records. Maurice did the melodies and Billy wrote the lyrics. Eventually they started their own company, Moby Productions ('Mo' for Maurice and 'By' for Billy).

Often when I went away Billy would stay with Mo and keep him company. He was also supposed to keep him out of trouble, but often the best laid plans . . . One afternoon Mo crashed his Bentley convertible after a long boozy lunch at San Lorenzo with Roberto Bassanini, who was soon to marry Cynthia Lennon.

Kinnerton Street was only a few minutes away and Mo made it almost all the way home before he clipped another car and drove head on into a deep gutter. He was only travelling at a few miles an hour, but it was enough to snap the chassis and write off the Bentley.

Mo hit his head on the windscreen and had blood leaking down his face. He ran inside the house before the neighbours arrived to investigate. He also had a quick brandy to calm his nerves.

The hospital was just around the corner. A nurse cleaned up the cut and it didn't seem so bad. Mo was more concerned about the Bentley. 'What car should I get next?' he asked.

I was tempted to say, 'A toy one.'

The Bee Gees' first two albums had produced a string of hits on both sides of the Atlantic – songs like 'To Love Somebody' and 'Massachusetts'. I was amazed by the cheques that would arrive for Mo, some of them for hundreds of thousands of pounds. He would leave them lying around the house or shove them in a drawer.

Mo didn't care about the size of his bank balance – he loved 'things'. Money was only important because it meant he could buy hi-fi equipment, cameras, projectors and editing devices. Every new gadget and new piece of technology had to be his.

Despite their success, The Bee Gees were always on the verge of splitting up. The rivalry between the brothers was obsessive, but at the same time there was a bond between them that was impossible to break. One couldn't have something without the other wanting it, whether it be a house, a particular car, or even a dog. Barry finished up getting his own Pyrenean mountain dog, which he called Barnaby.

Days after we married, Robin announced that he was quitting the band. The Bee Gees' next album went ahead without him. For the next eighteen months the brothers tried various solo projects, with mixed success, before being reunited in the summer of 1970.

They were a lovely family, but all of them had their problems. Even Robert Stigwood had private nicknames for them. He called them Pothead, Pillhead and Pisshead (Barry, Robin and Maurice). Their problems stemmed partly from sibling rivalry and partly from the pressure of being in the public eye from such an early age. It distorted their reality.

The best creative partnerships are often generated by tension, which can bring out the very best – and worst – in people; even more so if the partnership involves members of the same family.

The Gibb brothers were all talented, creative and highly strung. They had been performing since they were very young. They could say anything they liked to each other, whatever the criticism, but heaven help anybody from outside the family who did the same. The boys would immediately leap to each other's defence. I could understand this. I felt the same way about my family.

My own recording career seemed to be stuck in a rut. Mickie Most had turned me into a pure pop singer and it wasn't the only sort of music I wanted to be credited with. Given the choice, I wanted to go back to my first love – the rhythm and blues songs of my childhood.

The success of 'Shout' had given me enormous credibility as a rock singer. I was the girl with attitude. Nobody else sang like I did. Then I began making pop songs, which were successful in the charts but didn't lead to big album sales.

The music industry had fundamentally changed since the early sixties. Hit singles were OK, but the serious money was being made by best-selling albums, or bands like The Rolling Stones and Led Zeppelin who could fill huge stadiums. This was partly tied into the drug culture. Certain albums were almost made to order for people who wanted to kick back and chill out: albums like The Beatles' *White Album*.

The decision to go with Mickie had seemed like the right one. He was the proven hit-maker. However, songs like 'I'm a Tiger' and 'Boom Bang-a-Bang' were rinky-dink and lightweight. It drove me mad. I used to fight with Mickie, trying to convince him to do material that was more soulful and took advantage of the raw power of my voice.

When my contract with Mickie expired I didn't renew it. It was time to move on.

Jerry Wexler of Atlantic Records in America was quick to sign me. He thought I had a soulful voice and he wanted more songs like 'To Sir With Love'. I was tremendously flattered. Atlantic had released people I idolised like Ray Charles, Bobby Darin, Aretha Franklin and The Drifters.

I flew to Miami in 1969, taking Mum with me. We had to change planes twice and were completely exhausted by the time we arrived. It was Mum's first trip to America and she was very excited. Dad wouldn't come. He rarely left Glasgow, unless we dragged him.

Mum had turned her life around in the previous few years. Having never really been happy with her lot, she began searching for something more – something that was missing. It wasn't simply about love, or family, or the certainty of knowing her roots. She knew there had to be a better reason for living.

It still came as a total surprise when she announced that she was becoming a Mormon. I thought immediately of young men in suits knocking on doors.

'You didn't open the door did you, Mum?'

'Yes, I did. I had turned them away many times, but one day I invited them in. They were wonderful. What they said struck a chord inside me.'

Mum missed me terribly, but now she had another interest in her life. She had calmed down and didn't goad Dad into fights any more – or at least not as often. She had also given up alcohol, coffee and tea – even Coca-Cola. The withdrawal symptoms had given her terrible headaches, but these eventually faded.

For a long while she tried to convince me to accompany her to a service. She wanted me to understand her beliefs, but I think she was also hoping that she might convert me. Mormons are encouraged to bring their families into the church, which led to some colourful dialogue with Dad. As far as religion was concerned, he was best described as an abstainer, which is not the same thing as a non-believer.

Jerry Wexler met us at the airport and took me straight to the studio where I went over some songs that he hoped I might like. The plan was to review material and then come back to record the album at a later date.

A few days later I met Arif Mardin and Tom Dowd, who worked with Jerry. I felt both intimidated and flattered when I considered that these men had worked with people like The Drifters, Eric Clapton, Patti Labelle, Aretha Franklin and the Young Rascals. Jerry took us out to dinner and out fishing on his boat. He told stories about playing tambourine on several Ray Charles tracks and of hearing Aretha sing when she was only fifteen years old. I was in awe.

These men were consummate musicians. When we began recording at Mussel Shoals in Alabama, they would sometimes debate for hours as to whether a chord should change to a flat or a minor. I sat listening, unable to be involved, but amazed by their creative desire for perfection and their attention to detail. They would spend all day going through one part for the rhythm section, whereas in London I was used to recording three songs in an afternoon.

We did two albums together, *New Routes* and *Melody Fair*, both of which were well received in the States. Sadly this success didn't translate to the UK. Some people said I alienated myself from the British public by becoming too 'American' in style. Perhaps that's true. More likely I couldn't shake the 'pop star' label that had been attached to me.

The architect, designer and builders said it would take nine months to finish 'Woodley'. It took twice that long. No expense had been spared. Every piece of fabric and furniture had been carefully chosen.

One bedroom had become a walk-in wardrobe and another a billiard room. There were new bathrooms and a chef's kitchen, where I planned to cook roast lunches every Sunday.

Surprisingly, we already knew one of our neighbours. At a Beatles TV special in Manchester I had started chatting to Ringo Starr about houses. He had just married his long-time sweetheart Maureen Cox. They were living in the Surrey stockbroker belt, but Ringo wanted to move back to London.

I told him about 'Woodley' and said there was a house up for sale in the same quiet cul-de-sac. As it turned out, Ringo and Maureen moved in before we did.

Everybody seemed to gravitate towards 'Woodley'. I would often arrive home from rehearsals and find a crowd of people in the garden or the living room. Mo would be entertaining John Bonham, Keith Moon, Robert Plant, Ringo and Rod Stewart. Sometimes I invited whoever was on my TV show back for a drink – stars like The Carpenters, Harry Nilsson and Kenny Rogers.

We sat around, drinking and chatting, until invariably somebody picked up a guitar or sat at the piano. The jamming sessions sometimes lasted all night and featured some stunning performances. I wish I had recorded some of them.

Dudley Moore came round a lot. He would astonish everyone

with his brilliance as a pianist and then have us all in stitches by playing an entire song with a few perfectly placed notes off-key to create discord.

Later I did a TV series where Dudley was my guest every week. We used to go out filming silly sketches for the show. In a crowded restaurant one lunchtime he started doing his classic Derek and Clive routine. 'What are you fucking looking at? Don't you fucking look at me like that! You're a fucking . . .'

I started 'effing' and 'blinding' back at him, using every four-letter insult I could think of. The entire restaurant fell silent, listening to us. In the end, I couldn't keep a straight face. I was crying with laughter.

Mo was the perfect host for any party because he never wanted anybody to go home. He had turned a room downstairs into a 'cinema', with a big screen and projector. He would hire the latest movies from a shop in Bond Street and have film nights for all our friends.

At the same time he was making his own movies. The old air-raid shelter in the garden had been transformed into a makeshift film studio for all his camera equipment. He loved coming up with scripts and storylines. The sun would just be coming up and he and Ringo would be out in the back garden shooting a film. Maureen would be in the kitchen making fettucini for us all. Those are the mornings I remember best.

It was wonderful having friends like Ringo and Maureen living so close. We used to joke about building a tunnel between our houses to save us having to cross the road.

Mo could keep going night after night, but I needed to rest. I had rehearsals for my BBC TV series and couldn't perform without sleep. The doorbell would sometimes ring at three in the morning. Mo would go down in his dressing gown and open up the bar for Ringo or Rod Stewart.

At other times we'd all go out to Tramp or some other nightclub.

We always bumped into people we knew. Peter Sellers would be sitting next to Roman Polanski, who'd be next to George Harrison, who'd be next to Michael Caine.

For my twenty-first birthday in November 1969, Mo bought me a beautiful eternity ring and a diamond bracelet from Cartier. He organised a party at the 'Barracuda' on Baker Street. Tom Jones was there, as well as Little Richard, The Bee Gees, Roberto Bassanini and Cynthia. Mo ran proceedings, passing drinks, starting the singing and carrying the birthday cake.

When The Bee Gees were touring we saw less of each other but always tried to leave Sundays free. We slept until lunchtime and then I'd do a roast for family and friends.

I wasn't a genius in the kitchen, but I could do very basic wholesome food. Thankfully, Mo, like his brothers, had simple tastes. He could live on steak and chips or bacon and eggs.

Every time I flew to America I suffered from separation anxiety. I think this was a legacy of when I first left home and cried myself to sleep at night. I wanted Mo to come with me, but he had his own projects.

He was doing a stage show with Barbara Windsor called 'Sing a Rude Song' – a musical based on a cockney sparrow singer called Marie Lloyd who became a big music hall star. It opened at the Greenwich Theatre on the day before our first wedding anniversary.

Robert Stigwood picked me up and drove me to the theatre. I was nervous for Mo's sake. He needed a few drinks before, during and after to calm his nerves, he said. The show was good, although the first half was too long. Mo didn't let anyone down, but he needed more confidence.

The next day I wrote in my diary:

FEBRUARY 18TH 1970
Married a whole year today. Mo didn't have to be at the theatre until one, so we had a lovely breakfast. I gave him a

small portable TV that he wanted and he will buy my
present later. I don't know what. I do love Mo so much. I
finally got out of the house at about 3. I went to see
Marian.

Princess Alexandra and Angus Ogilvy came to the second night
of the show. I was there again, of course, trying to show Mo that
he had my love and support. I also knew I was leaving him for a
while. I flew to Miami the next day to finish vocal tracks for my
new album.

From there I went to New York to appear on *The David Frost
Show* and do a magazine interview with *Rolling Stone*. A week
after leaving London I was in Toron to to begin filming *The Andy
Williams Summer Replacement Show* for American TV.

Andy Williams was so popular in America that even his
replacement show was named after him. It was filmed in Canada
and my co-hosts were Ray Stevens, Mama Cass and the comedian
Steve Martin. It was produced by the same team that did *Laugh-in*
and *The Andy Williams Show*.

I had an enormous dressing room and there were stylists for my
hair and clothes. A lighting engineer actually asked me how I
wanted to be lit. Nobody had ever done that in Britain. It reinforced my opinion that in America management works for the
performer, while in Britain the performer works for management.

We started early in the morning and often didn't finish filming
until after ten at night. Then we'd all go to a restaurant or Ray
Stevens would arrange a party. Not surprisingly, it was sometimes
difficult to get my voice working next morning. At one point I was
singing 'Feeling All Right' and completely forgot the words.

Mo joined me for a few days when 'Sing a Rude Song' was
transferring to the West End. It was our only chance to see each
other for a month. Mo loved being around celebrities and was in
his element at the after-show parties and dinners.

On the last day of filming in Toronto – 30 May – Ray Stevens gave us each a gold pendant and we had a champagne party. Everybody cried. I flew back to London without telling Mo. I wanted to surprise him.

'Sing a Rude Song' had opened at the Garrick Theatre. Princess Margaret and Tony Armstrong-Jones came to the opening night party.

Mo was on a performance 'high' after the show and I was coming down from one. This is what happens when you live on a diet of applause and adrenalin. The impossible 'highs' have a bumpy ending as you come back down to earth.

# 10

# 'We Want Ruru!'

After two years of marriage, I still didn't feel grown-up or ready to start a family. Mo and I were like kids in the biggest candy store imaginable. We went to great restaurants, took holidays in the sun and bought presents for each other and all our friends.

Both of us loved shopping. We could spend hours in South Molton Street, Bond Street and King's Road. We discovered Gucci before it became hip and were regulars at Cartier, Aspreys and Garrards. We had clothes and boots made for us and thought nothing of flying to Paris for the day to shop.

Apart from cameras and recording equipment, Mo loved cars. He once bought a Rolls-Royce, took it back a week later and exchanged it for a Bentley. A week later he drove home in an Aston Martin.

Mo spent money without even thinking, which used to worry me. Eventually I introduced him to my accountant in the hope he would encourage Mo to keep track of his money and not fritter it away.

His brothers were equally compulsive. At one point Barry and

Robin questioned Robert Stigwood about how it was that Maurice could afford a big house in Highgate and they couldn't. It had to be explained to them that the house belonged to me. I had bought it with *my* money because I had taken care of my finances and been given the right advice.

Mo's parents, Barbara and Huey, had a house in Ibiza, and they loved company almost as much as they loved the sunshine. The first time I went with Mo, Barry and Linda. I couldn't remember ever having been on a holiday where I lived with a family. It was like an open house, with people coming and going. All the rooms opened on to the swimming pool and whatever time you dragged yourself out of bed there would be eggs and bacon cooking in the kitchen.

During the day we swam and sunbathed or rode scooters around the island, visiting bars and beaches. At night we played guitars, sang songs and made films.

Mo's parents were keen for their boys to buy houses in Ibiza, but none of them seemed very interested. I fell in love with the place and found a villa for sale that had been built by an English writer. It was set back from the road on the way to San Antonio, just on the other side of San Raphael. In those days San Antonio was tiny, with a couple of bars and discotheques.

Ibiza was then a hippy island, full of dope-smoking drop-outs, sailors, artists, poets, musicians and expats. Billy loved the place. He was always taking over my villa and inviting his friends. Even today I run into complete strangers who say, 'I once stayed in your house in Ibiza . . . with Billy.'

Jo Spoons, an Irish bar, was one of our favourite hang-outs. Another was Can Pau, a Catalan restaurant in the centre of the island, run by Jordi and his family. It had the same menu year in and year out. It reminded me of San Lorenzo – another family-run restaurant – and it too became a home away from home.

In late February I flew to Glasgow to perform at the Pavilion, one of the most famous venues in the city. Billy came with me and we ran the gauntlet of photographers and reporters at the airport. We went straight home to see Mum and Dad at their house in Mt Vernon. I then did the rounds of the relatives, visiting my aunties, Lizzie, Jeanie and Annie.

I was nervous about the show. Glaswegians are renowned for being the toughest audience in the world. 'If you can make it here, you can make it anywhere,' people used to say, and they weren't wrong.

There were lots of reasons why it was important for me to be accepted in Glasgow. There still are. For all the hardship, I remember my childhood with enormous fondness. I have a real need to belong to these people, because they raised me and discovered me and set me on my way. The older I get, the more emotional the journey home becomes. Loyalty is important to me, particularly when it comes to Scotland.

There were lots of friends in the audience. Neighbours and old schoolfriends had managed to find tickets; people who still called me 'Marie' and could remember me as a cheeky schoolgirl rather than a pop star.

They gave me a huge welcome, which made me feel very emotional. During the show I began singing an old Scottish song, 'My Ain Folk'. The audience took over and left me standing there with tears in my eyes. It was a wonderful moment.

After the concert I went to the City Chambers for an official reception. Willie Waddell, the manager of Rangers, was among the guests. Gordon, a huge fan at age eight, looked at him in awe. Willie shook his hand and I doubt if Gordon washed it ever again.

Being back in Glasgow made me think about how far I'd come in such a short time. Someone once said to me that our destiny is not about chance but about choice. In reality it is both. I had been blessed with a talent that could take me into concert halls around the world, but I had a choice about whether to leave Glasgow. And as much as I hated leaving home and cried myself to sleep, I never considered going back. I knew what I wanted.

Until recently I have never considered myself to be ambitious. I didn't like the word. It sounded like something to be ashamed of. Maybe this comes from growing up where I did. It wasn't wise to get ideas above your station.

At the same time, I must have had a hunger to succeed. I don't know if I dreamed of the fairytale – the big house in Highgate, buying jewellery at Cartier, eating at fine restaurants, flying first class and living in luxurious hotel suites. At first it was just about singing. Everything else seemed to come along with it.

I wasn't afraid to work, but I think a part of me was frightened of stopping working. Having tasted success I didn't want to lose it. In addition to this, I had inherited responsibility for a whole string of people.

When Marian and Gerry divorced I became Marian's major source of income. Consequently, it was important for her that I keep working. The same was true of drivers, secretaries, musical directors, my band, producers . . . everyone working closely with me. I was also helping Mum and Dad financially and supporting Billy, Edwina and Gordon at various times.

To me it seemed natural. All my life I had been taking responsibility for people – ever since I was five years old and would look after Billy. Now it was simply on a much larger scale and my successes and failures were magnified.

Late that night, after the reception was over, I caught a plane back to London. The following morning I caught an early flight to Los Angeles to catch up with Mo, who was touring America with The Bee Gees. Robin was back with the band and all three brothers had a house in Malibu, which had been rented for the Californian leg of the tour.

Mo had been away for five weeks – the longest we had ever been separated since we'd been married. In the past we'd always tried to limit our trips to ten days. To keep this promise I had gone on tour with The Bee Gees to Germany and also Japan.

In Tokyo I caused quite a stir because of my profile. I was in the audience at The Bee Gees concert when the crowd started chanting. It sounded like, 'We . . . wan . . . Ruru! We . . . wan . . . Ruru!'

The sound rolled forward in waves. 'What are they saying?'

'They're calling for you,' said Linda Gibb.

The chant grew louder and louder, but I knew I couldn't go on stage. This wasn't my tour. I had to stand back and play the dutiful wife.

Another potentially awkward moment happened in California when we came across Davy Jones and his wife. By that stage the popularity of The Monkees had started to wane and the TV series had been axed. Davy and the band were trying to make it on their own.

All the Gibb boys were really pleased to meet him. 'Look, it's Davy Jones. Come and join us.'

'You and Lulu know each other, don't you?' said Barry.

Davy and I looked at each other and I gave him a very abrupt, 'Hi!' I couldn't completely forgive him for what had happened.

After the final concert of the tour in late February, Mo and I flew back to London. Arriving in Heathrow at 7.30 a.m., we immediately caught a flight to Zurich. Then we waited two hours for a train and didn't reach San Moritz until late afternoon. I was shattered.

Ringo and Maureen had organised a skiing holiday and San Moritz was the place to be seen. After tea and a shower we were dragged off to a party thrown by Gunther Sachs, a multi-millionaire and the ex-husband of Brigitte Bardot. Christina Onassis was there, along with a host of European playboys and debutantes. Sergio Mendes and his band played. I didn't get to bed until 4.30 a.m.

Ringo woke Mo at ten to go skiing but I couldn't get out of bed.

By the time he came back to the hotel he had bought himself all the gear. I was annoyed that he was heading off without me so I stayed in the hotel in protest.

Next morning I finally bought some ski gear and made it on to the slopes. We were all beginners apart from Ringo, but the instructors lavished us with praise, telling us we were all destined to be champions.

I don't know how we managed to ski at all considering the late-night parties and drinking we did. We danced at the discos until midnight and then did a circuit of the parties. If none of them was any good, we went back to the hotel and jammed until the early hours.

After six days of this we had another horribly long journey back to London. That didn't stop us going straight to Tramp and staying out until four in the morning. We were young and had boundless energy.

A few weeks later a visitor turned up at 'Woodley'. It took me a few moments to place him. It was Hans, our ski instructor from San Moritz. I suddenly remembered that we'd invited him to visit us in London.

One of the few pieces of unsolicited advice I would ever give to someone is never take your ski instructor out of the mountains. Don't even invite him to dinner. What seems like a good idea when you're sharing schnapps in front of a log fire in an alpine bar is disastrous when transferred to sea-level.

To begin with, once you take snow out of the equation you have absolutely nothing in common. I struggled to even understand what Hans was saying. It was as though his accent became broader the further he got from Switzerland. Having taken up residence in our spare room, he emptied the fridge, took long baths, ran up a huge phone bill and kept following me around the house like an overgrown puppy dog.

*

Barry and Mo were always writing scripts and playing around with cameras. During one of Robin's periodic absences, they decided to make a TV special called *Cucumber Castle*. It was filmed at Robert Stigwood's mansion in Stanmore, with the interiors shot in the barn. The director was Mike Mansfield, who was well known for his pop videos.

The plot takes some explaining. Set in medieval times, two brothers, Frederic and Marmaduke, inherit their dying father's kingdom. One takes over the Kingdom of Cucumber and the other the Kingdom of Jelly. Basically the film consisted of their brotherly squabbles (rather true to life), and included a duel, a classic string quartet, a concert and a tennis game.

The dialogue was just plain silly. Open the script on any page and it contained exchanges similar to this:

'Here we go riding through the castle grounds. Is that you, Frederic?'

'Yes, it is, Marmaduke.'

'Look! What's that I see on yonder hill?'

'I think it's a damsel in distress.'

'Good gracious! I think we should save her, Frederic.'

'Good idea, Marmaduke.'

Then they'd burst into song. It was almost parody. I was the fair maiden, of course, and spent my time wearing wench-like dresses and being rescued. It was such a laugh.

*Cucumber Castle* featured five new Bee Gees songs and was shown on BBC TV in 1971. Since then it has gained a sort of cult status on Internet web sites and chat rooms.

My other experience of movie-making that year proved equally disastrous. I agreed to appear in a film called *The Cherry Picker*, starring, among others, Patrick Cargill, Spike Milligan, Terry-Thomas, Jack Hulbert and Wilfrid Hyde-White.

My leading man, Bob Sherman, played a hippy drop-out who

tries to commit suicide but is rescued by a young girl – namely me. The most embarrassing moment was a bedroom scene that we filmed on a wet little boat in Spain. It had been pouring with rain for days and everything was damp.

The scene wasn't explicit – at least not by today's standards. All Bob and I had to do was some passionate kissing and rolling around. The rest was left to the audience's imagination. Even so, I worked myself into a blind panic in the days beforehand.

'How can you do a love scene with someone you don't fancy?'

'That's what you call acting,' replied Marian. 'But don't ask me to do it.'

In truth, it would probably have been worse if I'd fancied Bob. I would have been shy and clumsy.

On the night before filming the love scene I barely slept. I arrived on set with dark rings under my eyes and an outbreak of nervous acne. About a dozen people were crammed into the cabin, with camera equipment taking up the rest of the room. The only spare space was on the bed.

I had a towel around me and was allowed to wear underwear underneath. It certainly wasn't *Last Tango in Paris*.

The two-minute love scene took all day to film. It was painstakingly slow, with lots of stopping and starting as shots were taken from different angles. My mouth hurt from kissing and I had Bob slobbering in my hair. I kept asking myself, Why am I putting myself through this? I'm not an actress. Stop trying to be something you're not.

The indoor scenes were filmed in Britain. Most days I travelled to and from the studio with Wilfrid Hyde-White, a marvellous character actor. I adored his twinkling eyes and wonderful sense of humour. He told me amazing stories of working on the London stage and going to Hollywood in the thirties.

*The Cherry Picker* ran out of money before it could be finished.

One of history's worst love scenes sank without trace – which is probably best for all concerned.

Thankfully, my music career was on a firmer footing. Almost without noticing, I had started concentrating more on cabaret work and TV series, rather than trying to find hit singles. I wasn't the dangerous-sounding teenager who had emerged from Glasgow six years earlier. (Marian used to say that I was the first punk.) I had grown up a lot since then and it was time to prove my versatility.

When I did 'Shout' all the young kids loved it, but a lot of the older generation – my mother's era – said, 'Is that all she can do? "Shout".'

This was like a red rag to a bull. 'What's wrong with them?' I said. 'Don't they know how difficult it is to sing that song?'

Clearly, I still had something to prove. Cabaret and TV appearances gave me the chance to sing many different songs. I also worked with wonderful international stars like Kenny Rogers, Glen Campbell, Jack Jones, Wilson Pickett and Stevie Wonder.

Very few people had made the jump from pop star to family entertainer. Cilla Black, Cliff Richard and Pat Boone were among them. Billy, for one, thought I was making a mistake tying myself in to television. He wanted me to concentrate on a recording career and worried that I would lose touch with the music scene. I thought I could do both.

At that moment I felt invincible. Everything I touched turned to gold. I had people fighting to book me and offers coming in from around the world. Nothing seemed beyond me.

I began 1971 with a new TV series for the BBC and followed up with a cabaret season at the Flamingo Hotel in Las Vegas. I had heard so many stories about Vegas but had no desire to go there.

Marian made the decision. Like most things in Vegas, it came down to money.

I will never forget flying over the Nevada Desert and looking down to see all those neon lights plonked in the sand. It was the middle of the day and the sun was shining, yet the lights were still flashing.

I don't know what I expected. People talked about Vegas like it was the Holy Grail of entertainment. It was synonymous with Frank Sinatra, Dean Martin, the Rat Pack and Elvis.

The place I discovered wasn't just seedy at the edges, it was cheap and tacky right to the core. The theme hotels were fairgrounds lit up with incandescent lights of livid pink, cyanic blue, methyl green and fuchsia. Yet behind the garishness and fake glitz there was a poverty of spirit and a nasty smell.

I had star billing at the Flamingo Hotel, one of the oldest on the strip. The cabaret facilities were amazing and the technical staff had a slickness that is a typical feature of working in America.

My show had been produced in the UK especially for Vegas. I had a lighting plot and full musical arrangements, as well as a wardrobe of costume changes. The expensive dresses and miniskirts had been hand-sewn with bugle beading and designed so that I could dance in them.

Finishing my second show one night, I came back to my suite and found three messages from Tom Jones. Each was a little more insistent. He was having drinks with Frank Sinatra. Did I want to come?

I couldn't believe it! Sinatra was the king. Nobody could touch him. All of my relations were mad about him and, growing up in Glasgow, everyone had tried to sing like him – even the women. They would tilt their heads the way Sinatra did and put their hands in their pockets.

'When somebody loves youuuuu. It's no good unless he loves youuuuuuu. Aaaaaall the way . . .'

I grabbed Mo and we took a taxi to Caesar's Palace. Tom and Frank were in one of the bars, sitting in a quiet corner with a young Chinese woman and a few other people. Halfway across the floor, I bounced off someone's chest.

'Excuse me, lady, where ya headin?'

'Um, well, we're here to see Mr Sinatra and Mr Jones. We've been invited.'

Mo had gone rather quiet. Right at that moment Frank stood up and beckoned us to the table. He kissed me on the cheek and motioned for me to sit down next to him.

I can't begin to explain what it felt like to meet my idol. Sinatra was the biggest star in the world. He was a god-like figure, with a reputation that was almost too large to fit into a human being. He had performed a single concert in Glasgow in the fifties and I had grown up hearing people say, 'I was there the night Sinatra sang.' Others would react with envy or awe.

Now I was sitting next to him. I kept telling myself to be cool and not say anything foolish. I had this image in my head of Mum and Dad. I wished they could have been there. We started talking about star signs and he said he was a Capricorn. I couldn't remember what that signified, although I remembered that Scott Walker and Davy Jones were both Capricorns.

Frank asked if I'd ever had singing lessons, or if I did vocal exercises before going on stage. I told him no.

'Well it's important that you do. I can show you some.' He had a voice like honey.

I still kick myself that I didn't follow up his invitation. I should have called him but I was too shy. I had this big thing about not over-stepping the mark. I didn't want to be pushy. It was stupid of me.

Marian was the sort of woman who believed that nobody should be taken by surprise. 'Shock is not a good look,' she used to say, which is probably why she never left the house without putting on her make-up and making sure every strand of hair was in place.

With this philosophy in mind, she took me aside one day and explained that I had to keep a very big secret. On 10 May 1972 I was to wear my best clothes and have my hair done.

'Why?'

'I can't tell you.'

'Do I have a meeting?'

'Yes . . . in a manner of speaking. A TV producer wants to see you.'

I knew something was up, but Marian wouldn't tell me any more. After rehearsing for my show that day, she ushered me to a waiting car and we drove to another studio. We arrived at the back entrance and she followed me up some steps.

Suddenly I was caught in a blaze of light. Eamonn Andrews held out the red book. 'Marie McDonald McLaughlin Lawrie, this is your life!'

I did my best to look absolutely stunned. In a sense I was. I was twenty-three years old, for goodness sake! Why would anyone want to know about *my* life?

I thought the whole idea was ridiculous, but I played along. Mo was there, of course, along with Mum, Dad, Billy, Edwina and Gordon. The researchers had even managed to find the Punch & Judy man from Rothesay Bay. It's a wonder anyone watching understood a word with all the Scottish accents.

Sidney Poitier filmed a lovely tribute. 'I'm sure you'll live for ever,' he said. They also played the record I made at the age of eight at the recording booth in Glasgow.

Some of the people they rolled out were very obscure. Eamonn would say, 'Do you remember this voice?'

And I'd think, Not a bloody clue.

Then I'd have to look surprised and pretend it was the most amazing reunion. Throughout the show I looked as though I was constantly on the verge of tears. Everyone assumed I was extremely emotional, but in reality I had a blocked tear duct, which was very annoying.

Afterwards I made the entire family vow that they would never do this to me again. They will *not* be forgiven.

Later in the year I began rehearsals for the Christmas production of 'Peter Pan' at the Opera House in Manchester. I was a surprise choice for the role, because this was the play, not the American musical. The lead role was coveted by serious dramatic actresses and had never been offered to someone like me.

I was flattered but also daunted. The list of serious actresses who had played Peter Pan read like a page from *Who's Who* and included the likes of Maggie Smith, Dorothy Tutin, Julia Lockwood, Sylvia Syms, Nina Boucicault and Sarah Churchill.

'Peter Pan' had been produced for the stage every year since 1904, with only two exceptions during the war: 1939 and 1940.

We did some of the rehearsals in London and the rest in Manchester. The first time I put on the harness to practise flying, I almost demolished the scenery, but quickly learned how to be more accurate.

Every so often I'd make the mistake of referring to the show as a pantomime. The director would inform me in no uncertain terms, 'It is *not* a pantomime! It is a children's play.'

I don't think I had any idea what I was getting myself into. My previous acting experience had always been in minor roles. Now I had to capture the essence of this small, ethereal character, who was so mercurial that he couldn't be tied down.

I knew people would question having a pop singer in the role, but I took up the challenge. I can't remember what the critics had to say about the play, but I do know that we broke the box office records that had stood for sixty years.

*

Very rarely are there single defining moments in life. Normally a whole combination of things will lead us in one direction or the other. The drip, drip, drip of knowledge and experience weighs on the scales until the balance is tipped. That's how it was with my marriage to Mo.

For all the parties, presents, tearful partings and reunions, we didn't know how to get along with each other. A lot of the time we fought like cat and dog and then made up again. Tears before bedtime would become kisses afterwards.

Mo was a fantastic, gentle and loving man, but he was also very young and he drank too much. Every night we either went out or had people over. I normally went to bed by one or two in the morning, but Mo kept partying until the last person had gone. He was rarely out of bed before mid-afternoon.

He often had his first beer with breakfast.

'Do you have to start so early?' I'd say.

'It's already the afternoon,' he'd reply.

On the days Mo went to the office, he would immediately take Billy over the road to the Beer Cellar for a few pints and shots of schnapps. They drank whisky and dry back in the office while they worked. Mo would get home at five or six and carry on drinking until Ringo came over and they broke out the bourbon.

Mo wasn't an angry or a sullen drunk. He was a lot like my father in many ways – he needed a few drinks to loosen up and overcome his shyness.

Sometimes I joined him, but only up to a certain point. I had been around alcoholics all my life and, like my mother, I knew when to stop drinking and I didn't *have* to start.

APRIL 25TH 1972
Watched two horror films until 3.00 a.m. Mo was drunk
and stoned. I wanted to go to bed early. We argued which

has been happening a lot lately. I feel tense (when he
drinks). Then we made up.

To the world our marriage seemed perfect. I didn't try to
change that perception. I didn't want anybody to know what it
was really like. I was exhausted a lot of the time and increasingly
prone to bronchitis and throat infections. Sometimes I fell asleep
in the dressing room before a show.

The stress of work and the arguments with Mo took their toll
on me physically. At one point I was suffering from terrible
cramps and none of the doctors knew why. It was diagnosed as an
infection and I was confined to bed for weeks. Mo wanted to stay
with me but was in the middle of recording an album. At times
like that I knew I was still in love with him.

I felt guilty. What did I have to complain about? I was married
to a man who adored me. I holidayed in Ibiza and San Moritz. My
friends were successful, creative and talented. My mother and
father had managed to sustain a marriage with far more serious
problems. I was being selfish and immature.

At the same time, I promised myself I would never go through
what my parents did. Their fighting and aggression had impacted
upon the lives of their children. I didn't want that to happen if Mo
and I started a family.

As much as I loved Mo, he could be extremely frustrating. He
used to tell fantastic stories, but some were based more on truth
than others. This didn't bother him at all. During interviews I
would sit beside him and listen to him tell anecdotes about how we
met or the people he knew. All the while I'd think, What on earth
is he saying? That didn't happen.

I remember him telling a story in a radio interview about the
time we spent the weekend with John Lennon and Yoko Ono.
Afterwards I said to him, 'We never did that.'

He simply shrugged. It didn't matter to him.

Billy confronted him one day and accused him of telling stories. Mo looked surprised. 'What do you mean?'

'What you're saying didn't happen.'

'Yes it did.'

'Come on, Mo, you don't have to make things up. The truth is interesting enough.'

Mo wouldn't back down and Billy became so angry that he wanted to hit him.

Another time it was John Bonham who stopped Mo in mid-story and called his bluff. Again Mo simply shrugged it off.

I don't know why he felt the need to embellish or exaggerate incidents. Maybe it had something to do with the influence of Robert Stigwood, who never let the truth stand in the way of a publicity coup for The Bee Gees. If you do this often enough there must come a time when you start forgetting what's real and what's invented.

If we hadn't both been so busy, the truth about our marriage would probably have emerged sooner. Instead we papered over the cracks and carried on. I hated giving in or admitting that my marriage was failing. I desperately wanted to make things work.

During the summer I was back in Las Vegas doing a season at the Riviera Hotel, where Dean Martin was a regular. Stewart Morris came over to produce the show, along with Alyn Ainsworth, my musical director.

The BBC wanted to get some footage for the new series, *Lulu in Vegas*. I went to see Dean Martin performing on the first night, along with Marian and Janey, who had come with me. Mo had stayed in London, but was hoping to join me in a week's time.

Ray Stevens was also doing the Riviera. It was like old-home week as we reminisced about our time in Canada, working with Mama Cass and Steve Martin.

I stayed in Vegas until the end of June with Mo, and then we both flew to LA where Mo caught a flight to New Zealand to meet up with The Bee Gees.

I wrote in my diary:

> When he looks at me the way he does, I feel I never want to leave him. There is so much love and I am very lucky. When I dropped him off at the plane I wanted to run after him. I don't want to be on my own.

I had no role models when it came to marriage – certainly not my parents or any of the people around me. Marian was already divorced and John and Cynthia didn't last. A lot of other music marriages were also destined to fail.

The crucial moment for me came late in 1972 when I went to see my gynaecologist, George Pinker. He was a lovely man, who later delivered both of Princess Diana's babies. He went grey overnight when he became involved with the Royals.

During a regular check-up at his Harley Street office, he said, 'So now you've been married for a while, are you thinking of having children?'

It was a simple enough question, yet I burst into tears. I couldn't believe it and neither could he.

'Oh, my goodness,' he flustered, 'I'm sorry if I upset you.'

I was convulsing with sobs. It was almost like a release. He handed me his handkerchief and waited until I calmed down.

'I can't have children yet,' I whispered.

'Why?'

'I'm not sure . . . right now things are difficult. Maurice and I are . . .' I couldn't finish.

'Well, if you have difficulties in your marriage I know someone you can talk to,' he said gently. 'She is a psychologist and a marriage guidance counsellor . . .'

I went to see her a few days later, feeling anxious and frustrated.

I didn't think I'd be able to talk about Mo, but she spoke very calmly and gently.

'I don't know if I can have babies,' I said, tearfully. 'I don't know if my marriage . . . I don't know . . . I just . . .' I couldn't get the words out. They stuck in my throat.

She asked very pertinent questions and I told her about Mo and the fights and how unhappy I had become. How could I possibly have a child? It would be a disaster.

After two hours of pouring my heart out I was exhausted. I looked at her, hoping for an answer.

'You know exactly what you should do,' she said.

'What do you mean?'

'You know the answer already.'

'Are you saying I should leave the marriage?'

'Only you can make that decision. You're only young. So is Maurice. If you decide the marriage can't work you both have plenty of time to find someone else . . .'

'Can't we just split up for a while . . . have a trial separation?'

'You could do that,' she said. 'Maybe things will get better. At the same time, it could also mean that you're avoiding the inevitable. The first thing that you must decide is whether there is something *worth* saving.'

I was in tears again. At that moment I realised my marriage had to end. How was I going to tell Maurice? 'Oh, my God! He'll go mad. He's still in love with me.'

'Would you like to send him to me?' she said. 'I'll talk to him.'

At home that evening I told Mo what the counsellor had said. He wouldn't listen.

'There's nothing wrong with our marriage. You're just feeling run-down. We should take a holiday. Let's go to Ibiza . . .'

'I can't. I have to work.'

'Cancel the concerts. You need a break.'

I begged him to see the counsellor, but he continued to refuse until I issued an ultimatum. For the next two weeks I called her and asked, 'Has he made an appointment?'

'No.'

'He said he was going to call you.'

'He hasn't.'

When I confronted him about this he spun another story about why he hadn't called. This became a habit. He was always witnessing terrible accidents, or having to rescue cats from trees. I knew it was all fantasy.

'Do you think I'm stupid?' I screamed. 'Do you really expect me to believe that?'

He looked hurt and questioned why I was being so hard on him.

This went on for weeks. I started checking out his stories so that I could prove he was lying. Still he persisted with them and I became even angrier. I hit him and physically shook him, wanting to rattle the truth from inside him. Mo was such a gentle soul he would hold me off and he never once retaliated. He knew I was half crazed.

I had aches and pains all over my body. I went to the doctor and had dozens of tests, convinced I had some mystery illness. It turned out to be frustration. I was so tense and coiled up inside that everything ached.

Billy was living with us through most of this time. He was a distraction from the fighting, but also found himself being dragged into the middle. It was very difficult for him because he and Mo were business partners. At the same time, he could see that I was unhappy.

Most evenings we were surrounded by so many people that Mo and I didn't have to relate to each other and could avoid the issue. It wasn't a marriage – it was party planning.

I was asleep by the time he crawled into bed beside me. And in the morning he was still sleeping when I left for rehearsals. Of an afternoon I'd come home determined to confront him. I pleaded with him to see the counsellor. 'I'm not the one who needs help,' he argued. 'You're the one who's nuts.'

I wasn't begging him to go because I *wanted* to end our marriage. Quite the opposite. I clung to the hope that the counsellor would discover some detail that would save it. Perhaps she could help Mo to find his truth and something would just click. Our marriage would be turned around.

If not, then I wanted Mo to hear the truth from someone who was objective and qualified. I knew he wouldn't listen to me.

Finally he promised to go and I vowed to accept no more excuses. That afternoon I phoned the counsellor. 'Is he there?'

'No.'

I waited fifteen minutes and called again.

He still hadn't arrived. I wanted to kill him. An hour later he turned up. Meanwhile, I waited at home, sitting on a sofa, clutching my knees and biting my bottom lip. What would Mo say? What would he do?

When he came through the door he shrugged off his jacket and poured himself a drink.

'What did she say?' I asked softly.

He shrugged. 'She said to me there is nothing wrong with our marriage, but you definitely need help.'

I was in shock. Had she really said that? I picked up the phone and called her, repeating word for word what Mo had said to me.

'Of course I didn't say that,' she said. 'I told him exactly what I told you: you're both very young, things haven't been working out and you should seriously consider whether your marriage has any future.'

'And what did he say?'

'He was perfectly reasonable.'

I couldn't stay married to Mo after that. I was at risk of hating him, which he didn't deserve. For weeks I walked around in a daze, crying at the drop of a hat. I fluctuated wildly from wanting to stay with Mo and realising it was impossible.

Over Christmas we put on a brave face for our families. I kept saying in interviews that everything was fine, not wanting to have my private life dissected in the pages of magazines and newspapers.

Early in the New Year Mo was due to tour America and I was going to Hong Kong for an arts festival. We decided that by the time I returned he would have left the house. Neither of us mentioned the word divorce. For the moment we would simply stay friends.

The official announcement took everyone by surprise. Photographers and journalists set up camp outside the house and followed me to and from the studios. Mo and I had agreed to say as little as possible and not give interviews. I fixed a smile and tried to ignore the questions.

A few days later Mo flew out of London to join his brothers. He broke our agreement and spoke to journalists, saying that he was upset and confused. 'I don't want to leave her. I'm still in love with her. I've done everything to please her. I should have loved us to have a baby, but she was always working.'

I was furious. I issued the one and only statement I ever made about my marriage, denying the split had anything to do with my career.

'He's a terrific guy. I love him dearly but we cannot live with each other.' The statement ended: 'Typical of Maurice is his reported remark that if we met now we would go out and get drunk.'

# The Man Who Sold
the World

My first public appearance after the announcement was at the Talk of the Town nightclub in Southend. I looked at the audience and asked myself, What do they really think about me? Do they blame me? Was it my fault?

I felt responsible for Mo. I had hurt him. Stupid me for getting married! I should have listened to my brother and brother-in-law.

Mo and I had been two spoiled little pop stars, with too much money and not enough sense. Everybody said 'yes' to us. Nobody told me where to get off. We were too young and bound up in ourselves to get married.

Each night at Southend I managed to get through the show. I realised that no-one was judging me or accusing me of anything. Couples break up every day, although perhaps not quite so publicly.

My parents were upset. Mum asked me if I was making the right decision.

'I wasn't happy,' I confessed.

'It's not all about happiness.'

She was talking about her own marriage, of course, but I still felt angry. The idea that people *have* to stay married regardless of how much pain they cause each other is madness. Apart from their own misery, they blight the lives of their children.

A lot of people were taken by surprise by the break-up because I had kept my unhappiness secret. Most of my friends understood. Some couldn't believe that Mo and I had stayed together as long as we did. Paul and Linda McCartney took the opposite view. They reprimanded me at a party one night, saying that marriage was for keeps. This is absolutely true, of course, but it's an easy thing to say when you make the right choice first time round. What if you make a mistake?

My sadness lasted for months. It was like a black cloud that only ever lifted when I was performing. For those few minutes, or hours, I could forget everything else and let the songs carry me away.

Mum always said I had an 'old soul' and was grown up before my time, but my success had created a bubble around me and now that had burst. The real world was a much harsher and lonelier place.

I threw myself into work. I had a new ten-week TV series, *It's Lulu*, as well as regular cabaret bookings at clubs around the country and overseas. In many ways I had two separate careers – one in America and one in the UK. Audiences on each side of the Atlantic expected something different.

It was a lot quieter without Mo around. I still cooked Sunday lunches and invited people back for drinks or dinner. Slowly I began to relax and enjoy being single again. The press speculated whenever I was seen out with a man, but most were just friends. David Frost took me to the West End opening of *Live and Let Die*, the new Bond film. It was never going to be a romance from my point of view, but he was funny, intelligent and I loved his company.

Being single second time around was different. For one thing I had lots of offers. I could have sown entire fields of wild oats, but I stopped short of becoming a wild woman. On the other hand, I didn't let the grass grow under my feet.

For years I had been having my hair done at Leonards of Mayfair in Grosvenor Place, around the corner from the American Embassy. Finding the right hairdresser wasn't just a matter of life and death – it was more important than that. Every time I changed my style it was written up in magazines and newspapers. I went from long to short, flick in, flick out, bob . . . and back again. With me it was all about the hair. My mother had been just the same.

Clifford Stafford had initially cut my hair, and then I began using Leonard. He was very sweet, but he occasionally made me nervous with some of his suggestions. He once cut my hair so short I looked bald. It might have looked great on someone else, but on me it looked ridiculous.

Leonard's other exasperating trait was taking long lunches and not being available when I needed him. I told him that I wanted somebody who would be there for me. He suggested John Frieda.

John had been one of Leonard's star pupils and had become a brilliant hairdresser in his own right. His attention to detail was astonishing. As a junior he had made himself indispensable at the salon. He would polish, shine and clean every implement, making sure it was always at Leonard's fingertips.

John barely said a word the first few times he cut my hair. He was average height, with dark hair and a serious demeanour. He gave me the impression of being shy but quietly intelligent.

I was still married to Mo at that stage and I didn't think of John as anything other than my hairdresser. We talked a lot about people and the problems of the world. We had similar tastes in music and were both interested in spirituality and Eastern mysticism.

John's grandfather had been a barber in Fleet Street and his father had followed in his footsteps. He worked at the Hyde Park Hotel and later opened his own hairdressing salon in Ealing.

His family had been Polish Jews who came to England in the 1890s. He told me a story about how his great-grandfather had been given a piece of land in Poland when they emancipated the serfs. He neglected it, but his son Samual, who was only nine years old, took over the land and made it productive.

Another relative, a great-uncle, had been foreman at a steel mill in Middlesbrough and was the first person in England to 'roll the beam' – a procedure which removed all the imperfections in the metal. John liked to think of himself as being a combination of these two men.

It wasn't until a year after Mo had left that I began to look at John in a different light. I can remember the moment. He was styling my hair and he said that he didn't want to be a hairdresser all his life.

'What would you do?'

'I don't know. Maybe I'll go and live on a mountaintop in Tibet.'

I know that might sound a little corny, but it completely caught my attention. I thought it was a wonderfully romantic image.

The last thing I expected or wanted was to fall for someone again. I couldn't believe what was happening between us. It was electric.

When I was touring or doing a cabaret outside of London, John would often travel long distances after work just to see me for a few hours. Once or twice he almost fell asleep at the wheel on the drive home.

It wasn't until fourteen months after the split with Mo – on 9 June 1974 – that the *Sunday Express* ran the headline: 'HAS LULU FALLEN IN LOVE WITH THE MAN WHO DOES HER HAIR?'

They were only speculating but it did make me think: Am I in love with him?

Sitting in a hotel lobby in Sheffield, I was discussing the details of my next TV series with John Ammonds of the BBC. I had worked with John many times before and he was a typical producer-type, with corduroy trousers, a cardigan and a bushy moustache.

A splash of orange caught my eye. I looked up and saw David Bowie – or more precisely Ziggy Stardust – waiting at the reception desk for his key. He looked like a painted stick insect with his white face, carrot-coloured hair, thin limbs and platform boots.

He turned and grinned like a Cheshire cat. 'Lulu!' Next moment he was sitting down with us. I thought John was going to choke on his pipe.

I loved Bowie. I remember first hearing his music at Billy's flat off Marylebone High Street. 'You have to hear this album,' Billy had said, turning the volume up loud on *Hunky Dory*. It blew me away.

Not long after that I met David at a recording studio in Los Angeles. I arrived to put a vocal on a track and noticed a weird-looking, emaciated character sitting in one of the studios. It was Iggy Pop.

David walked in and we were both excited about meeting each other. Iggy kept looking at me really dangerously. If looks could kill I would have been a goner. Maybe he regarded me as competition.

In Sheffield David was nearing the end of a sell-out nationwide tour.

'Come to the gig tonight,' he said. 'I'll send a car to pick you up.'

The concert was amazing – the best I had ever seen. It was pure theatre and I think John Ammonds was almost in shock. I doubt if he had seen anything like it in his life.

After the concert I had to do my own show at a club in Sheffield. Arriving back at the hotel, I found a note: 'Come upstairs. We're having a party.'

David's band, road crew and entourage had taken over the upstairs bar. Angie Bowie was there, along with her American boyfriend. People were drinking, smoking dope and singing around the piano. David wanted to show me videos of his recent concert tour of Japan. He talked about Kabuki make-up and showed me what he'd learned.

Although I had never thought David looked particularly sexy, there was an aura about him. It was the way he moved and measured people up. When he focused on me I felt like the only person in the room . . . in the universe.

He was very charming and not at all fey. Instead he was like a chameleon. He could be 'Jack-the-lad' – very manly and tough-talking – and then suddenly become attentive and flirtatious. This fascinated and excited me.

When the party began winding down, he asked me to stay. Some people have beautiful hands or beautiful necks, but I discovered that night that David had beautiful thighs – the best I had ever seen. I had my own private viewing – up close and personal!

At some point in the early hours I went back to my room. I had a phone call from David. 'I want us to work together,' he said. 'Let's make a hit record.'

Yeah, yeah, I thought. Let's see if he's all talk.

'I'll give you a call next week.'

I didn't expect to hear from him again. We'd had our little fling and that would be that. But it wasn't. He followed through – not once, but again and again.

In late July he called to invite me to the last gig of his Ziggy Stardust tour at the Hammersmith Odeon in London. An amazing cast of people turned up, including some of the biggest names in rock music.

During the show David announced his retirement to the crowd of 3,500. 'This has been one of the greatest tours of our lives,' he said. 'I would like to thank the band. I would like to thank our road crew. I would like to thank our lighting people . . . Of all of the shows on this tour, this particular show will remain with us the longest because not only is it the end of the tour, but it is the last show that we'll ever do. Thank you.'

There was a shocked silence. Then people began crying and calling out, 'No!'

David had been touring and promoting his albums for nearly a year without a break. He was exhausted. Even so, how could he contemplate retiring?

Only later did it emerge that he was 'retiring' Ziggy Stardust. He was sick of touring and wanted to concentrate on movies and recording instead.

The retirement party at the Café Royal in Regent Street was labelled 'The Last Supper' by music journalists. People were invited at the last minute, but still turned up, including Paul and Linda McCartney, Keith Moon, Peter Cook and Dudley Moore, Cat Stevens, Ringo and Maureen, Mick and Bianca Jagger, Jeff Beck, Lou Reed, Barbra Streisand, Ryan O'Neal, Marc Bolan, Sonny Bono, Elliott Gould and Britt Ekland.

Someone had organised a velvet-covered throne for David, who enjoyed being the centre of attention. Later he slipped away from the head of the table and sat down next to me. We talked about working on a single. He liked the idea of producing me singing one of his songs.

The following week I went to see him at the Hyde Park Hotel. He played several tracks for me. We couldn't decide between 'Watch That Man' and 'The Man Who Sold the World'. In the end we agreed to do both of them.

I was thrilled. This was definitely going to surprise people. Had there ever been an odder couple? I was perceived as the girl-next-door, while David Bowie was a weird, androgynous 'alien' and the hottest star in the world.

In early July I flew to France where David was recording at Château D'Herouville, just outside of Paris. He and the band were working on his new album, *PinUps*. The château had two sixteen-track recording studios, one in the stables and the other in the main house.

An endless stream of visitors came and went – DJs, singers, photographers and models. I arrived just as Twiggy was leaving. She had come to shoot a *Vogue* cover with Bowie.

The photographer, Justin de Villeneuve, had a problem because Twiggy was all tanned from a holiday in the Bahamas while David's skin was snow white. He had a make-up artist draw masks on each of them – brown for David and white for Twiggy.

The final photograph was amazing. It was never used in *Vogue*, but instead graced the album sleeve of *PinUps*. It has become one of the most famous rock album covers of all time, with Twiggy looking straight at the camera while Bowie seems to be staring straight through it.

I loved the château. It had once been owned by Chopin and had also been home to the famous female writer, George Sand. It was sunny and romantic, with high stone walls and iron gates. There were ducks, chickens and rabbits roaming round the gardens and a moat full of goldfish.

The rooms were like dormitories and very basic, but the food was amazing. The kitchen stayed open all hours and there was always someone in the dining room. At dinner we sat around a long table lit with candles and loaded with delicious food. Afterwards we worked in the studio until dawn. Then we'd sleep in late and lie around the pool (everyone except for David and I, who didn't like the sun).

He told me I should lose weight.

'Thanks a lot,' I said, pretending to take offence.

I knew what he meant. He wasn't suggesting that I should lose weight because he fancied me more that way. It was more a professional observation. He was one of the pioneers of the emaciated, heroin chic look and he thought it would help my career.

It was typical of David. He could be charming one moment and blunt and forthright the next. Regardless of this, he was *totally* seductive. He had that magnetic sort of personality that was intoxicating to be around. Sometimes I would hear women say, 'Oh, I couldn't fancy him – he's weird looking.' And I'd think, 'Not to me.'

He had a reputation for being very sexually adventurous and I'm sure it's true, but with me he stayed within fairly normal territory. It wasn't wild or anything like that.

What did he see in me? I don't know. We were drawn to each other. He loved my voice. I was flattered and excited. Creative and talented people have an air of confidence. They are high on life and sometimes you want to be close to them so you can breathe the same air.

During the recording sessions David encouraged me to experiment with my voice and discover my limits.

'Why aren't you smoking?' he asked one day.

'Because I have to sing.'

'I want you to keep smoking. Smoke more. Take a cigarette with you into the booth.'

Of course, David smoked like a chimney – French cigarettes made with dark, strong tobacco. He wanted my voice to sound husky and more decadent. He wanted the darkness in me to emerge.

David's band, including Mick Ronson on guitar, played on 'The Man Who Sold the World'. David played the sax and also sang the backing vocals. The final result was a funky, sax-driven song that sounded incredibly cool. I thought the lyric was about Jesus, but David would probably have said it was about something completely different.

It was another six months before the single was released. In that time I saw David every few weeks. If we found ourselves in the same place at the same time, the sexual chemistry drew us together. Angie knew but she didn't seem to mind. She and David both had their lovers and sometimes shared them. If she was interested in me, I ignored the signals.

As part of the launch campaign for 'The Man Who Sold the World' I did *Top of the Pops* on 10 January 1974. David came along for the recording session and sorted out the sound. Billy filled in doing the backing vocals and harmonies for him.

I came up with the idea to dress like a man, wearing a tight-fitting black suit with wide lapels, a black waistcoat, white shirt, a tie, and a white fedora hat with a black band, shielding my eyes. I looked like a Chicago gangster. I also had the complete opposite: a white suit, black shirt and black hat.

The bizarreness of the collaboration intrigued the media. When the record company sent out preview copies they recommended that DJs listen to the song more than once. It seemed to work. Radio One made it 'Record of the Week' and it entered the charts at No. 27. By early February it was at No. 3 in the UK and a Top 10 hit throughout Europe.

One critic wrote: 'I felt Lulu has been rather scratching round for a direction with her recent releases. This is a good direction to be in . . .'

I was hip and cool again. I toured the Continent doing TV and radio appearances. David was particularly happy with the success. Partly I think it fed his ego. He had set out to be my Svengali, determined to make a hit record with me. The idea had seemed crazy at first, but he pulled it off. God bless him.

We discussed doing more songs and perhaps even an album. It

was difficult because we both had so many commitments. We managed to do a few recording sessions at a studio in Olympia in London, and early in April 1974 I flew to New York where David was preparing for a tour of America. He had written a song for me, 'Can You Hear Me', which he wanted me to record.

He was working very hard on his own album and seemed preoccupied. New York was the turning point in our collaboration. In a sense I had the opportunity to become part of the amazing circus that followed David. We could do more songs, perhaps even an album. I could be a huge rock star.

Yet already I could feel myself backing away. I don't know why. I think it had something to do with the incredibly decadent and hedonistic life that he led. David excited and intimidated me at the same time. He lived on the very edge, sometimes not eating or sleeping for days a time, experimenting with anything and everything.

I was drawn to him, but I knew it was never going to last. It wouldn't have worked out in a million years. David wanted the darkness to emerge in me, and if I had hung around with him long enough I could easily have become lost in it. I simply didn't want to go there.

In London I had been seeing a lot more of John Frieda. The more time I spent with David, the more I thought about John. He was safe and steady. Wholesome isn't the right word . . . that makes him sound staid and boring. Maybe it was more about me, what I wanted.

At one point in New York I was on the telephone to John when David overheard us. He wrinkled up his nose and said, 'Hairdressers are all poofs!'

I looked him up and down, as if to say, 'Have you seen yourself in the mirror lately?'

He laughed.

We didn't see each other after New York. I think David realised that I wasn't going to drop everything for him. In truth, I don't think he cared that much. It wasn't as though either of us had fallen in love, and he was heading down a dark road.

Soon afterwards he split with his manager, Tony DeVries. There was a lot of acrimony about recording and publishing contracts and as a result the songs we recorded were never released.

# 12

# *A Prince Maybe,*
# *But a Hairdresser?*

A lot of my friends couldn't understand what I saw in John. He seemed so quiet and withdrawn, while I was bright, chatty and outgoing. They failed to realise that John had a lot going on upstairs. He was a real thinker.

Marian said to me, 'How do you get that miserable boy to talk?'

'You just have to spend some time with him,' I said defensively.

Mo had loved going out to showbiz parties and to restaurants with well-known people. John was different. He could take them or leave them. Sometimes I wanted him to be more outgoing. 'You *have* to talk,' I'd say. 'They think you're peculiar.'

He replied, 'I talk when I have something to say.'

I took him to the villa in Ibiza. Billy came too. The island had changed a lot since the mid-sixties. The hippies had gone and been replaced by rich Europeans, who were very chic and trendy. Euro-trash. Can Pau was still going strong. As soon as I walked in the door, Jordi yelled in a gruff voice, 'Hey, Lulu! Elton John was here. It was fabulous. We did some great stuff. We stayed up for four weeks.'

The old town of Ibiza had a Moorish influence and was full of dark-skinned French Moroccans. Thursday was couscous night and afterwards we went dancing at a nightclub, Pasha.

By midnight we were all smashed. John went wild on the dancefloor. He let his hair down, pretending to be Mick Jagger, strutting and preening. Billy really warmed to him that night. The two of them were mad about music and were both interested in cricket.

Mum and Dad weren't so sure. Mum used to say things like, 'How can he afford to buy those silk shirts? He's a hairdresser.' I think she feared he was a gold digger, only interested in my money.

They had liked Mo because he was completely crazy about me, but John was harder to warm to because he was so quiet and reserved. Mo had been an open book, who was always doing sweet things for my mum. John was far more restrained. He was always thinking . . . and calculating.

Publicly, everyone still assumed that he was my hairdresser. If anybody asked why he was always around, I said he was a friend of Billy's. It wasn't a case of trying to hide him. Mo had been so distressed about the break-up that I didn't want to openly publicise my new romance.

In April 1974, just before I went to New York, we talked for the first time about the possibility of getting married. 'Maybe in a year or two,' I said, hoping that Mo would have found someone by then.

When I told Billy of our plans he was thrilled. He had known that Mo wasn't right for me, but John was different. He was hard-working and level-headed – exactly the sort of man you'd like your sister to marry.

Being linked with Bowie gave my recording career a boost. One of the things I was asked to do was the title song for the new James

Bond film, *The Man With the Golden Gun*. Don Black wrote the lyrics and I did publicity shots with Roger Moore.

At that stage I was being produced by Wes Farrell and recording on the Chelsea label. Wes also produced David Cassidy and later married Tina Sinatra. He was warm, enthusiastic and energetic, as well as having a great pop sensibility, with an American rhythm and blues take. We made some great records, which didn't quite make it, perhaps because the record label didn't have enough faith.

In December I began rehearsals for another production of 'Peter Pan', this time the musical rather than the dramatic version of the story. Tessa Wyatt played Wendy and Ron Moody was an inspired choice as Captain Hook.

Ron had just returned from Hollywood where he had recreated his famous performance as Fagin in the film version of *Oliver Twist*. In truth, Ron seemed to bring a little bit of Fagin into Hook, but nobody minded because he was such a wonderful actor.

During the show, Jean Rook of the *Daily Express* arranged to interview me. Amid all her other questions, she came out and asked me point blank if John Frieda was the man in my life. I didn't deny it. Jean took this one small acknowledgement and wrote an article devoted to my love life.

When the news broke it launched a thousand headlines about 'Lulu marrying her hairdresser'. Some of the comments were quite cruel. My first marriage had been one of the biggest celebrity couplings of the decade, but now I was somehow perceived as having gone backwards. I had fallen in love with someone who, by comparison, was totally anonymous. The general reaction seemed to be, 'A prince maybe, but a hairdresser?'

What people failed to realise (or chose to ignore) was just how good a hairdresser they were talking about. John was the best. He worked with photographers like David Bailey, Norman Parkinson, Clive Arrowsmith and Barry Lategan. He was in constant demand and celebrity clients would beg for an appointment.

I didn't care what other people thought. I loved John. Nobody knew him like I did.

It wasn't until the summer of 1976 that we decided to marry. Mo had made it to the altar before me, which is what I wanted. He met Yvonne when she walked into a club where he was playing, six months after we separated. I was happy for him and also relieved.

John and I purposely waited until after he had opened his first salon before we married. This was important to him because I think he wanted to show people he was his own man, and independently successful.

When I first met him he didn't express any interest in having his own salon. It wasn't until Clifford Stafford, another Leonard stylist, suggested the idea that John began to think about it seriously.

They went into partnership and rented a small shop in Blandford Street, decorating it inexpensively. Clifford's wife Joan had some contacts and organised help with the décor.

It was a very small salon because Clifford and John decided they wanted somewhere that was packed and buzzing, rather than empty and echoing.

The day before the opening we were all on our hands and knees scrubbing the floors, cleaning toilets and polishing fittings. It was all very exciting. John was so nervous his stomach was churning and he barely slept.

From the very first day the phones rang off the hook. John and Clifford worked incredible hours because they didn't want to say no to anyone. This was the message they wanted to send to clients – 'we will always fit you in'.

The two of them complemented each other. Clifford was a brilliant in-house hairdresser, whereas John had the patience and the eye for detail that made him perfect to work on photographic shoots.

John and I married on 8 October 1976 at the Hampstead Register office. Bill Gibb, a very successful Scottish designer, did my dress. He had grown up on a farm near Edinburgh, yet became one of the most sought-after designers of the sixties, dressing people like Twiggy, Elizabeth Taylor, Bianca Jagger and Joan Collins.

He created an Arabian-style gown in pale cream wool, delicately embroidered with pale peach, lilac and cream bugle beads. The dress had an Empire-line bodice from the bust down and very fine pleats all the way to the ankles. Coupled with a matching coat and turban it looked like something out of *Lawrence of Arabia*. (Someone by now will have noticed the correlation between a *Dr Zhivago* look at my first wedding and *Lawrence of Arabia* at the second. Perhaps I should have been marrying David Lean.)

The dress was very neat over the bustline and had to be fitted perfectly. Bill Gibb was a real artist and we did three fittings to make sure everything was absolutely right.

It was delivered the day before the wedding. On the morning, I tried it on. It was gorgeous, but to my surprise it was tight. I couldn't understand why I had to squeeze myself into it. What had gone wrong? To make matters worse, I had heavy circles under my eyes and felt queasy.

Of course, it didn't even occur to me that I was pregnant, which would have explained my ballooning breasts.

John had to go to work on the morning of the wedding. I had arranged to visit the salon to have my hair pinned up beneath the turban. There were photographers camped outside the house and I didn't want anyone to catch me until I was properly dressed. I ended up lying on the floor of a car and being driven past them like some fugitive.

The register office ceremony was very short and matter-of-fact. Afterwards we paused on the steps to let everyone get their pictures. I look like a Cheshire cat in the photographs. It's amazing how hard a person can smile.

We had a lunch at 'Woodley' for our immediate families, and that evening the party began. I took off my turban and let my hair down. Guests included Bill Wyman, Bruce Forsyth, Elton John and Kiki Dee. It was still going at six the following morning and would have lasted even longer if Robert Plant and his wife hadn't announced that it was time for everyone to leave.

John and I had talked about finding somewhere new to live. We both thought 'Woodley' was too big, and it also held too many memories associated with Mo. We hoped to find somewhere smaller – a place to call our own.

All this changed within two months. I was rehearsing for 'Aladdin' in Oxford, when I began to worry about my weight gain. I thought it was a sign of how happy I was, but decided to see George Pinker.

'Well, young lady, I hope you're ready for it this time.'

'Ready for what?'

'You're having a baby.'

He was thrilled and I was shocked. We had only just married and John had just opened his salon. It was a lot to happen in a short space of time.

'Poor John,' I said to his father, John Snr. 'He starts a business, gets married and has a baby all within a year. I feel for him.'

'It will turn him into a man,' he replied.

My mother was out of her mind with excitement. This was to be her first grandchild. Within days she was planning to be in London for the birth and shopping for baby clothes.

Publicly, at least, I decided to keep the pregnancy a secret for as long as I could. It meant letting out a few of my costumes in

'Aladdin' and fobbing off questions about why I wasn't drinking alcohol or coffee. The news finally broke in February, four months before the baby was due.

I can honestly say that pregnancy was the happiest time of my life. My hair shone, my skin was clear, I had no cravings. Colours, sounds and smells were more intense and vivid. I remember driving home along Fitzjohn's Avenue in Hampstead, which was lined with blossom trees in full bloom. It was the most beautiful scene imaginable. Like the blossoms, I felt like bursting with happiness.

I wrote in my diary:

I don't know when I have ever felt so good about my life. I think it is contentment. Mind you, I now worry that it is too good to last. How stupid! This week I feel very tired, but my temperament is good. I feel very happy.

John had seen a TV programme about the Leboyer Method of childbirth and then read the book. Full of enthusiasm, he declared that I should have a completely natural birth, without painkillers.

'Is that right?' I said, raising my eyebrows. Isn't it amazing how men know just what's right for a woman when it comes to having children?

The Leboyer Method was conceived by a French obstetrician and is basically designed to minimise any stress and trauma on the newborn. The idea is to keep the delivery suite in semi-darkness and very quiet. Doctors and midwives make no unnecessary intervention in the birth and afterwards the baby is placed on the mother's tummy so it can still hear her heartbeat.

I explained all this to George Pinker, who smiled wisely. 'Well, if you need any help it will be there.'

The morning sickness disappeared after two or three months and the pregnancy went like clockwork until the last few weeks.

Up until then we'd all been hoping the baby would turn, but instead it wanted to come out bum first.

George discussed the options with us and recommended that I have a Caesarean. John and I agreed. We put ourselves in his hands. I didn't care about the scarring or the fact I wouldn't get to experience childbirth. I just wanted my baby to be safe.

I knew a few weeks in advance when I was going into hospital. Mum had come down from Scotland to stay with me. I packed and repacked my suitcase and we went shopping in Harrods for a pram and things for the nursery.

We were still trying to come up with names. For a girl we had Alexis, Amber and Chloe, but a boy's name was more difficult.

The weather for the Jubilee Holiday was horrible. It didn't stop raining. Not that it mattered to the millions who celebrated at street parties and fairs. I felt quite melancholy, but also very proud to be British. Had it really been twenty-five years since I sang to the Coronation party in Soho Street? I could barely remember it, yet it had become one of those family stories that are passed down and retold so many times that even Gordon and Edwina, who weren't even born then, could imagine they were there.

On the night before I went into hospital I couldn't sleep. I finally dropped off at about 2.00 a.m., only to be woken by a tremendous crack of thunder and lightning. It didn't bother John. He slept right through it. I went upstairs to see if Mum was all right. Together we sat watching the amazing lightning display that seemed to freeze-frame the London skyline and then plunge it back into darkness again.

The following afternoon I checked into a room at St Mary's Hospital in Paddington. They ran a few tests and monitored the baby's heartbeat.

'Well, you can go out for dinner if you like,' said the nurse.

'I'm going nowhere,' I replied. 'I've come here to have a baby and I'm not leaving until I get one.'

She laughed. 'It's perfectly OK. You won't be having the baby until the morning.'

It seemed very odd. Having come so far I just wanted it to be over. John was at work. I called him at the salon and he came to the hospital when he finished. We went to a restaurant, but neither of us felt much like eating. All we could think about was the operation in a few hours' time.

John arrived early the next morning, 17 June, after celebrating most of the night with Billy. George Pinker suggested he might prefer to wait outside the delivery suite. John was relieved. His stomach was doing back-flips already. At moments like this we become almost childlike and willing to be directed.

Having been wheeled into the operating theatre, I was totally knocked out and, consequently, I can't remember a thing about the birth. This saddens me because I didn't get to see my baby son at the moment he came into the world.

George did a wonderful job. I ended up with the smallest scar, low down, where it isn't noticeable.

It was strange waking up and being told that I had a son, weighing 7lb 3oz.

'Can I see him?'

'No, not at the moment,' said a nurse.

'Why? What's wrong?'

'Nothing. He's perfectly OK.' She explained that Jordan had conjunctivitis, which is very contagious. He was being quarantined in the nursery.

'Can I go to him?'

'You have just had an operation, Mrs Frieda. You're not supposed to move.'

John had gone to Lord's with Billy to see the second day of the Jubilee Test Match between Australia and England. I knew the two of them would be celebrating, drinking champagne and toasting the new arrival.

All through the day I kept asking about the baby. Nurses kept putting me off, saying that I had to stay in bed. When John finally arrived I was almost beside myself.

'Please, I have to see him,' I said.

John took charge and commandeered a wheelchair. He wheeled me through the corridors until we found the nursery. Our newborn son was swaddled and lying in a tiny crib. His eyes were swollen and red with conjunctivitis. We both burst into tears, it was so emotional. My throat began to close. I couldn't talk.

At the same time, I struggled to comprehend how this tiny thing could belong to me. My abdomen was no longer swollen. Something had come out of me, but was it really a baby? I had missed being at the birth. It was as though I'd been left behind and was now struggling to catch up.

George thought I was exhausted and wanted me to sleep. He put a sign on my door saying, 'No visitors without matron's permission'. This didn't stop dozens of people getting in, but I didn't mind. My mind was buzzing and I enjoyed the company.

Right up until the final weeks we had wrestled with possible names for a boy. Eventually, Marian said to me, 'What about Jordan?'

I turned to John. 'What do you think of Jordan Frieda?'

His eyes lit up. Our baby had a name.

I left hospital after six days. George wanted me to stay longer, but I recovered very quickly from the operation and physically felt fine. Apart from having Mum to help me at home, I had also hired a maternity nurse, Carol. Her mother had been my dresser on 'Aladdin' and had told me how her daughter helped new mothers in the first few months after the birth. Carol turned out to be about six feet tall with a jolly personality. She immediately took charge of any situation and didn't get flustered.

Despite her presence, I couldn't shake the sense of being unqualified and ill-equipped for motherhood. On the drive home from the hospital I had a strange feeling that everything looked different. The world had somehow changed.

Initially, Jordan slept in the room next door to John's and mine. He had a Moses basket and a musical mobile. Carol told me to have a sherry before his last feed, which would help him sleep.

I wrote in my diary:

I have never known what it feels like to be so happy. I consider myself to be truly blessed. I know that I have a wonderful life . . . I think John has great gentleness, strength and courage. I love him and my little baby Jordan. We are now a family.

The impact on our lives couldn't have been greater. Nothing seemed important any more except for Jordan. Nothing else interested me. I had listened to baby bores and always promised myself that I would never be like that. Ha! I was the worst, and John not far behind.

A few weeks after taking Jordan home, we were invited out to a party. I would love to have cancelled, but told myself that we should at least make an appearance. We stood there, drinks in hand, making small talk. It seemed so inconsequential and unexciting.

I caught John's eye just as he caught mine. One look was all it took. No words were spoken. We slipped out of the party and drove home at breakneck speed. We opened the door and ran up the stairs two at a time. Jordan was asleep. We looked at him and then at each other. Why bother going out? We didn't want to go anywhere. We wanted to wrap ourselves in the warmth of our little threesome and keep the world at bay.

I didn't expect to be thrown by Jordan's birth. I had grown up looking after babies. I was changing Billy's nappies and feeding him when I was only four. I was taking care of everyone in my family by the time I was eight. There was no question of me coping.

The reality couldn't have been more different. I was completely overwhelmed by the responsibility and the love. How could I possibly look after this tiny, helpless human being? I thought I knew everything . . . but realised I knew nothing.

John had never been busier. The salon was booked solid and he was doing session work with fashion photographers and TV companies. He would leave home at seven each morning and not finish until late in the evening.

We talked on the phone constantly. We'd call each other to get updates about Jordan and to make small talk. Sometimes it drove me mad when he worked late. Highly emotional, I would call him up and say things like, 'Are you coming home or what? Dinner has been ready for hours.'

He would apologise and bring home flowers. He knew I was very passionate and vocal.

John had a plan. He didn't do anything without thinking it through. He told me that when everything was up and running he wouldn't have to work so hard. I believed him. I wanted to.

On 17 July, I wrote in my diary:

Today is Jordan's birthday. He is one month old and weighs 8lb. John came home at five o'clock. (Hooray!) He sent me flowers and a card saying, 'I have loved you in all my lifetimes.'

7TH SEPTEMBER 1977

I am going to Nottingham for a show. I cried this morning when I looked at Jordan and thought of not seeing him for four days. Why did I say yes? I should be at home . . . with him.

From the moment I became pregnant, I made sure to tell everyone that I'd be going back to work. I planned to take a couple of months off and then slowly ease myself back into work. I even imagined taking Jordan with me a lot of the time. I had visions of us having naps together in the afternoon.

As it turned out, it was easier to leave him at home rather than cart him all over the country, upsetting his routine. The moment I arrived at the studio or the venue I would call home.

I recorded six shows with Les Dawson and also went into the recording studio to lay down a single, 'Your Love is Everywhere', which was released in January 1978. In the months that followed I did cabaret seasons in London, Glasgow, Dublin and smaller centres.

I made a point of trying to be home each morning, even if that meant driving through the night. Thankfully, I had a nice car – a top of the range Mercedes, with an extra long wheelbase, which was the height of luxury and perfect for long journeys. I also had a driver, which meant I could fall asleep on the back seat and wake up as we pulled into the driveway at 'Woodley'.

I could kick myself for going back to work so soon. I wish somebody had said to me, 'Don't you think you should spend more time with your family?'

It wasn't as though I had signed cast-iron contracts or had prior commitments. I could have stopped work completely. Unfortunately, none of those things was clear in my head. I just had this innate understanding that I *had* to keep working.

With hindsight I can see it was a mishmash of Protestant work ethic, a sense of responsibility for people and a desire not to be forgotten. I didn't ask myself what I could do differently. That sort of introspection came years later when I learned how to get in touch with my feelings and look after the world inside me, not just the world outside.

For Jordan's sake, I wish I had done this sooner. I would have stayed at home and not gone back to work. I would have kissed him goodnight every evening and made his breakfast every morning.

John was working harder than ever. He had a growing client list and was making a real name for himself as a celebrity crimper and 'top London hairdresser'as the papers referred to him. I used to get annoyed with him for never being home. I wanted more of his attention.

Maybe I thought that one celebrity in the house was enough. And from John's point of view, maybe he was driven by the need to cast a bigger shadow. In his own field he was becoming a giant – respected by other hairdressers and adored by clients.

In the very early days he hated anyone referring to him as 'Mr Lulu'. He quickly outgrew that. Now he was succeeding on his own terms, proving something to himself as well as other people.

We still found time to be together. Sometimes he would come with me to Manchester or Newcastle if I had to do a show. We would talk in the car and then he'd return to London. We also made sure that Sunday was our day. We had a proper roast lunch, inviting friends and family, or we accepted an invitation for lunch.

Jordan was only three months old when we first took him to Ibiza. John had fallen in love with the villa and it was one of the few places that he could truly relax and forget about the salon. Eventually we extended the pool and had a paddling pool built for youngsters. John also had plans for a tennis court. He had a real eye for design and would have loved to be an architect.

## 7TH OCTOBER 1977

John and I have been married a year tomorrow. I am so happy. He has bought me a beautiful gold heart and chain from Cartier. I love him more and more.

Robert and Maureen Plant came over with Phil Carson and Jenny. [Phil was Head of Atlantic Records.] Jordan has moved out of his Moses basket and into his own cot and his own room. He is teething and dribbling everywhere . . .

I filmed a TV series in November and did a season at Bournemouth before Christmas. I had also become a disc jockey, with a regular stint on Capital Radio every Sunday for two hours. The best part was being able to choose the music. I tried to balance the new material with plenty of classic rock, soul and blues tracks. I even threw in some Pavarotti.

I left my gift-buying until the last minute and had to rush around, generally wearing myself out. There were hundreds of presents under the tree on Christmas morning. Mum and Dad helped with the cooking and cleaning.

For Christmas lunch, David Bailey and his wife Marie Helvin came around, along with David's assistant John Swannell and a crowd of other people. I went to bed at 1.00 a.m. but John kept entertaining until four. The best thing about the whole day was that Jordan enjoyed his first Christmas. He sat in his new high chair and put all his presents in his mouth, tasting each of them.

# 13

# *Who's Foolin' Who?*

My life had completely changed because of Jordan. All the empty space in 'Woodley' was suddenly filled, along with all the space in my heart.

I loved the fact that he made us a family, but I still struggled under the burden of responsibility. The fantasy of having a child doesn't reveal any of the fear that comes with the joy. Every infection, every cough, every grazed knee became something to worry about.

Like a lot of parents, I would sometimes sit beside him at night and listen to him breathing. He seemed too fragile to survive. I wanted to protect him and keep him safe.

I had always wanted four children. John talked about having six. We both liked the idea of a large family and a bustling home. Unfortunately, the gap between the idea and the reality only grew after Jordan was born. The birth itself hadn't been difficult, and Jordan was a dream baby, but at the same time I didn't feel like having any more children.

More significantly, I actually felt frightened of having any more. It is difficult to describe because it sounds so implausible. Why should I be so terrified? And why did the fear get worse rather than diminish?

Whenever John raised the possibility of having another child, I made excuses. At the same time I felt guilty. I felt as though I had made him a promise which I didn't want to keep. I had shared a dream with him.

In total denial, I pushed it down. I told him that I wasn't quite ready. 'Maybe next year,' I said. In the meantime, I hoped some miracle would happen and my fear would go away.

Ever since the Lux soap deal, I had promoted lots of different products, such as tea, shampoo, hair gel, make-up remover and Lulu hairspray. Since 1968 I had also been the Freemans girl, doing twice-yearly fashion shoots for the company's mail order catalogue.

I was very flattered to be asked to model – after all, I was hardly 'model' material at five foot one. I have to be honest, however, and admit that I wore very few Freemans fashions.

I could afford to buy clothes by the world's top fashion designers or have them made for me. My wardrobe was full of expensive, beautifully tailored clothes that were at the cutting edge of fashion. Bruce Forsyth used to joke with me, 'Are you wearing Freemans?' I always smiled wryly and declined to answer. He knew the truth – as did most people.

My association with Freemans lasted twenty years, and it suited both of us when it ended.

It was a difficult time to be buying anything in Britain. The economy had crumbled and trade unions were holding entire industries hostage. Images appeared on TV showing garbage piling up on the streets and violent confrontations on picket lines. There had been forced power cuts and heating shortages throughout the winter. Fewer people were going out and seeing shows. Theatres and clubs were barely surviving.

Dad was made redundant from the Glasgow Meat Market in 1978. It was a sign of the times. Scotland had 200,000 unemployed workers and people were considered to be 'over the hill' in their early fifties.

'That's the tragedy in this country – writing people off because of age,' I told the *Daily Express*.

For years I had been trying to convince Mum and Dad to move down to London. Billy and Edwina were already here and, like me, wanted to have them a lot closer.

Billy was still working in the music industry and had married. His wife, Susan Harrison, was a model, and sister of Stephanie Maclean, then girlfriend of motorcycle champion Barry Sheene.

Edwina, then eighteen, was about to make her stage debut in a rock musical called 'Elidor'. Later she sang in a pop group, Reflections, and became one of the original VJs (video-jocks), hosting a show for TV-AM.

Jordan's arrival and Dad losing his job became the spur they needed to move. Being a proud man, Dad wanted to have a job before he came south. I offered to help them buy a shop, but he found work in a Jewish meat market in North London. He lived on his own in digs for two months until Mum joined him and they moved into a house in Chingford, Essex.

It must have been very difficult to leave Glasgow. All their friends were there and they had reached an age where it is hard to start again. At the same time, they wanted to be close to their children and grandchildren.

Mum and Dad couldn't get over how huge London was and how long it took to get anywhere. In Glasgow you could go from one end of the city to the other in twenty minutes.

Mum doted on Jordan. She was as obsessed with him as she had once been with me, and the two of them had a tremendous bond.

Neither Mum nor Dad could drive. I offered to buy them a car and help them get a licence, but they had no desire. Instead Mum would take two or three buses and spend two hours travelling to reach 'Woodley' so that she could see Jordan. Then she would travel home again on the bus.

Dad worked for two more years before retiring. He became friends with Terry Venables' father, who was a publican in North London. Dad would knock on the pub door at the crack of dawn and have a 'constitutional' before he started the day.

Mum found a Mormon church in central London and became a regular. She was always trying to convince her children to go along.

I had high hopes for Margaret Thatcher. Although not a political animal, I didn't have to be an expert to see the country was in trouble.

Like many people, I was worried for the future. We all want a leader: someone to look up to, to respect; someone we know will follow through. So many politicians seemed to be too ambitious or in it for themselves. Maggie reminded me of a strong and confident nanny like Carol, who would sweep us all up in her arms and take care of us.

During the 1979 election campaign I had no hesitation about supporting her. When I was invited to appear on the same platform I said yes immediately. I wanted to see a woman in charge. I loved her strength and her conviction.

I appeared on stage with her, along with the likes of Nigel Davenport, the singer Vince Hill and the disc jockey Pete Murray. I will never forget when Mrs Thatcher declared, 'I am here to bury Mr Callaghan, not to praise him.'

She was elected Prime Minister in May 1979 and it didn't come a moment too soon. She gave us hope. Although I didn't always agree with everything she did – particularly in later years – I still believe she restored a lot of pride in Britain.

From June to September I was booked at the Winter Gardens in Margate. I was really looking forward to spending the summer with Jordan. He loved the seaside. Edwina was one of my backing singers.

I rented a house in Herne Bay, about twenty minutes from Margate, and Mum came down to help look after Jordan. John was opening a new salon in London and joined us each weekend.

At the end of August, Mark Corne, my driver, took a few days off. I drove myself home after the show at about 11.00 p.m. I remember sea mist drifting across the hedgerows and stone fences.

I don't remember anything about the accident. I think I swerved, but I can't be sure. The next thing I remember I was lying in a pool of blood on the road, with a very sweet girl asking me, 'Are you all right?' I had a four-inch cut on the top of my head, which had severed an artery.

The accident happened at a notorious black spot called Brooksend Hill. My Chrysler Rancho collided head-on with a Ford Capri on a tight bend in dense fog. I was thrown against the steering wheel and into the windscreen, which shattered. Semi-conscious, I either stumbled from the car or someone dragged me out. Whoever raised the alarm must have held their hand against my head to stop the bleeding.

By the time I reached Canterbury Hospital I had been unconscious a few times. I remember lying in the ambulance and looking across at the other car driver. His name was Laurence Broadley, a twenty-year-old trainee hairdresser. He had cuts to his face and a fractured pelvis. Both of us were lucky to be alive.

I kept asking the ambulance officer about him.

'Calm down. He's going to be OK. Just relax.'

Marian received the phone call at two in the morning from

Margate police. She telephoned John and they drove immediately to Canterbury. Surgeons operated on my scalp. I needed thirty stitches to close the wound. Marian loves telling a story about how I was wheeled from the operating theatre, covered in blood and barely conscious, but still managed to sign an autograph for a cleaning lady.

Apparently, I also told someone that I'd be back at work the following Monday, which was a wee bit optimistic.

I was shocked when I saw my face in the mirror the next morning. I had two black eyes and bits of glass were embedded in my forehead and cheeks. For years afterwards I would come across tiny splinters of glass that had gradually worked their way back to the surface of my skin. Laurence looked even worse.

John Lennon was among the hundreds of people who sent me get well cards. I also had thirty-four flower arrangements – too many to fit in my room so I distributed them throughout the hospital.

After a week in hospital the doctors gave me permission to leave. John very gently washed the blood from my hair, careful not to wet my sutures. He had a gentle touch and it was a quality I loved in him.

I wore big sunglasses and needed a walking stick as I left the hospital. The pictures were all over the newspapers the next morning. Even with the sunglasses and heavy make-up, I couldn't hide my bruised eyes. It was another four weeks before I could walk without a stick.

I went to Ibiza to recuperate and it was another two months before I made my next appearance. Doctors had advised me to take things easy.

By far the most remarkable part of the whole story was that nobody knew who had saved my life. I didn't even realise myself how lucky I had been until a doctor explained what had happened.

'You would have bled to death in minutes,' he said. 'It doesn't get much more serious than a severed artery. Someone was looking after you.'

'I know,' I answered, without realising exactly what I meant. Only later did I realise that someone *up there* was looking after me. But who was the good Samaritan who had saved my life? And why had he disappeared before the ambulance arrived?

For weeks there was a media search. All sorts of crazy people claimed the credit, but the genuine hero remained a mystery.

A couple of summers later I was at a flower stall in Sloane Square on a very hot day. As I turned to walk along the footpath I noticed someone coming towards me with bare feet. In truth, I noticed his feet first because it was quite odd for anyone to have no shoes in Sloane Square. My eyes travelled up to the most beautiful black face. He gave me a huge smile.

'Lulu?'

'Yes.'

I was expecting him to say, 'Oh, my mother loves you', or 'Can I have your autograph?' Instead he said, 'I saw you that night on the road.'

'I beg your pardon?'

'When you had the accident. I saw you bleeding. I called the ambulance.'

I was taken aback and didn't know what to say. I think I mumbled a thank you, but his statement was still sinking in as he turned and disappeared into the crowd.

I walked towards my car, still thinking about the barefoot man. So many people had come forward claiming to have made that call, yet there was something about this man. He had a serene and knowing face.

Suddenly I realised that I believed him. *He* was the one. I ran back to look for him. There were too many people. Then I drove around the block half a dozen times, hoping to spot him. He had disappeared.

I could have kicked myself. If only I had realised sooner, I would have embraced him. I would have thanked him properly.

It had been five years since my last hit record. The cabaret seasons and TV specials blurred into one another. The adrenalin still surged when I walked on stage – otherwise I couldn't have kept going – but it was harder to reach the highs that once came naturally.

I had grown to hate cabaret. Once it had been exciting and new. Now it was almost a dirty word.

I had no regrets. Marian had made the right decisions. She had wanted to prolong my career rather than leave me relying on pop records and the fickleness of public taste. I had opted to take the comfortable road and become locked into it. I was stuck in the comfort zone – no longer moving forward, creatively or spiritually. I had also lost touch with younger audiences – the kids who spent their pocket money on records. Instead I was someone that Mum and Dad listened to.

Many of my friends and peers from the sixties had become the elite of the music business, earning millions of pounds in album sales and concert receipts. I looked at The Beatles, Led Zeppelin, The Rolling Stones and The Who, as well as artists like Eric Clapton and Stevie Wonder. They had stayed with the music and a part of me wished that I'd done the same.

I realise now that I should have taken time off. I had the sort of career I could put on hold and then pick up when I wanted to. Unfortunately, I didn't appreciate that at the time.

My diaries show my frustration. I would swing from happiness to anger to sadness in the space of a day. I would be angry with John and then desperately in love with him. I would accuse him of being a workaholic and then accept even more work myself.

Life on the road was no longer a pleasure. Although I had a dedicated team of people around me – a musical director, backing singers, members of the band and the road crew – I found myself worrying about their problems as much as my own.

I wrote in my diary:

I feel my career is stagnant. The Musicians' Union doesn't help. For the past two years they have steadily been putting up the prices for musicians and my fees don't go up. They are almost crippling me.

   Also everything else in this country is going to the dogs, partly because of the unions so it's not unexpected that life is hard and getting harder. Thank God John seems to be really doing well. He has most of his staff problems sorted out (for this week anyway). Mind you, he seems to think of nothing but his bloody salon.

Jordan started nursery school in January 1980. He joined a little playgroup in Hampstead Garden Suburb. John and I both took him on his first day. My heart ached a little, but Jordan didn't look back. He waved goodbye and took the teacher's hand.

Parents were encouraged not to hang around, but we both desperately wanted to find out what happened. Outside the nursery was a small window high up on the wall. John lifted me up so I could look through it.

'What's he doing now?'

'He's holding a red block and waving it in the air. Now he's picked up a green block . . .'

'It's my turn. It's my turn.'

I lifted John to the window. 'What's happening?'

'He's gone over to a little girl . . .'

'What's he doing? What's he doing?'

'It's *sooo* cute.'

'It's my turn. It's my turn.'

'But you had longer than me.'

'Yes, but you're heavier.'

Jordan was only at the nursery for two hours. Most of that time we spent staring through the window. Thankfully, the novelty wore off. I'm sure it's the same with all new parents.

Jordan's best friend was a little girl and he became besotted with her. He came home one day and announced that he wanted to wear pink socks.

'Why?'

'Because Jessie wears pink socks.'

He was adamant, so I made a special trip to the shops. From then on they wore matching socks. Although only four, it was love.

In the summer I recorded a new album and did a TV series for the BBC. I also did a 'made for America' series called *Let's Rock*, which was produced by Jack Good.

Jack had been a BBC producer and the undisputed champion of rock 'n' roll on British and American TV in the fifties and sixties. He looked and sounded like a very pukka public school boy (which he was), but had a famous unbridled enthusiasm and energy that whipped audiences into a frenzy. He also created enormous excitement by having audiences crowd around performers.

Working on *Let's Rock* gave me a new sense of purpose. It got me pumped and made the adrenalin flow. Jack knew all about music and created shows that were held together intelligently by a theme and by the energy he created.

We recorded six shows in six weeks at Elstree Studios, outside London. The other regular members of the cast included Shakin' Stevens, Joe Brown and Alvin Stardust. We got to sing lots of rock 'n' roll songs, with hundreds of teenagers dancing around us.

One minute I'd have a ponytail and sticky-out frock as I sang, 'Darling, youoooo send me . . .', and the next I'd be dressed in leather, singing, 'Devil in the blue dress, blue dress . . .'

Working on *Let's Rock* really lifted my spirits, but the feeling didn't last beyond the summer. I was struggling to find a direction for my career and it was affecting everyone around me.

Clearly I was going through a bad patch. Not even Ibiza offered the same comforts. The recession was keeping people away and several of our holiday breaks proved to be wet and cold.

John and I spent a weekend at Marian's cottage, 'Snuff', in Gloucestershire. I told him that he was working too hard and I felt neglected. I needed more of his time.

'I remember smiling at you the other night,' he said, trying to make a joke of it.

'Why can't you be warmer and more affectionate?'

'That's the way I am.'

The following week he sent me flowers and arranged to take me to dinner. He seemed to make a conscious effort to be home at a reasonable hour.

I wrote in my diary:

I really think the talk I had with John worked. He is attentive, warm, almost affectionate. Marian and I had a long talking session after the show in Bo'ness, Scotland. She told me that for a long time, up until a few months ago, a lot of people thought I was on the verge of a nervous breakdown. I was stunned. I suppose I have been a bit edgy.

I have so many people relying on me. Then there's John being so involved with his work and going into his shell . . . not to mention Jordan's continuous croup.

In December the gloom deepened when I turned on the radio one morning and heard that John Lennon had been shot dead outside the Dakota apartment building in New York. It was a gut-wrenching moment. I thought about Yoko, Sean, Julian and

Cynthia. I couldn't analyse or rationalise why someone would do this. What had John Lennon ever done to them?

Downstairs in the hallway at 'Woodley' I had a beautiful antique love-seat which John and Yoko had given to me. A few years earlier, I had given Julian a guitar for his seventh birthday. We'd had a party at Cynthia's house in Holland Park. John and Yoko were there.

Cynthia's mother loved buying antiques and hunting out bargains. 'My hallway needs a big piece of furniture like a love-seat,' I told her. 'Keep your eye out for one.'

John said, 'We have one. You can have it.'

'No, no, I couldn't.'

'We don't use it,' said Yoko.

It was during their 'white period' and the seat didn't suit their plans. They organised to have it delivered. After John's death I couldn't look at that lovely piece of furniture without thinking about him.

A lot of stars changed their lifestyles as a result of what happened. They hired bodyguards, drivers and installed expensive alarm systems. Whereas once they signed autographs when stopped in the street, they now looked at fans in a different light.

I didn't consider myself to be vulnerable. I wasn't in the same league as John Lennon. Even so, I found myself taking extra precautions and becoming even more protective of Jordan.

A few weeks later we spent Christmas at the Royal Crescent in Bath. Over lunch on Christmas Day John and I talked about having another baby. As always, he was all for the idea, but I was against it.

'There's so much to do now,' I said, feeling confused.

'Jordan would love a brother or a sister. If we wait any longer the age difference will be too great.'

'Yes, I know, but I feel I should *want* another baby. Right now I don't.'

'But you'll think about it?'

'Please, don't pressure me.'

I felt guilty for not being more maternal and for not wanting more children. When I was expecting Jordan I had yearned for a child. I wanted to wait until I had that feeling again.

In truth I was still frightened, but I didn't know how to tell John. I just wanted all our friends and relations to stop dropping hints and looking at my tummy for signs.

John is the sort of person who wanted to plan everything. Even when Jordan was just born we were already talking about schools, piano lessons and possible careers.

I am passionate, volatile and spontaneous. I have big emotions and I'm used to living my life to extremes. John isn't like that. He can't just say what he feels. He has to think it through, work it out and find the right words.

Part of me admired this, and part of me was irritated as hell. I think sometimes I wanted him to just react rather than calculate every move and utterance.

Anger can be a positive thing as long as you don't try to bottle it up or hold it in. I have always had a short fuse, but in my defence I don't bear grudges. When an argument is over, it is over. Cross words and accusations are forgotten.

In the summer John played cricket every weekend for Tim Rice's Heartaches XI, which was sprinkled with celebrities and friends. To please him and spend time with him, I would go along to watch.

John wanted me to love the game, but I couldn't go that far. Instead I read the weekend papers and watched Jordan playing with the other children.

I was becoming a thoroughly modern mum – soon to be doing school runs, swimming lessons, cricket practice, school plays and sleep-overs. The eighties had arrived and I wore suits with padded shoulders and big hair. I was the wife of an upwardly mobile businessman in Margaret Thatcher's Britain.

When Jordan first started school I think I was a bit of a curiosity. Other mothers would try hard not to stare at me as I waited at the school gates. Jordan had very little idea that he had a famous mum, but he began picking up on things. He wanted to know why my photograph was in the newspaper and why people kept asking me to write my name on bits of paper?

He *really* understood when Adam Ant took the country by storm. Jordan was besotted by him and had an Adam Ant outfit – black leather trousers, a wide belt and buckle, a black shirt with puffed sleeves, braided waistcoat and a black cape. He looked adorable.

At the Royal Variety Show that year, I sang the Beatles song 'Yesterday' in a show that was billed as a tribute to British rock and pop music. Adam Ant was on the same bill and we discovered that we were born on the same day.

Adam asked me to be in the video for 'Ant Rap', his new single. I took Jordan along to the filming and he had his photo taken with his hero, both wearing their outfits. Jordan kept it on his bedroom wall.

From then on he *knew* his mother was a celebrity, but I still managed to shield him from that side of my life. It wasn't until he was eleven, for instance, that he realised that I had once won the Eurovision Song Contest. Watching the contest that year on TV, he heard a commentator mention previous winners. Jordan turned to me in amazement when he heard my name.

'How come you never told me?'

'You never asked.'

In truth, it seemed like a lifetime ago.

Marian had been my guide, protector and surrogate mother for seventeen years. I had started off as her 'hobby' and become a full-time occupation.

She didn't always make the right decisions, but I have no complaints about not being consulted. We often talked to each other a dozen times a day on the phone. It drove John crazy. He felt as though my career was stagnating and could see I was frustrated.

After divorcing Gerry, Marian had married Mark London, who had written the music for 'To Sir With Love'. In the late seventies Mark branched out into producing, publishing and management. We did an album together. Mark's songwriters provided many of the songs and he published the music and acted as producer.

This harmonisation worked well. Things were 'kept in-house'. In retrospect, however, I don't know if I would do it again. It is far more dynamic and exciting to work with different creative people than to be tied too closely or work for too long with one team.

Some of the people I most admired felt I hadn't fulfilled my potential. Pete Townshend was one of them. We had both started off at about the same time and I can still picture him sitting in my parents' front room in Glasgow when I invited The High Numbers back to Garfield Street.

In the early eighties I appeared on a show with Pete. Afterwards, having enjoyed a few drinks, he turned on me and said, 'What the fuck are you doing, Lulu? Why are you doing this crap? You should be on the road, kicking ass. What happened?'

The criticism stung me and I reacted angrily. 'What would you rather me do – finish up like Janis Joplin? Should I drown in a bottle of bourbon, or stick a needle in my arm? I have a family and a son. The mortgage has to be paid. Don't lecture me!'

Pete felt as though I had taken the easy way out – that I had sold out and gone fuzzy at the edges. He was right. I had. I should have been in a band, still roughing it on the road. Instead I had become a Highgate mum, doing school runs and playing Mrs Frieda. Not quite wearing Laura Ashley yet . . . but it was coming.

I knew Pete was right, but that didn't stop me feeling hurt and angry. I wanted to lash out. I wanted to say, 'Oh, yeah! Oh, yeah! Is that what you think, Mr Pete-bigshot-Townshend? What would you know? Don't judge me!'

I realise now, of course, that he really cared. That was the thing about the sixties – there was a genuine respect and love between musicians. I know it probably sounds soft, but we were all part of something that was much bigger than we were.

Some took a path that led to heroin addiction and alcoholism. Some found fame and made amazing fortunes. I took a safer path in between. You only have to look at my family background to see why I did this. My father was an alcoholic. I had started with nothing.

Decisions were made for me with my best interests at heart. At the same time, I know that people in the recording industry – including Billy – felt as though I had sacrificed my credibility for the sake of a regular income.

'Shame about Lu. What's she doing now?' they would ask Billy.

'The same old thing,' he'd answer.

Heads would nod and silence follow.

For Christmas and New Year we all flew to Bophuthatswana in South Africa for the 'Million Dollar Challenge' golf tournament at Sun City. I had been booked to perform for a week and I took a full entourage – tour manager, musical director and my band and backing singers, including Edwina. John and Jordan came too, along with our nanny.

The place was full of famous golfers and showbiz personalities, including Johnny Mathis, Glen Campbell, Telly Savalas, Ernest Borgnine and Sean Connery. Many of them I'd known for years, having performed on the same bill or appeared on the same chat shows.

The Sun City concerts also featured The Beach Boys, and it was great to see them again. Edwina struck up a real friendship with Dennis Wilson, who was gorgeous, but alas an alcoholic. Sadly he died soon afterwards.

Brian was as big as a house and Bruce could talk the leg off a table. Carl was my favourite. There was a bit of mystery about him and he, more than anyone else, held The Beach Boys together. I always felt the Wilson family was too sensitive for this world.

It was nice travelling with John and Jordan, although poor John had the flu when he arrived and then proceeded to crack his head in the pool and needed two stitches in the wound. I did a show each night and most of the golfers came along.

On the final day of the tournament, the rain began falling. It stopped just long enough for Johnny Miller to beat Seve Ballesteros. I had a final show that night and we flew home from South Africa the next day. The weather was so bad, with thunderstorms buffeting the plane, that Seve threw up in the seat behind us before passing out.

Three days after getting home, I flew to Los Angeles. It was a whirlwind trip to promote my single 'I Could Never Miss You (More Than I Do)'.

The song had been the fastest-selling single in America when it was released in early July. The same sales in the UK would have given me the number one position for more than a month.

In late July it reached No. 18 in the Billboard Top 100 and spent eighteen weeks in the US charts.

For a while it looked like a major breakthrough. I was back and forth to the States, doing TV, radio and press interviews, including an appearance on *Dick Clark's Bandstand*.

In mid-January I had rehearsals for a BBC series and more work in the recording studio, but within weeks I was in Los Angeles again. This time for the American Music Awards and *The Billy Crystal Show*.

At the Grammy Awards I was nominated for Best Rock

Performance by a Female Vocalist for the song 'Who's Foolin'
Who?'. I didn't win, but I had a great night.

Afterwards I wrote in my diary:

> I miss John and Jordan. I hope I get another hit record then
> maybe we can come here [to LA] to live for a few months.
> Please God, give us all help to cope. John is away at a
> hairdressing convention in Europe. We lead such busy
> lives . . .

Almost in the same breath, I wrote:

> I am so lucky to be able to do everything I want. When I
> think of women who have tough or domineering husbands
> or I think of lonely career girls . . . I have the best of both
> worlds . . .
>
>   I feel guilty about not giving enough time and attention
> to John and Jordan. I could say the same about my mother
> and father . . . and so on and so on. There just isn't enough
> time . . .

# 14

# *When the Student is Ready, the Teacher Appears*

I had never contemplated doing a West End musical. To be honest, I thought they were too old fashioned and full of sugary sentiment and moralising. Very few of them were gritty and topical.

It wasn't as though I didn't have offers. When Linda Ronstadt appeared in 'The Pirates of Penzance' on Broadway – a big success for her – she told the producers, 'If you're going to London, you *have* to get Lulu.'

When the idea was put to me I said, 'No way! What do I know about singing light opera?'

Cameron Mackintosh was another who tried to convince me. 'I read somewhere that you said you wanted to play Annie Oakley,' he said one day, picturing me in 'Annie Get Your Gun'.

'That's right,' I laughed. 'But I've grown up since then.'

As a guest on a Harry Secombe TV special one evening, I met up with Julia McKenzie who I had known for years. She had just finished playing the role of Miss Adelaide in the award-winning National Theatre production of 'Guys & Dolls'.

I went to see the show and even managed to drag John along, despite his workload. He was often so exhausted that he didn't go out during the week. During the intermission, several people, including Marian, said to me, 'You know, Lu, you would make a perfect Miss Adelaide.'

I said nothing at the time, but for the rest of the show I pictured myself as the nightclub dancer, desperate to marry her long-time boyfriend, the gambler Nathan Detroit.

Backstage afterwards I bumped into Marcia Hunt, who was in the midst of rehearsing for 'A Midsummer Night's Dream'. Her first words to me were, 'Why don't you play Miss Adelaide?'

I guess you could say the seed of an idea was planted in my mind. For the first time I really began to think about doing a musical. I was thirty-four years old and had been working since I was nine. I wasn't getting the same enjoyment from doing cabaret. My audiences were getting older. Maybe it was time to broaden my range and try something new.

'Song & Dance' the Andrew Lloyd Webber musical, had been playing successfully at the Palace Theatre in London. Gemma Craven was leaving the show and I had a call from Andrew asking if I'd consider taking over the role.

I hesitated. This was a light soprano role. My roots were rock 'n' roll and black American music. Did they really think I could do it? I talked it over with John and Marian.

John didn't hesitate. 'I think you should do it.'

'What about the workload?'

'We'll manage. We always have.'

'Song & Dance' had started its life as a one-woman show, written by Lloyd Webber and my old friend Don Black. It was about a girl arriving in New York and her relationships with various men.

It had become a surprise West End hit in the early eighties, when Lloyd Webber and Cameron Mackintosh could do no wrong.

Apparently, it is supposed to be easier taking over in an established play. I'm not so sure. I felt like a teenager again, I was so nervous. I even had singing lessons to prepare for the role – something I had never contemplated before, but singing light soprano was a whole new kettle of fish.

Although it was challenging vocally, that didn't bother me as much as the acting side. 'Song & Dance' is a tour de force and I was on stage virtually the entire time. Gemma Craven was a wonderful actress and I didn't want to suffer by comparison.

I worked very hard with the director, John Caird, who was focused and patient. He knew the part inside out. John had come from the RSC and I had never worked with someone like that before.

For almost the entire first half of the show I had to be on stage alone. It was incredibly nerve-racking. If I had been doing a concert as Lulu it would have been fine, but I was expected to be someone else – a girl from New York, with a Bronx accent, who could reel off witty one-liners.

Wayne Sleep had the lead dancing role. He told me to relax and enjoy myself. I tried to follow his advice, but when I walked out on the stage I felt tiny in front of that huge set.

Next morning I knew the reviews were in the newspapers. I wanted to read them and at the same time I didn't want to read them. Marian called and began quoting certain paragraphs. I dashed out and bought my own set. The reviews were wonderful. I was relieved and excited. After all these years I could still learn something new.

I did eight shows a week, including matinees, and loved every minute of it. Lots of friends and family came along to watch, including Freddie Mercury (three times), John Reid and Elton John, as well as Maurice, Robin and Barry Gibb and their wives.

Soon I had offers of stage work on both sides of the Atlantic. 'One show at a time,' I told myself.

A month into the run, during a mid-week show, the sound system malfunctioned. The fold-back failed and I couldn't hear myself singing. At that point I was standing on scaffolding, high above the thirty-piece orchestra, belting out a song. I began forcing my voice, trying to hear myself.

The sound engineer came to my dressing room afterwards to apologise. A tiny microchip had blown, she explained, showing me the offending chip. It seemed ridiculous to think that such a small piece of equipment could have created such havoc.

A few nights later I noticed that I had a slightly sore throat. I thought it was a cold coming on – an occupational hazard. In twenty years I had only twice had to cancel an engagement. Soon my voice became hoarse and, for the first time in my life, I couldn't hit my top notes.

Clearly, this wasn't just a sore throat. My doctor referred me to a throat specialist, who advised me to rest for a few weeks and be totally quiet. Hopefully the damage would repair itself.

Andrew Lloyd Webber and Cameron Mackintosh were very understanding when I dropped out of the show. Hopefully, I could return within a week or two. It didn't even occur to me that my career was in danger. Of course I'd be able to sing again. I took that for granted.

I wasn't allowed to utter a sound, which ranks as a form of torture for someone like me. My mother always claimed that I hadn't been silent for more than eight hours my entire life . . . and only then when I was sleeping.

I had to jot things down in a notebook, but could never write fast enough. Either that or nobody could understand my scrawl. I grew more and more frustrated as each week passed.

With no sign of improvement, I went to see one expert after another, seeking second, third and fourth opinions. All agreed that I had damaged my vocal cords. One said that I had abrasions on my throat. Another described them as blisters.

Of all the specialists, one impressed me most with his honesty and professionalism. He recommended that I have an operation on my throat. Showing me the process, he produced a very long, thin pair of scissors and drew a picture showing how the scissors would go down my throat and slice off the blisters.

It sounded straightforward so I agreed to go ahead. John couldn't believe that I could be so calm.

'How can you take a chance like this? Why aren't you flying to clinics in Switzerland or America? I'd be looking everywhere for another opinion.'

'Because I trust this man. I think he knows what he's doing.'

The operation was over within a few hours. Afterwards I was under strict instructions not to utter a sound for seven days. Again, it seemed like an eternity. Even after a week there was no question of trying to sing until my throat had healed properly.

During the days of waiting I began to feel the first flutters of anxiety. I picked up a newspaper one morning and saw the headline: 'LULU MIGHT NEVER SING AGAIN!' Suddenly, my voice was being discussed on the radio and all sorts of experts were quoted on how risky throat surgery could be.

This fed into my anxiety until eventually it turned to panic. What if they were right? What if I couldn't sing again?

I tried to imagine what it would be like *not* singing. My voice had kept a roof over my head, helped my family out of the tenements and taken me around the world. I had always taken it for granted. I was born with it. It was a gift from God. It had always defined who I was – the wee girl from Glasgow with the big voice.

On the morning of my visit to the specialist, I woke early and paced through the house, trying to push the dark thoughts away. I drove myself to his office. John offered to take me, but I knew he was busy.

'How will I know if my voice is OK?' I asked the specialist.

'Because it will feel just like it always did.'

'What should I do?'

'Go away, be quiet and let it heal. Come back and see me in a week.'

'Can I sing?'

'Not yet.'

It was another four weeks before I could tentatively sing a few notes and do vocal exercises. I started slowly and warmed up beforehand. It was during this time that Marian read a story about a singing teacher who had worked with George Michael. I contacted Helena Shenel and arranged an appointment.

'I'm not going to teach you how to sing,' she said. 'You can do that already. But I can teach you how to protect your vocal cords and make the most of your gift.'

Over the next few months Helena taught me how to make the vowel sounds like an Italian and to breathe naturally. With her help I began to open my mouth more, dropping my jaw and lifting the soft palate. This opened my throat wide and let the sound just 'happen' rather than forcing it.

The effect was amazing. In the studio I became more accomplished. I had been given a wider vocal range, which was like being handed new tools. I was more skilful and had a better technique. And over time my voice became rounder and richer.

Certain singers have the most unbelievable instruments available to them. People like Christina Aguilera, Mariah Carey and Whitney Houston – all of whom I love, as long as they don't over-sing. Although born with these remarkable voices, they still had to do a lot of work to become technically brilliant.

With my voice now repaired, I went back to work. Sadly it was nothing as grand as a West End musical. I was in Lewisham doing a pantomime with Bonnie Langford, Tony Brandon and Jeremy Beadle.

They were lovely people, but it still felt like one of the low points of my career. It wasn't quite the chicken-in-a-basket circuit, but I was getting closer.

John could see I wasn't happy. He also felt I had given my power away when I let Marian become a fifty-fifty partner. At the same time, her husband Mark produced and his writers were providing many of the songs on my albums.

John could see that my career was stagnating and he wanted me to do something about it. But what? I had been with Marian right from the beginning. How could I leave her?

In 1984 I received two offers which illustrated perfectly how differently Marian and I viewed my career. The first was the chance to play Adelaide in the new National Theatre production of 'Guys & Dolls'. I loved this musical and everybody had said the role was perfect for me. It would also, hopefully, make up for the disappointment of having to leave 'Song & Dance'.

At the same time I was approached by Granada with a TV project. *Some You Win (Some You Lose)* was totally different to anything I'd done on TV before. To begin with it wasn't a variety show. Instead of having to sing for my supper, I got the chance to interview people and learn about their lives. The aim was to find guests who were celebrated winners (and losers) in their fields. It might be a champion sportsman like Daley Thompson, or a perennial loser like Eddie the Eagle.

Marian wanted me to take the TV offer. 'This is something new,' she argued. 'The stage can wait.'

My co-hosts were Kenneth Williams of 'Carry On' fame and a newcomer, Ted Robbins. Each week Kenneth told legendary stories of embarrassing blunders, while I interviewed well-known people about the highs and lows of their careers.

For example, Liberal leader David Steel described getting caught in a room at the British Embassy in Moscow with David Owen while they were both changing their long johns. Denis

Healey burst in and chortled, 'Ah, so that's what the Alliance is all about.'

I flew to Hollywood and interviewed, among others, Larry Hagman, who I hadn't seen for years, and his *Dallas* co-star Charlene Tilton. Larry admitted to twice forgetting the words when he was singing for the Queen Mum at a Royal Variety Performance. 'If you're going to blow it, blow it big,' he advised.

I met some fascinating people, including Muhammad Ali, Zsa Zsa Gabor and Olivia Newton-John (another old friend). I spent a wonderful day with Rock Hudson, sitting beside a swimming pool at a beautiful ranch-style house in the Hollywood Hills, sharing a bottle of wine. We watched the sun go down and listened to his stories about working with the likes of James Dean and Elizabeth Taylor.

Doing the Hollywood interviews was the highlight of the series for me, and much more fun than being back in the studio. As it turned out, *Some You Win* never really worked for Granada. I don't think the makers knew what sort of programme they wanted it to be.

Having turned down the role of Miss Adelaide I thought I'd missed my chance of ever playing in 'Guys & Dolls', but the opportunity came up again. Just before my thirty-sixth birthday in 1984 I had a call from Richard Eyre, who had been asked to direct the musical again. This time I didn't hesitate. It felt like my destiny.

It was a privilege working with a director like Richard. I loved him. Right from the outset I told him that I wasn't an actress and I needed his help. He committed himself to be there for me – just as John Caird had done.

Highly intelligent, gifted and very gentle, Richard drew the most amazing performances from people. He proved to me that a great director can turn almost anyone who wants it into a good actor . . . and if they happen to have any talent they can become a great one.

The plan was to take the show on tour and then return to the West End. We opened in Bristol in March 1985, before playing in Manchester, Edinburgh and Birmingham. We toured for three months, doing over 100 performances. It was lovely staying in hotels, with only myself to think of when I dressed in the morning and undressed at night. Best of all, John and Jordan came to visit me every weekend. It was one of the happiest times of my life.

Richard had never done a production outside of the National Theatre and it was a great coup for the producers to get him. Here was the man who had blown everyone away with his production of 'Guys & Dolls'.

In July we came back to the West End for a season at the Prince of Wales Theatre. I had committed myself to the show until December – eight shows a week for seven months.

At weekends Jordan would often stay with me at the theatre while John played cricket. We'd meet up before the evening show for a Chinese meal and then John would take Jordan back to 'Woodley'.

I didn't get home until late. They were usually both asleep. It was hard to unwind after the rush of performing. Normally I watched TV or read a book. In the morning I would often sleep in.

Ever since the late sixties I had been interested in Eastern philosophy and the various spiritual teachings that I had heard about. When I met John he had shared the same interests. Soon after we met he was given a book by Ringo's wife, Maureen, called *Autobiography of a Yogi*. It had first been published in the 1940s and became one of the most widely read and respected books ever published on Eastern mysticism and spirituality.

It relates the life story of Paramahansa Yogananda, who had trained as a yoga master in India and later lived and taught in America. In a remarkable life he met people like Mahatma Gandhi and many of the most admired spiritualists in the East.

In the early days, when John and I were getting to know each other, he would spend hours on the phone reading me sections of the book. I think he probably read the whole thing to me.

When The Beatles went to India, I remember John Lennon coming back and telling me that I really should learn how to meditate. Not long after that I went to a TM (transcendental meditation) centre in London with Patti Boyd and Cynthia. I was given a mantra that I was supposed to repeat when I meditated. For some reason, I thought it would be magical. Nothing happened.

I was quite cynical about the whole thing and dropped it very quickly. I was still very interested in meditation, but I hadn't found the right teacher.

Later, when I was recuperating from my throat operation, I tried to meditate again. I felt as though, when I damaged my voice, I had broken something deep inside myself which was fundamental to my entire well-being. For this reason I looked for ways to relieve my tension and anxiety. Again I couldn't meditate.

I have always known that timing is very important. I simply wasn't ready.

While I was in 'Guys & Dolls' John went to America to do a major hair show in New York. He met a choreographer who impressed everyone on the show with her attitude and demeanour. She seemed to have an indefinable quality about her that made her easy to be around.

She told John that she practised Siddha meditation and said there was a centre in London. He came back and began going to the meditation programme, which was on one evening a week. Unfortunately, because of the show, I couldn't go with him.

One night, unable to sleep after a performance, I picked up some of the literature that John had brought home. I began reading a book, *Where are you Going?* by Baba Muktananda. Even when I grew tired, I couldn't put it down.

There is one line I will always remember: 'All the answers are on the inside, not the outside.' That night I had a classic spiritual awakening.

The following Sunday I went along to the Siddha Centre and listened to one of the talks. I really enjoyed being there. Nobody wanted anything from me, or cared about who I was. At the same time they were so respectful of who I was – as an individual, not as a celebrity.

When I finished 'Guys & Dolls' I went to the centre regularly, learning about Hatha yoga and the principles of meditation. I could do the breathing and the exercises, but it just didn't click. As hard as I tried, I couldn't reach that place that I needed to reach for me to meditate deeply. This didn't bother me. I enjoyed the energy and loved the chanting.

All this changed when I met Gurumayi Chidvilasananda, the spiritual head of the Siddha Yoga Foundation. She was passing through London on her way from the US to India and I was asked if I'd like to meet her.

John was busy, Jordan had school and I had the show to do. Yet for some reason we all woke very early that morning and we were almost carried there.

Gurumayi was coming through Heathrow, but only for a few hours. I expected to find a handful of people waiting for her, but instead discovered more than 600. We waited. There was incense burning and people chanted. The air was filled with a wonderful sense of anticipation. It was such a divine feeling.

I was drawn to these people. I wasn't the focus of anyone's attention. They were waiting for someone far more important.

All of a sudden the hair on the back of my neck stood up. I

turned around and Gurumayi walked in. She stepped on to a low raised platform and sat in the lotus position on a chair.

I had seen a lot of people with presence walk on to a stage – some of the biggest names in the history of popular music – but this woman had a presence beyond any of them. She looked around her as though she was soaking up all the love in the room. And when she looked at me I went red hot. My spine tingled and I had tears running down my face. I wasn't crying.

I remember very few of her words, but one statement stuck in my mind. 'Where I have come from it is a particular time of the day,' she said. 'And I have arrived in London and it is another time. And where I am heading is a completely different time again. None of this matters. Because we are all here now, the *time* is right.'

Afterwards, when I arrived home, I went to the place where I normally tried to meditate – a little corner that I had set aside, with a picture, a candle, a flower, a little bell and incense. My sacred place.

I did my yogic breathing and a bit of hatha yoga stretching. I sat down, lit the candle, and then suddenly it happened. I went into a deep state of meditation for the first time. At the same moment, I was totally aware of what was happening around me. I was conscious of a plane flying overhead. I had the sense it was Gurumayi.

An energy had been woken inside of me. Whatever path I was looking for, whatever I was seeking, now became clear. I could see the way ahead.

I was thrilled. How many books had I read? How many years had I wanted to do this? Finally, it had happened.

I know some people are sceptical. They think meditation is weird. They are right to question things. It is very important to do this. But meditation has had a profound impact on my life. It has refined me and worked on me. It has been like putting on a new pair of prescription glasses and going, 'Woah, my God, I can see . . . myself and the world.'

I used to be very self-critical. If I made a mistake I would attack myself. I had a fearful temper and would just explode. Now I have more patience. I can see my faults but I don't hate myself for them.

I also used to spend my days worrying about other people – especially my younger brothers and sister. Now I've learned to let go somewhat and let them get on with their lives. I'm learning to slow down and to laugh more. I appreciate other people for what they are.

The more I learn about Siddha yoga, the more there is still to learn. And the more informed I become, the more subtle the truth turns out to be. These things are impossible to explain in words, but at the heart lies an eternal truth and understanding that God dwells inside each of us.

I am still learning.

# 15

## *I Don't Wanna Fight*

When I first met John he told me that he didn't want to be a hair-dresser all his life. In a sense that was true – he became a businessman. One salon was never going to be enough. He opened his second in Aldford Street in 1979 and had plans for a third. He and Clifford parted ways and John carried on under his own name.

Soon he had plans to launch his own hair-care range and began talking to banks about financing. It was a very expensive plan. At one point I went along to the head office of Barclay's Bank and supported John as he discussed a loan. The bank wanted him to have more equity in the business, which meant finding more money.

Property prices in North London were booming and 'Woodley' was worth almost ten times what I paid for it in the late sixties. We decided to sell the house and invest some of the equity in John's business. We'd buy a place closer to the salons and the theatres, cutting down on our travelling time.

I wasn't bothered about selling 'Woodley'. It was only bricks and mortar, and my family came first.

John's father had retired from hairdressing but he still helped John with the books. John Snr had been buying and selling houses all his life and the family had moved around like gypsies when John was growing up.

Once we had a buyer for 'Woodley' and a settlement date had been agreed, John Snr helped us find a house to buy in Eaton Terrace by Sloane Square, and we put Jordan into a good local school – Eaton House. On the day of completion the buyer failed to show. The sale of 'Woodley' fell through, leaving us with two houses and a massive mortgage. The stress almost killed John. He was now taking care of all the joint finances. We took out a bridging loan and moved back into 'Woodley' for another year. Jordan stayed at the same school and John would drop him off on his way to work each morning. I picked him up some days and Mum took care of him on others.

It was a terrible time for John because he felt totally responsible. He wanted to fix everything – all our problems – but they just compounded. The pressure was unbelievable and ultimately it affected his health.

In early July 1986 I wrote:

> This week I feel so worn down. Jordan has whooping cough and I haven't been getting my proper sleep. John has been coming home exhausted. Now I'm off to Germany and Switzerland. John feels it is all too much. He can't cope. Can I help him and myself too? I don't know. Maybe I've taken on too much.

I knew John had stomach problems when I married him. He was a worrier. Sometimes it played up badly and I could see the pain on his face and knew that he wasn't sleeping well. I tried to be sympathetic but it infuriated me when he ignored symptoms and refused to see a doctor. Instead of comforting him, I was more likely to say, 'Oh for God's sake, this business is making you sick, tell them all to get lost.'

'Be serious.'

'At least go to the doctor.'

'I'm fine.'

Like a lot of men, he was his own worst enemy – refusing to seek help, or slow down. He would work all day at the salon without eating because he was so busy. This only made his stomach problems worse.

One Saturday morning in mid-July he told me about the bleeding. I begged him to go straight to a doctor, but he said that Monday would be soon enough. Instead he went off to play cricket with the Heartaches XI, ignoring the pain.

He didn't make it through the game. The ulcer had perforated and was bleeding into his stomach. The doctor admitted him straight into the Princess Grace Hospital near Regent's Park. He underwent surgery within hours. It all happened so quickly that it was almost surreal.

Everything seemed fine and John seemed comfortable. I visited him every day, taking Jordan with me. Then suddenly his condition deteriorated. I found him lying in bed, with a tube up his nose and another in his arm. His skin was wax-like and pale.

He had caught a secondary infection and the antibiotics seemed to have little effect. Whenever he coughed he was in agony. I could have cried at the sight of him.

John's father was amazing. He hunted down the right doctors and insisted they help. He wouldn't leave the hospital unless someone else was there to sit with John.

For the next ten days John seemed to hover on the edge. At times I thought I was going to lose him. It scared me. What would I do without him?

He spent two months in hospital. The ordeal drained us both, but eventually he pulled through. He had lost so much weight that he had to recuperate at home, regaining his strength. He never complained. When John was sick he didn't want to be comforted. He shut himself off.

I think this stemmed from his childhood. When quite young he spent a long time in hospital with heart problems. His father found the best care possible, but this meant that John had to be looked after miles away from home. His parents would visit whenever they could. John told me that it was a very difficult time. They were a very close family.

Later, when I married John, his mother took me to one side and said, 'Don't let him get colds.'

At the time I thought, Oh my God. What might happen? I should have replied, 'That's all very well, but he won't take care of himself.'

We finally sold 'Woodley', as well as the house in Eaton Terrace. It was a relief to get rid of both of them. John's father helped us to find a large fourteen-room flat in Mayfair, over the road from Green Park and around the corner from John's salon in Aldford Street. We spent a lot of money doing it up, with marble in the entrance hall, big fireplaces and a chandelier.

I threw myself into work. In particular I had to prepare for a new TV role. The director Peter Sasdy had asked me to play Mrs Pauline Mole in the second series of *The Growing Pains of Adrian Mole*.

The fact that I was taking over the role from Julie Walters wasn't something I even considered. She is such a brilliant actress that I didn't want to go there, otherwise I don't think I could have said yes.

Pauline Mole was a wonderful part. She was Adrian's loud, insensitive mum – hair by Worzel Gummidge and wardrobe by Oxfam. Considering how vain I can be, it was quite a transformation to let my roots show through and have frown lines pencilled on to my grey make-up.

The new series revolved around the arrival of a new baby sister in the Mole household. Adrian was still lusting after his girlfriend Pandora and fantasising about seeing her nipples, but his life became even more complicated with a baby in the house.

In the first of the six episodes I had to wear a pregnancy suit, which didn't make me feel broody at all. The babies certainly did. There were three of them used in the filming, including one that was only four hours old. The mother had just given birth at Harrow Hospital and stood watching in her dressing gown.

'What is her name?' I asked.

'Hannah.'

'She's beautiful.' My heart went out to this tiny, fragile thing in my arms. I struggled to do the scene.

'You're being too sweet,' said Peter. 'You're supposed to be loud and brash.'

As hard as I tried to be Pauline, I didn't want to scare little Hannah. I managed to get through the scene, but I felt a pang of regret as I handed the newborn back to her mother. I wanted one just like her.

Until Jordan was six I felt physically handcuffed to him. It was a mixture of maternal love and constantly watching him. Then he was a little person – a real individual – who became my friend.

I have always been maternal. That has never been a problem. I adore my nieces and nephews and love all babies. At the same time, I never lost the fear of having another. It just goes to show that you can want something very badly, but still be afraid of it.

Having made the decision to try to get pregnant, I totally embraced it. I felt my life wouldn't be complete without another baby. At the same time, I tried to be philosophical and say, 'If it happens, it happens.'

I told a magazine journalist, 'I hope you forgive me if I take a little time off next year. John insists that I have another child.

He's been insisting for some time but I've always found excuses. Now I have given in and I'm actually looking forward to it . . .'

*The Growing Pains of Adrian Mole* was broadcast in January 1987. John, Jordan and I were in India at the time. We spent Christmas at the Siddha Yoga Ashram in Ganeshpuri, two hours north of Bombay, whilst Gurumayi was there.

During the filming of the series I had made a point of not looking at the rushes. Even to this day, I have only seen snippets of myself as Pauline Mole.

I have never liked seeing myself on screen. I also find that it's best to be totally detached or you risk getting too involved in the outcome.

Of course people were going to compare me to Julie. It couldn't be avoided. As it turned out, the reviews were mostly positive and the second series was a ratings success.

In March 1987 I began rehearsals for 'The Mystery of Edwin Drood', a musical based loosely on the last unfinished Dickens novel.

It had been a huge hit on Broadway, winning nineteen American awards, and was now transferring to the Savoy Theatre in London's West End.

When the American producers first approached me, the role they had in mind was that of a girl who dresses up as a boy. Having played Peter Pan three times already, I wasn't very interested in another chapter of cross-dressing. 'Princess Puffa is much more interesting to me,' I said.

They were shocked. I don't think they could picture me as an ageing madam and opium dealer, with my waist cinched in and my tits hanging out. Cleo Laine had played the role on Broadway.

I sang a few of the songs and managed to convince them. Bottom line, they wanted me for the musical, which gave me a lot of leverage.

'The Mystery of Edwin Drood' was an unbelievably sumptuous production, with an elaborate set and wonderful costumes. I wore a ringlet wig, high-heel shoes, lacy pantaloons and a bustle.

It was a singing murder mystery in which the audience got to choose the murderer each night. This meant we had different endings rehearsed. It was a very complicated show and I loved the challenge. I had to stretch myself to do credit to the role of Princess Puffa.

Sadly the story didn't resonate with audiences in the UK. It didn't quite hit people in the heart because it wasn't different enough for them.

I was disappointed but philosophical. There isn't a magic formula that guarantees success. If there were we'd all be rich and theatre seats would never be empty.

John always used to say he would retire at forty. I believed him at first, but slowly began to realise that his ambitions were far greater than I ever imagined. I had never known anyone who worked so hard or was so focused on a goal.

By 1988 he had three salons and his own hair-care range. Selfishly, perhaps, I wanted more of his attention. I became more demanding and we argued. It must have been very hard for him.

Most of our arguments were about working too hard or having more children. I used to find it very difficult to get involved in John's work. The politics of looking after staff and sorting out their personal problems would get him stressed, which annoyed me. I would see him playing the psychologist, nurturing them and bolstering their self-esteem.

'Tell them to go shove it,' I'd say.

'That would be clever.'

'I can't stand it – the way you are now – you're a nervous wreck. You can't sleep . . . you're not eating properly . . . your stomach is churning . . .'

What I really meant to say was, 'Why can't you give me the same attention?'

John would have liked me to take more of an interest in the salons. He wanted me to listen without being critical. He loved the challenge of sorting out someone's troubles.

Whenever we argued it was all over in five minutes from my point of view. I would get angry, air my views and then be sweet again. John would take longer to forgive me. We're different in that way. If I trust and feel safe with someone I say what I think and then try to forget it.

I find it strange how often the things that most attract us to someone will eventually drive us crazy. I think this happened with John. He once loved my spontaneity and eventually it got on his nerves. I used to make him laugh with almost anything I did . . . and then I didn't.

For years we had talked fifteen times a day. It didn't matter where in the world we were. I don't know what we talked about – little things that were domestic, everyday and ordinary. We had always communicated on a deep level, but all of a sudden this stopped.

I wrote in my diary:

My poor John is feeling so much pressure. God, please find someone to relieve him of some of the pressure and responsibility. I am not capable of doing that. I hope he won't leave me because of this incapability. Help him find someone to guide him like Marian guides me . . .

My prayer was answered, but not quite in the way I had planned. John was doing a hair show in Italy when he met Gail Federici, a brilliant marketing manager, who worked for Conair – an international hair product company.

I think they sized each other up and saw the same thing in each other – a fierce drive and ambition.

Gail is very tiny but hugely single-minded. Like John, she has an analytical mind and is a powerful force when she puts her mind to business.

She once said to me, 'If you can't get in the front door, you use the side door. And if you can't get in the side door, you go to the back door. There will *always* be a way in.'

Gail was American and lived in New York with her husband Jimmy and her twin girls. She loved music and was fascinated when John told her that he was married to me.

The two of them decided to do a hairdressing book. From my point of view, I saw it as even more work for John. Not only was he spending twelve hours a day at the salons, he was coming home and spending another four on the phone to Gail as they discussed ideas and corrected proofs. Can you believe it? Four hours!

Not surprisingly, I was jealous of how much time he spent talking to her. I had so little of him already.

I can't remember how I discovered I was pregnant. I know it seemed like a miracle. We had been trying for more than two years and I had started to think it might not happen. I was also beginning to regret having announced my intentions to everyone. All that did was draw attention to the fact that nothing had materialised.

John seemed to be over the moon. I remember when he first set eyes on Jordan he described the moment as 'an awakening'. He told me he had never felt such pure joy. I wanted him to experience that again.

Jordan was in America on a holiday with friends. I told him the good news over the phone. Sometimes you forget how grown up your children are. 'Mum, I just don't believe it,' he said, astonished. There was no hint of jealousy. He was full of questions.

'Have you got a lump yet? Are you eating funny things? When is it due?'

I laughed. 'Not until next June or July.'

'Maybe it will be on my birthday,' he said, hopefully.

Looking ahead, I cancelled plans for an autumn tour in the title role of 'Peter Pan'. A heavily pregnant woman flying through the air on a wire was hardly going to impress an audience, or my obstetrician.

I wanted to keep the news a secret, but couldn't help myself. I was appearing in Bournemouth in the 'All Wight Laughter Show' with Michael Barrymore. I told the cast during rehearsals that I was ten weeks pregnant. Next morning I made all the papers.

'LULU'S IN THE CLUB FOR A BABY AT 40!' declared the *News of the World*. There were feature stories and columns written about 'older mothers'. It seemed to trigger a national debate about late pregnancies.

I was walking on air. I realised that I could and should have done this earlier. John came down to Bournemouth whenever he could get away. The new salon took up more of his time and his thoughts. He seemed distracted and not really there. Ten days after the announcement, I was on stage during the show when I felt the twinges of a cramp. I started bleeding. Even then I didn't realise I was losing the baby. The thought didn't even enter my head.

John had gone to see a movie and I couldn't reach him. I was rushed to hospital and taken into casualty. I still didn't think it was serious. I must have been in denial. My health was something that had never let me down.

When the doctors broke the news to me, I knew instinctively that I would be strong. I called Edwina. She heard my voice start to break. Then I stopped myself.

'Stop being so sensible, Lu. Let yourself go. You need to cry.'

She was right. I couldn't keep it bottled up.

John arrived and I burst into tears. I thought a baby meant everything to him. What would he think now? I also kept wishing that I hadn't told anyone. Then we could have kept the miscarriage a secret. It would have been a family thing.

'LULU LOSES BABY,' declared the front page of the *Sun* on 27 August 1988. The headlines were even bigger and bolder than when I announced my pregnancy. Tragedy is more newsworthy than joy.

Although heartbroken, I kept telling myself that a miscarriage is a natural thing; it's nature's way of getting rid of something that wasn't quite right. Yet that didn't stop me crying at the drop of a hat. I could be absolutely fine one minute, then burst into tears the next.

A lot of people expected me to pull out of the show in Bournemouth. However, I didn't want to sit at home thinking about what had happened. Work had always been my saving grace. It was the most natural thing in the world.

My doctor said it was OK, so a week after the miscarriage I went back to Bournemouth believing that it was all over . . . done . . . finished, if not forgotten. On the first night I stood at the side of the stage, ready to make my entrance. Then something strange happened. For the first time in twenty-five years I began to shake with nerves.

Everybody in the audience knew I had lost the baby. What were they going to think? I shouldn't be here. I should have stayed at home, but it was too late to back out.

I heard the announcement. 'Ladies and gentlemen, Lulu!'

The band struck up and I walked out into the spotlight. Before I could start singing I noticed that the audience was standing. I remember thinking, 'What are they doing?' Then I heard the applause. They were giving me a standing ovation.

My throat closed and I couldn't get any words out. I wanted to thank them. I wanted to embrace every one of them. At the same time I was incredibly embarrassed. I hated being so publicly in pain. I stood there, out of respect for them, and allowed them to give me their sympathy and love, but all I really wanted to do was run back to my dressing room and shut the door.

'What am I doing here?' I asked myself. 'I'm in pain. I should have stayed at home. This is madness.'

My face was wet with tears and a kind woman in the front row passed me a handkerchief. It was another five minutes before I could sing.

John and I decided to wait until we saw Jordan before breaking the news to him. How do you tell an eleven-year-old boy something like that? When I finished in Bournemouth we flew to America. Jordan was staying with friends just outside New York. It was supposed to be a family reunion and celebration, but first we had to break the news.

I had it all worked out – exactly what I wanted to say – but I couldn't get the words out. I let Jordan chat happily about his three weeks away. Finally I blurted it out. 'I'm not having a baby any more.'

For a second Jordan said nothing. Then his face changed to an expression of pain and anguish. I tried to explain that miscarriages happen to thousands of women during the first three months of pregnancy. Often it's for the best just in case something might have been wrong.

'It doesn't mean I won't get pregnant again,' I said. 'We're going to keep trying.'

John and Gail had finished the book and now had new plans. John's product range was doing well, and they decided to launch it again on a huge scale into the UK and America. After months of discussions, Gail left Conair and began working full-time with John.

She and the twins flew to England, along with her assistant,

Ann. John rented her a house and her husband Jimmy planned to come and go when work permitted.

John's ambitions had always been grand, but Gail cemented them and gave them momentum. She was brilliant at marketing strategies and product placement. Whereas once John had spent hours on the phone with her every night, now he seemed to spend every spare moment with her. He kept telling me how brilliant she was and really wanted us to be best friends.

That's exactly what happened. I really liked Gail and I think the feeling was mutual. I would sometimes baby-sit for her or we'd go shopping together.

At the same time I was jealous of her. John seemed to be obsessed with her. I know what John's like. When he focuses on a person he gives them 100 per cent. He looks right into their eyes and they feel like the only person in the room. But eventually he moves on and focuses on someone else – someone who can teach him something.

John and Gail's plans were expensive. We sold the apartment in Mayfair to raise money and moved into a rented garden flat in Maida Vale. John said it would only be for six months to a year.

I was quite happy to sell the apartment. It was too formal. Instead I wanted to buy a maisonette in somewhere like Randolph Avenue, with a communal garden for Jordan to ride his bike around and play football.

The garden flat was nice enough, but it had low ceilings and was quite dark and pokey. Mum and Dad were a little concerned. They had seen me go from a spacious seven-bedroom house in Highgate to a small rented flat. What was happening?

My doctor was still optimistic that I could have a child, but as the months and then years passed I began to realise that it wasn't going to happen. I tried to be philosophical, but it hurt.

John and I still loved each other, but like most marriages the attraction had changed. There wasn't the same tremendous excitement in our relationship as when it first started. It was settled, steady and deep. At least that's what I told myself.

My career was a completely different story. In October 1988 I played Peter Pan for the fourth time, this time in the musical version, with Eric Sykes as Captain Hook. We opened in Manchester and then moved to Wimbledon in London.

Marian didn't seem to understand that I was on a treadmill. I had to lift myself for each performance when in reality I was often exhausted, unhappy, and most of all bored. Nothing excited me. Even worse, I was doing things that made money but killed my credibility.

Sadly we weren't on the same wavelength any more. Marian could picture me hosting a TV game show, or doing showbusiness interviews for arts programmes. She wanted me on the stage, in films, doing musicals, promoting products – you name it. 'You can do it all,' she used to say proudly.

'Yes, but what if I don't want to?' I'd reply.

Although Marian worked very hard to find opportunities for me, she was struggling to deliver on the things that I wanted. To be fair to her, I didn't know exactly what these things were. I knew, however, what I *didn't* want – the same old stuff.

In my heart I wanted to record again. Unfortunately, this was an area that Marian found difficult because the industry changed so rapidly. Unless you focused on it completely, the way John was doing with his business – almost to the point of making it an obsession – you quickly lost touch. Marian had chosen, for all the right reasons, to keep many irons in the fire, but it meant she didn't have the contacts or the sway to open doors at recording companies.

John could see I was unhappy. I was going through the motions, struggling to lift myself for more of the same. I needed to be challenged.

*

I didn't want to fall in love again, but with John Frieda I couldn't help it.

We married in October 1976 . . . not a moment too soon.

No wonder my wedding dress was tight!

A baby boy, Jordan, born in June 1977.

I had never felt such joy, or such trepidation.

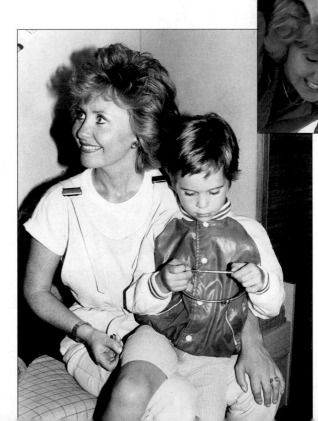

A thoroughly modern mum, doing birthday parties and sleepovers, as well as the odd holiday.

Music filled our lives. Jamming at home with Andy Gibb.

Adam Ant and I were born on the same day. Jordan was a huge fan, and had his own Adam-Ant outfit.

Third time lucky! I finally got to play Miss Adelaide in *Guys & Dolls*.

Smiling through the pain of a break-up.
John and I split in 1990, and I relaunched
my recording career with *Independence*.

In New York, to do a new
version of 'To Sir With
Love' with Soul Asylum.

My first UK
No 1. Take
That helped
relight my fire!

With Mum and Dad,
in 1994.

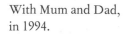

Elton John
and David Furnish –
two angels in my life.

Jordan, all grown up.

It's all about the hair!
From the sixties . . .

... to the nineties, and beyond.

My loyalties were torn. Marian and I had been together for twenty-five years. We were emotionally dependent upon each other.

As my frustration grew, it became obvious to Marian and began affecting her confidence. Finally she challenged me.

'This thing isn't working,' she said.

'No, it isn't.'

Silence followed. Both of us knew what was coming, but neither wanted to be the first to say it.

She sighed and straightened her skirt. 'Well, it just seems like we can't work together any more.'

I said nothing.

'My mother hasn't been well, you know. She needs someone to take care of her. I've been thinking about retiring and spending more time with her . . .'

I was so proud of Marian. Even though bitterly disappointed, she maintained her dignity and found a way of gently slipping into the background. She had been like a mother to me, as well as a best friend. Through my marriages, the birth of Jordan, the craziness of the sixties and the years of TV and cabaret, she had been a constant in my life. Now it was ending.

'I'll be here if you need some advice,' she said.

I was devastated. Even knowing it had to happen, and accepting and wanting it, made no difference. This was like a death. I felt abandoned. I had cut my lifeline and gone drifting off into space.

Part of me was racked with doubt. Had I done the right thing? Even though the answer always came back as 'yes', I still felt empty inside.

For those first few weeks, whenever the phone rang I expected it to be Marian. Similarly, out of habit, I would start dialling her number and then realise that she wasn't my manager any more.

Initially, I didn't accept much work. I sat back and tried to take stock, before deciding what to do next. In reality, I felt like a bird with a broken wing, unable to fly.

John was never around. He was spending all his spare time with Gail. They were on a mission.

John worked around beautiful women every day but this had never worried me. He had always been a flirt, but I knew there would have to be something more than beauty or sexual attraction to capture his interest. There had to be more. Gail was different. This was a meeting of minds. She caught his imagination. They shared the same vision. Even more importantly, Gail knew how to make it a reality.

For the first time I felt my marriage was under threat. How ironic! I had prayed for John to find someone to whom he could delegate and who could take the pressure off him. Yet now that he'd found this person, I was jealous of her and feared I was losing him.

The end result was that I became more demanding and insecure.

I should probably have found myself a new manager. Instead, I decided to manage myself and filter things through an agent.

John suggested Gail be involved and perhaps even manage me. She absolutely loves music and thought I had a great rock voice. I remember sitting down with her and talking about the sort of things I had done and what I wanted to do next. We both agreed that what I did best was getting up on stage with a hot band and belting out songs.

As a result, Gail helped set up 'The Red Hot Tour', involving more than forty gigs, which started in October 1989. I realise now that Gail would have liked to concentrate on my career – she loved music more than she did hair products – but she was already committed to working with John.

All three of our lives were now completely tied up together, yet at the same time I felt left out. John and Gail could spend hours going over business plans and discussing tactics. I wanted him home, talking to me.

Whenever we argued, John would never raise his voice or become emotional. Instead he would frame his questions carefully and remember my answers. He waited for me to vary my story even slightly and then seize upon this. He could quote things back to me verbatim that I had said weeks or months earlier.

Sometimes he would get things wrong, but he would never admit to it. Instead, he simply wore me down, until I began to question my own mind. Maybe he was right. Maybe I was being irrational or demanding or hysterical.

The more jealous I became, the more insane it made me. I grew fearful and needy. When I confronted John he looked at me calmly, taking all this in. 'What are you on about? Why are you getting so worked up about this? You're hysterical. I'm just trying to run a business.'

All sorts of thoughts would go through my head. I had lost the baby. I couldn't fall pregnant again. John had always wanted another child. I couldn't give him one. What now?

None of this happened overnight. Everything seemed to feed into my insecurity and I spiralled downwards into depression. I lost my objectivity and clarity. When John wasn't home, I wondered if he was at Gail's house. Coming home late one evening, I drove past her house and saw John's car parked out the front.

'Shit! He's in there!' I muttered. 'He left home at six in the morning. Now it's eleven at night. He's still with her!'

I confronted John, but again he told me that I was over-reacting. I was jealous without any justification. 'Why are you making such a big fuss?' he asked. 'You're making a mountain out of a molehill.'

Others had begun to wonder, too. There were rumours, but John didn't see any reason to even comment on them. 'They're not true, so why should I bother?' seemed to be his attitude. It drove me crazy.

Finally I confronted him. He was in the bath. Vulnerable.

'John, I need to know. Are you having an affair with Gail?'

His eyes widened. I thought, my God, he looks guilty.

'No, I'm not.'

I accepted his word, turned and walked out. Inside I was shaking. What was I going to do? John's life was moving on. Mine was stagnating. I had supported him when he opened his salons and launched his product range. It was as though I had helped build a ladder and now I was watching him climb above me and away.

John wasn't having an affair. Gail would never have done that. She was totally in love with her husband and the twins. I was looking for someone to blame and she was in the middle. The truth is, I really liked Gail and Jimmy and I thought their children were gorgeous.

Early in 1990 I was still clinging to the hope of having a baby. My doctor had put me on a special diet, designed to flush toxins from my system. I was eating plenty of protein, fruit and vegetables, but avoiding wheat, yeast, sugar, coffee and cheese.

Apart from touring, I had also done another TV role, playing a gangster's moll called Gossamer Trouble in *Perfect Scoundrels* with Peter Bowles and Bryan Murray.

John and Gail were about to launch the product range in America and John was going to have to spend a lot more time there. We talked about moving. Perhaps I could kick-start my career in the US. I was still well known there.

As we had these discussions, I felt an odd sense of trepidation. I don't know why. I was quite looking forward to a change of scenery . . . a new challenge. At the same time, I had a warning voice inside me that I couldn't quite hear.

Jordan was easy to convince. He had been to America many times on holiday and loved it. One of his favourite songs was Kim Wilde's 'Kids in America'.

The plan was to find a good school for Jordan and get a house nearby – probably just outside New York. As part of the reconnaissance we rented an apartment in Manhattan for the summer of 1990 during Jordan's school holidays. We planned to spend a few months there while John and Gail travelled all over America promoting their new company.

Jordan loved New York. We had a great time exploring the city and going to the movies. Both of us became really excited about the move.

Towards the end of the holiday, Jordan went to stay with friends for a few days. John and I had the apartment to ourselves. He had been quite moody and withdrawn for days. I didn't know why. I thought he was worried about work. I was used to that.

One evening he suggested going to the Siddha Yoga Centre. Something was clearly troubling him. When we came back we sat in the lounge, watching the lights of Manhattan.

John wanted to tell me something, but he was struggling. At the same time, I could see he was very focused. He had gone over this in his mind. He had rehearsed what he wanted to say. He just had to get started.

I can't remember the exact words he used, because at the moment he uttered them my mind froze. His voice was emotionless.

'We're not getting along,' he said. 'We have nothing in common. We never did have anything in common. We don't communicate. We have never communicated. I would rather not be in a relationship unless it is just the way I want it to be . . .'

I was numb. My mouth opened but no words came out. I felt myself almost hyperventilate. I wanted to ask him why, but the words were lodged in my throat.

He was still talking. 'This relationship isn't working. I know exactly where I'm going and I know exactly what I want in my life. I have really thought about this. I want out.'

Each statement was like a body blow. It had never even entered my head that John might leave me. John, I thought, wasn't the type of person who would break up his family. He loved Jordan too much. I thought he loved me enough to work things through.

Finally I managed to say something. 'My God, how can you say those things? After all these years . . . how can you do this?'

'Because I'm unhappy. I don't remember ever being happy. Instead I've been lonely. You've never supported me . . . things have never been right. You don't listen to me . . . don't hear me.'

I tried desperately to reach him. Surely he wasn't going to give up without a fight. 'Let's see someone . . . a counsellor. We can get help . . .'

John shook his head. 'I have made up my mind.'

'You're not even trying. I want to fight for this.'

'I *have* tried.'

I was sobbing and shaking. All his accusations were filling my head . . . how I'd never supported him and he'd never been happy . . .

Only later – when I replayed things in my mind – did I realise that he wasn't being completely honest. I remembered all the times we were blissfully happy. I remembered the times he had driven through the night just to spend a few hours with me . . . the wonderfully romantic holidays . . . our joy at having Jordan . . . watching him grow up . . . We loved together, laughed together, shared our fears and our hopes. How could he say we had nothing?

And if what he said was true, what did it say about him? That he had wasted fourteen years of his life with a woman he never loved. It wasn't true. He was simply trying to justify his desire to get out.

I didn't sleep that night. I paced the apartment. It felt as though my entire insides had been dissolved and flushed out, leaving me empty.

In the morning I got up and dressed. I knew John was watching my every move. He made small talk as we went downstairs for breakfast. I could see in his body language that he was feeling unburdened.

'You're not eating,' he said chattily.

I couldn't eat. Nothing would go down my throat. It was a horrible feeling.

'We need to talk about Jordan,' he said.

I didn't reply. From the look on my face he knew it was not a good time.

Jordan didn't come back that day. John and Gail took off on a product tour. I was on my own. For the rest of the weekend I aimlessly wandered the streets of Manhattan. My family pleaded with me to get on a plane and come home. I couldn't. I had Jordan to think about.

When he came back to the apartment I pretended that nothing was wrong. I wasn't going to tell him. That was John's job. For a long while we kept it a secret. I regret that now.

A week later I flew back to London with Jordan. We were living in a small house in Maida Vale which John Snr had found for us when we left the garden flat.

I can't describe how I felt. Everything I held dear – the rock that my life had been built upon – had crumbled beneath my feet. I couldn't believe it had happened. I kept thinking – hoping – John would change his mind. Maybe he had completely lost his senses. Maybe he would realise his mistake and come back.

Soon it became clear, however, that he had planned even further ahead. As well as wanting to get out of the marriage, he wanted Jordan to come to America. Whether I came too was up to me.

The subject was always framed around Jordan's schooling. It was a decision about his education, not about custody or parenting.

'I don't know, I can't make a decision like that,' I told John.

'Well, in not making that decision, you've already made a decision,' he would say. 'This could affect our son's life.'

I didn't know what to do.

John called almost every day, pressing me for a decision. 'Are you coming? What about Jordan? We have to think of his education.'

School was due to start at the end of September. What should I do? Should I go to America? My marriage was over. I didn't want to spend all day sitting in some apartment by myself, while Jordan was at school. John didn't want me around. My family was here, in Britain. This country had been good to me.

Gurumayi was touring in Australia. I visited her for a month. Jordan came with me for a shorter visit. John phoned every day, always asking the same question. 'Is Jordan coming to America? We have to organise the school.'

I was torn. John had left the marriage. He didn't want to be with me, but at the same time he didn't want to lose Jordan.

At times this made me angry and I was determined to say no. But then I thought about how much I loved John. I wanted to hold us together – me, John and Jordan – not tear us apart with accusations and recriminations.

I had seen my parents do this. I had listened to them, night after night, abusing and beating each other. I couldn't do that to Jordan. And that's what would happen if I said no to John. He was not going to let go. I could see us locked in a tug-of-war for Jordan's affections and his life. Something would have to break.

If for one moment I thought I was losing Jordan I would have fought with my life. But I knew John wasn't running away with him. It wasn't a kidnapping or anything so dramatic. I even told myself it would be good for Jordan. He was about to go through puberty. Boys of thirteen and fourteen need their fathers.

Traditionally, in cultures around the world and throughout history, boys are initiated into manhood by being around other men. I tried to console myself with this thought.

I didn't want to be selfish. I bent over backwards trying to be fair and to rationalise my decision. John seemed strong, while I seemed to be the opposite. What was I going to *be* for Jordan? John's strength would be a good thing for him. Maybe I was the only one in pain. I certainly wasn't in a good place.

I meditated and prayed, asking for guidance. John hadn't mentioned divorce. It was only a separation. I hadn't given up on my marriage. By letting Jordan go with John, I would be keeping the possibility alive, I thought. It meant that I could keep in touch with John and Jordan on a daily basis. We would talk on the phone and see each other. Maybe he'd change his mind. There was still hope.

In late September I flew to America with Jordan. John and I looked at different schools and took Jordan for interviews. Eventually, we settled on Hackley, an exclusive private school in West Chester, New York. It took day students, as well as mid-week and full-time boarders.

I helped John find a house nearby, with a swimming pool and a nice garden. It was strange choosing a family home knowing that I wouldn't be living there.

I was already preparing Jordan. I dropped hints and filtered information about why I wouldn't be around. I told him about trying to get a record deal and how I'd be travelling back and forth between London, New York and LA.

I pretended everything was normal, just as John wanted. We thought we were keeping a secret from Jordan. Who were we kidding?

# 16

# *Washing that Man Right Out of my Hair*

I suffered all the classic symptoms of grief. I existed in a daze, shocked and fearful in turns. My family rallied around me. They, too, were devastated. They wanted me to fight for my strength.

Jordan took precedence. Any excuse and I jumped on a flight to New York. I was there to see him play football, on speech day, for parent/teacher nights.

Initially he was a mid-week boarder and later he began to board full-time. John encouraged his sister to move to America, bringing her children – Elliot, Duncan and Emily. They had always been close to Jordan and I hoped they would keep him company.

Within a month, journalists began to speculate on whether our 'long-distance marriage' was on the rocks. I lied and said that everything was fine. There was no way I was admitting something to a newspaper that I wouldn't admit to my son.

I told the *Daily Express* that it was Jordan's decision to go to school in America, although I added it was, 'Not from my choice, not with my advice, nor with my guidance. It will be five years of his life – he's off. That's it. But even that final day was nowhere near as bad as the month of anticipation.'

In November I again scotched the rumours. 'It's untrue. There is nothing wrong with my marriage. Why don't they leave us alone?' I told the *News of the World*.

In the meantime, I was slowly trying to kick-start my recording career. Because of Jordan I chose bookings that could be manipulated time-wise so I could go to America at short notice. I said no more than I said yes.

I saw Jordan every school holiday and spent a lot of time in America staying with friends. On weekends I would pick Jordan up from school and take him to Manhattan, where we'd stay at a nice hotel. We didn't do very much. I just wanted to be with him. I took him to buy clothes or we'd see a movie. We had a favourite pizza place.

At night I'd lie awake in a huge American hotel bed, counting how many hours I had left with him. I couldn't get my head around what had happened . . . what a surreal life I was leading.

Jordan understood that John and I had separated and he never asked me about it. We both had a lot of unspoken pain and just wanted to be close. The saddest moment was dropping him back at school on Sunday afternoons. I had to hold myself together until the car was out of sight. Then the tears started.

Eventually John told Jordan, but he already knew. He is brighter than both of us.

The split finally became public in November 1991. The media was looking for animosity and rancour. I smiled and told them it was all very amicable. 'We are not getting divorced. There is nobody else involved,' I said. Asked why Jordan was in America, I said I thought it best for a teenage boy to be with his father.

It was all a front, of course, but when it came to putting on a brave face, I had the best teacher in the world. My mother had been doing it all her life.

Music sustained me. I sat down with Billy and we began to talk about what I should do. How could I get back some of my strength . . . my self-esteem. I had lost touch with my roots and why I loved music so much. Now I wanted to go back there. I wanted my credibility back and to record songs again.

'Is it too late?'

'No,' said Billy. We were sitting downstairs in the house in Maida Vale. Billy had grown up and calmed down a lot since his youth. He too had battled his demons, with a divorce and a roller-coaster career. Now he was happily married and was managing songwriters and publishing music.

My success in 1964 had been a whirlwind that had picked me up and carried me along. 'This time around we'll have to make it happen,' said Billy. 'It's not going to be easy.'

'Where do we start?'

'It's about the songs. You have to find them and you have to write them.'

'I can't write.'

'Yes you can.'

For years Billy had been trying to get me to write songs. I refused to believe that I could do it. Don't you need to study or be trained or have a formal education? What did I know? The Bee Gees had very little formal education yet look at the songs they wrote! Basically, I think I was just afraid of failing or not being good enough at it.

Billy suggested that I write with someone who wouldn't intimidate me. He had a young songwriter that he was managing and he put us together.

I explained to Steve DuBerry what sort of melodies I liked and played him some songs. In particular I gave him some stuff written by Don Henley, the drummer and co-founder of the legendary Eagles.

'I've never heard of him,' said Steve.

'Well, you go away and listen. If you can come back with a chord structure that sounds anything like any song he's ever written, then you'll be giving me exactly what I want.'

Steve took the brief perfectly. A fortnight later he came up with a very classy melody. Billy and I listened to it a few times as we sat downstairs in the house in Maida Vale. It was open plan with a beautiful glass atrium and a piano on one side of the room.

'OK, you have to decide what you want to write about,' said Billy. 'The simplest thing is to take your own experiences.'

As the melody played I began to think about my childhood, my family, John, Jordan and the break-up. The previous six months had been some of the most painful of my life, and were still palpable. How could I put emotion like that into words? I had been keeping it hidden. Very few people knew how much I was hurting.

'What do you want to say?' Billy asked.

'I don't know. I'm tired. This whole thing has worn me down. I don't want to fight any more.'

'There's your title – "I Don't Wanna Fight".'

The melody was still playing and I sang the line, 'I don't wanna fight no more.' It fitted perfectly.

Billy kept asking me questions and I talked about my emotions. I remembered our childhoods, when we used to plead with Mum not to goad Dad into a fight. Then I thought of John and how sometimes late at night we'd start talking, trying to thrash things out. Sometimes I was exhausted and just wanted to sleep, but he kept talking. We would go round and round in circles. I just wanted it to end.

These were the thoughts that flooded my mind. My emotions spilled out and became the words of a song. The chorus went:

*I don't care who's wrong or right*
*I don't really wanna fight no more*
*(Too much talking babe)*
*Let's sleep on it tonight*
*I don't really wanna fight no more*
*(This is time for letting go)*

The rest of the lyrics were about the heartache and pain of breaking up. We had done too much talking and it wasn't about who was wrong and who was right.

Although it had started as an exercise in writing, Billy and I both agreed it wasn't a bad effort. Maybe it could be an album track, if I managed to shop a deal.

The first person we played it to was Edwina. She said she got goosebumps, and remembered the chorus after hearing it once. A week later I recorded 'I Don't Wanna Fight' in a studio. It was only then, as I heard it played back that I realised we had created something special.

Within a week Steve DuBerry called us. He was friendly with Sade and had taken the song to her. She loved it. Her manager, Roger Davis, was also looking after Tina Turner. Tina was the executive producer of a movie about her life called *What's Love Got to do With It*. It covered the early part of her career and focused on her disastrous marriage to Ike Turner, who created and nearly destroyed her with his jealousy and violence.

They were still looking for songs and Tina fell in love with 'I Don't Wanna Fight'. Within weeks we had struck a deal that would see it used in one of the biggest films of 1993.

A part of me hated the idea that the song was about John. I wanted to let go. Then I realised that it was much more. It was about hope and saying goodbye and being strong. I heard an interview in which Tina Turner said it was a song about *her* life.

'Oh yeah?' I said to myself. 'It's about my life.'

A lot of people had said the same thing. We had written something that resonated with other human beings. It was about anybody's life that contained sadness, turmoil and loss.

Tina did a brilliant job and turned the song into a huge hit. It was eventually nominated for a Grammy Award and an Ivor Novello.

Afterwards, a lot of people asked me why I had given the song away. Why hadn't I kept it for myself? I was looking at the big picture. This was Tina Turner who wanted my song. The film of her life was going to be massive, and so was the promotional campaign. The song was going to be played around the world. It was far more important as a vehicle for Tina Turner than it was for me.

While all of this was going on, I relaunched my own career. Billy and I had spent weeks and months planning how to do this. He had said to me, 'It is all about the songs.'

'You have to look for them,' he said. 'We'll do it ourselves. We'll go directly to the publishing companies, and show them that you're absolutely serious about this. You're going to walk the walk . . . That's when they're really going to *get* it!'

People with my profile usually don't visit writers or publishing companies. We get material sent directly to us, or via agents or managers who filter the wheat from the chaff.

I didn't have a management team behind me. I had also been out of circulation for so long that nobody was sending me material any more. But if the mountain won't come to Muhammad, then Muhammad must go to the mountain.

Billy started to put the word out, dropping hints in the right places. Then he began making appointments. The reaction from songwriters and publishers was amazing. They were quite shocked when I simply walked in. I think I made them nervous, but at the same time impressed them.

The plan was to get some good songs together before approaching record companies and trying to get a deal. Again I would do this in person. I had to show I wasn't just some relic from the sixties.

It didn't prove easy. Before I even arrived, the producers and executives would ask the same questions. 'Where has she been? How does she look? How is the voice?'

'You should see her,' Billy would say, being very cool about it. 'And you should hear her.'

Some people thought I was past my sell-by date. The culture of youth had taken hold. Teenage bands were all the rage. Performers had to look young, act young and be beautiful. Artists in their mid-twenties were considered over the hill. What chance did I have at forty-two?

Once or twice executives didn't even bother turning up for appointments. One in particular was a man who I thought should have known better. His father had written some of my early hits and I'd been a friend of the family. Billy and I sat outside his office and waited and waited . . . I would happily have stayed there until he was ready, but instead we were told that he couldn't see me. I was hurt and angry. I remembered him as a kid, trailing around after his dad. How could he ignore me now? Hadn't I earned even a little respect?

A rejection like this made me feel worthless, but at the same time it inspired me. I was hungry.

It took a year but I got my deal. Peter Robinson at Dome, a great A&R man, said I was exactly what he was looking for. The feeling was mutual. I had known Peter for a long time. Apart from a long and successful career in the music industry, he also played cricket for the Heartaches XI with John. One of the first people I spoke to was Barry Gibb, who said, 'It's about time you got back into the studio.' The Bee Gees wrote a song for me, 'Let Me Wake up in Your Arms', which became one of my favourites on the album.

Going back into the studio was quite strange after being away for so long. I felt a little cack-handed. The technology was changing every five minutes and I was out of touch with my recording skills.

It didn't take long to get over my nerves because people really believed in me. Peter knew I loved the soulful sound and we both liked the same kind of music. We didn't want to do some rinky-dink album. It was going to sound modern, with great dance tracks and soulful ballads.

I worked with hot producers like Errol Henry and Nick Martinelli, and had remixes done by the likes of Brothers in Rhythm. We did dozens of different mixes of each song, constantly tweaking things until we had exactly the sound we wanted.

It took almost two years to finish the album. Once it was ready, Dome and its parent label, EMI, began discussing the marketing and promotion. EMI wanted me to have a manager and suggested Tony King.

Oh my God, that's a blast from the past, I thought.

I had known Tony since the mid-sixties. He is a charismatic, funny, good-looking and outrageous personality, with invaluable experience and great style. Tony had a pedigree. He had started off as a record plugger at Decca in the mid-sixties. Then he went to work for Apple. Later he ran a dance label in New York before hooking up with the likes of John Lennon and The Rolling Stones. That's where he would normally have been, but The Stones were taking a year off.

Rupert Perry, the boss at EMI, spoke to Tony. 'How would you like to manage Lulu?'

I think Tony was almost as surprised as I was.

He listened to the album before he made his decision. It clinched the deal. Not only was it credible, he said, but stylistically it was on the money.

# 17

# *Perfectly Imperfect*

My comeback single was released in January 1993. Called 'Independence', it was a dance track with a classic soul sound. It was about a woman making her own choices for the first time in her life.

When the record company tested the track on young DJs in the clubs, the general reaction seemed to be, 'I thought she died years ago.' At the same time, they were surprised and suitably impressed.

As part of the promotion the record company arranged cameo appearances at Ministry of Sound and other trendy clubs. I'd be lying if I said I wasn't nervous. Most of the crowd weren't even born when I had the hit with 'Shout'. I wondered how they were going to take me.

I didn't have to worry. Once the music started they were soon dancing. I was back where I wanted to be.

Tony King was brilliant at working the media and understood how best to position me, organising interviews and TV appearances that reached exactly the right audience. From the beginning we set out the philosophy – 'less is more'. There would be no bubbly, smiley, cuddly shots of Lulu in bright colours and cheesy poses. Tony wanted more thought, muted colours, simple lines, a lot of black and a lighter touch.

I had matured. My face no longer looked round like a school-girl's. I tipped the scales at under eight stone, lighter than when I was fifteen years old. People were saying how great I looked, which made me feel wonderful.

It wasn't just about looks. I was a different person. After what I'd been through, how could it be any other way?

'LULU'S NEW DAWN,' declared *The Times* in January 1993. 'LULU'S BACK FOR MORE,' said the *Independent*.

One journalist described me as 'the great white soul voice that Britain forgot. The girl who sold her soul to light entertainment. Now it's time for a revival . . .'

All of the heavyweights from EMI (Dome's parent label) were in the south of France in early February. Billy was there too. That's where he heard the news. 'Independence' had gone straight into the charts at No. 12.

I was amazed it rose so high, so quickly. I had been telling myself for months that one single wasn't going to determine whether I succeeded or failed. Even so, I felt a huge sense of relief. I had started something.

'Independence' reached No. 1 on the UK dance charts and also became something of a gay anthem. My second single, 'I'm Back for More' – a duet with soul singer Bobby Womack – was released in April and reached No. 27 on the UK Top 40.

The album was launched at about the same time. Critics described it as having a strong flavour of soul and R&B, as well as disco and pop sounds. Some compared me to Lisa Stansfield.

Although I knew there was still a long way to go, I now felt that I had something to build upon. I told the London *Evening Standard*: 'Four years ago I took control of my career. I started saying no to things that I didn't want to do and began to concentrate on what I had a gift for. The result is "Independence". Now I'm going to bop until I get a bus pass.'

In America 'Independence' reached the Top 10 on *Billboard*'s club play chart. The *Los Angeles Advocate* wrote: 'Lulu sounds half her age and her music is as up-to-date as the latest Lisa Stansfield CD. Funny how a middle-aged Brit with a camp pedigree can record a soul album this classy . . .'

All through the promotion campaign I was asked questions about Jordan and why he was in America with John. I kept spouting the same line about it being important for teenage boys to be with their father. I also said it was a great thing for Jordan to be furthering his education in America.

My father had left home at fourteen. I had left home at fourteen. Now it was Jordan's turn. 'I know it was very hard on my mother. I understand this now more than ever,' I admitted.

I flew to America for Jordan's fifteenth birthday, planning to bring him back to Britain for the summer. He was really excited for me and had followed my newfound success.

I took him along to the MTV studios in New York, along with his cousins Emily and Duncan. The grunge band Soul Asylum was recording an MTV Unplugged concert. Soul Asylum did a rendition of 'To Sir With Love' in their concert sets. I had no idea. Now they invited me to sing with them. I ended up doing the hidden verse from the film that was never released on the single.

The band was very sweet and nervous. They treated me like some sort of living legend, which was embarrassing but nice. One of them explained, 'You have to understand . . . that song is part of American history.'

This was hammered home to me that same month when MTV organised an inaugural ball to welcome Bill Clinton to the presidency. 'To Sir With Love' was sung by Natalie Merchant and 10,000 Maniacs, along with Michael Stipe of REM.

Jordan had a great summer. I was in the middle of promoting the album so he tagged along, meeting lots of musicians and young stars. We also spent time catching up with my family and visiting friends he had left behind when he moved to America.

I had tried to come to terms with living apart from him, but the sense of loss had never left me. In my head I envisaged travelling back and forth to America for the rest of my life. Jordan would go to university there, find a career, get married and have children. My grandchildren would grow up on the other side of the world.

It didn't seem likely that John and I would ever get back together. He told the *Daily Mail* in April 1993: 'You are what you are. You do what you do. In life it is best to move on and not dwell on things.'

He said of Jordan, 'He hasn't been upset by the situation. He knows that Lu and I are still friends and we are not throwing rocks at each other. He knows that we still care about him and he is still the priority in both our lives.'

Being on the road again was almost like old times. I didn't have to travel in a battered van, but the days were just as long. I did radio interviews, talk shows, open-air concerts and gigs.

In August I found myself in a caravan at Bude, Cornwall, waiting to appear at a Radio One Roadshow. Tony King and the rest of the entourage had come with me. The phone rang for Tony. Peter Robinson had a message for him. The management of Take That wanted me to record with them.

My first reaction was, 'What would I do with a bunch of young boys?'

'They're doing a remake of "Relight My Fire",' said Peter, clearly keen on the idea.

I knew the song. It had been a disco hit for Dan Hartman in the late seventies. Loleatta Holloway, a black gospel singer, had featured on the original. Did they want me to sound like her?

'No, they want you to sound like yourself,' Peter said.

I knew very little about Take That, but I knew they were hot. The band had emerged from Manchester and Stoke and, after a few near misses, had just had a UK No. 1 with 'Everything Changes'.

It was an odd idea . . . almost as bizarre as the Bowie collaboration. I was torn. I had fought hard to claw back some credibility with 'Independence'. Would an alliance with a young boy band enhance or damage my career?

Nigel Martin-Smith, the manager of Take That, had championed the idea, and everyone from my record company, along with Billy and Tony, were right behind the move.

'Nigel has been telling the boys all about you,' said Tony. 'He gave them the album. They love it. They really want this to happen.'

Nigel, I discovered later, had pushed hard to get Take That's record company to agree. Initially, they had suggested a black dance diva, but Nigel and the boys had insisted on me.

Shortly afterwards, I went into a studio in Primrose Hill for the recording. My vocals only took a couple of hours. Gary, Robbie and Jason were there. Gary and I worked on vocals together.

My cameo was about two-thirds of the way through. It was a powerful section of the song and everyone seemed happy with the result. It wasn't until I heard the final mix that I realised why the producers were so excited.

We filmed the video at an empty club in London. There was only one Winnebago, but the boys decided before I arrived that I should have it. I thought that was really nice of them. At first I felt like the new girl at school, except they were all half my age. Jason was the first to break the ice.

I was standing just off stage when he walked up to me and said that I was sexy and he fancied me rotten. I couldn't believe he had said it right to my face. He certainly got my attention.

'Relight My Fire' was launched in late September with a performance on *Top of the Pops*. The song went straight to No. 1. I was at the top of the mountain.

Soon I had another decision to make. Take That was about to embark on a big UK tour and then head to Europe. Nigel asked me to go with them. Initially, I said no. I didn't think this was my audience; they wanted to see five good-looking boys, not me.

The band did a few lead-up gigs before launching the major tour. Nigel invited me along to Wembley Arena to watch them in action. For 'Relight My Fire' they were weighing up whether to have someone else singing my part, or to use a video. As I was heading for my seat the crowd erupted into a roar. They had seen me coming in. A chill ran straight up my spine. I must be stupid, I thought. Why am I saying no to this? This is about the music, not about my age. So I joined the second leg of the tour.

The first gig we did was in Glasgow, which was very appropriate. The roof lifted off the place every time I came on stage. Take That was obviously the main event, but I opened the show by singing 'Shout', 'Independence' and 'I Don't Wanna Fight'.

I then joined them on stage for the very last song of the show, 'Relight My Fire'. We all looked outrageous. The boys were half naked in skimpy thongs or shorts, with devil-like horns on their heads. I wore a figure-hugging, completely see-through red lace dress and a red wig that made me look like Medusa with my hair on fire. For the finale, amid smoke and fireworks, I came up from the middle of the boys and they hoisted me high above their heads. The audience went insane.

Being on tour was exhilarating and enormous fun. The boys were great. We travelled on a huge luxury bus or in private planes.

There were always hundreds of screaming girls outside the hotel or waiting at the concert venue. For me it was a case of déjà vu. I had seen it with The Beatles, The Bee Gees and The Monkees; now it was Take That.

Hanging out with five young boys did wonders for my ego. They had enormous energy. They began calling me 'Looby' as in 'Loobylu', which became a sort of pet name.

'Right, Looby, we're going to a club,' they'd say after the concert. 'You're coming with us.' There was no holding me back.

We'd pile into a car and go clubbing until the early hours. I felt like a teenager again.

At the same time I had to overcome one of the most sexually charged friendships of my life. Jason and I saw each other all day from nine in the morning. We were together on stage and afterwards at nightclubs. Then we went back to the same hotel and stayed in rooms only a few feet from each other.

He had a way of looking at me (really looking at me) that woke something in me . . . something I hadn't felt in a long time. At the same time it was quite intimidating. He was such a flirt! All of this was heady, exciting, frustrating and electric. It was a tonic and a distraction and a huge boost to my ego. When I'm seventy I'll look back and say, 'Why the hell didn't I sleep with him?'

At the time everyone was worried that I would. Tony King used to give me warning looks and tell Jason to behave. He would phone Billy and say, 'Please God she doesn't go there. She can't.' I don't know why he was so worried.

The European tour took up the rest of the year. It brought back memories of travelling with The Bee Gees. Although exhausting, I had a good fitness regime – jogging and working out at least three mornings every week. I also continued to meditate.

Whenever the boys arrived and smelled the incense they'd say, 'Oh, Looby's in.'

Instead of making fun of me they were fascinated, especially

Mark Owen, who began to meditate with me. Robbie would come and show me his poetry and lyrics.

They were all fascinated by the sixties and used to ask me questions about The Beatles, The Rolling Stones and The Bee Gees. What was it like? How did I keep my head? How did I last so long?

All of the boys admired Elton John, particularly Gary Barlow. When the tour reached London, Elton's agent, John Reid, invited me to lunch at his new house, which was just around the corner from mine. 'Why don't you invite the boys,' I said. 'And get Elton to come.'

At the lunch I had Elton on one side and Gary on the other. The rest of the boys were around the table. We had a really nice day, talking about music, clothes, houses and being on the road.

Elton asked me what I was going to do next. Songwriting was still quite new to me and I wanted to explore that further. Out of the blue he said, 'I'll write with you.'

My jaw dropped. I was stunned. This was amazing! Elton John – one of the greatest songwriters of all time – wanted to write with *me*!

That night he came to the concert and said afterwards that I sounded better than ever. We arranged to get together once I had written some lyrics.

Billy and I began beavering away, madly writing. We kept saying to each other, 'What would he like?'

It was hard. We had never worked this way. Elton is one of the few people who creates a song around the lyric. Most people have the music first, or do both side by side.

Eventually, I sent Elton a pile of lyrics and he picked one. His partner, David Furnish, was in the midst of making a documentary on Elton, *Tantrums & Tiaras*. He wanted to film us working, which was fine by me.

Elton was amazing. He sat down at the piano and created a

melody around the lyric. He wrapped music around the words. I was blown away. In twenty minutes it was finished!

Although I had known Elton for a long while, our friendship seemed to grow stronger from then on. We are both about the same age and have many things in common. He was in recovery from drugs and alcohol and I knew all about addiction and the damage it wreaked. Elton could see I had been through a lot. I think he liked what I had turned into and I felt the same about him.

Billy and I had also been writing other new material. The Grammy Award nomination had won us enormous respect and songwriters were keen to work with us. Bonnie Raitt, one of my favourite singers, took one of our songs, and another was recorded by country & western star Wynonna Judd.

I bumped into Wynonna while shopping in Beverly Hills. I walked past a woman wearing a baseball cap, which couldn't hide the reddest hair I had ever seen. I thought to myself, 'I know who that is.'

She walked into a store and I followed her. I kept peering over displays, trying to get a better look. Yes, it was definitely Wynonna. She was with her sister, Ashley. Should I say something or not? Famous people in America often get freaked out if approached in the street.

I walked very slowly across to her. 'Excuse me, my name is Lulu and I'm a singer. I wrote . . .'

Ashley smiled and Wynonna turned. 'There is only *one* Lulu,' she said.

It was a relief to be recognised. I told her what a great job she'd done with the song.

'On stage every night I sing it to my son,' she explained, telling me about her little boy. I told her that I had written 'My Angel is Here' about Gurumayi. Again it showed how a song could have different meanings for different people.

*They say there's a state of heaven*
*Somewhere way above the clouds*
*I know there's a piece of heaven*
*In every little thing that you do*
*'Cause every time you walk in the room, my angel is here.*

On that same trip to California, Billy and I were staying at the Sunset Marquee. In the middle of the night on 17 January 1994, I heard Billy's big, gruff voice.

'Lu! Lu! Lu!' He was hammering on the door.

'What's the matter?'

'Didn't you feel it?'

'What?'

'The earthquake.'

'Is that what it was?'

'Come on, we have to get out.'

'Let me get my shoes.'

'No, forget your shoes.'

'I'm getting my shoes.'

At least I wasn't alone. Gabriel Byrne, who was at the same hotel, also admitted to sleeping through the biggest quake in fifty years.

Guests were shepherded outside on to the street. Billy kept everyone entertained, telling them stories and jokes. There didn't seem to be much damage to the hotel. Being single-storey, it escaped relatively unscathed. I couldn't see what the fuss was about until later, when the images on TV showed buckled freeways, broken water pipes, fires and roads that had disappeared.

John and I divorced in 1995. In the end I urged him to get on with it. We were existing in a kind of limbo.

The break-up was still painful. I had spent countless hours trying to work things through and still didn't understand how we had drifted apart, although I realised I had lost him a long time before he physically left me.

In truth, I think John left me in 1988 when I lost the baby. I was in denial of my marriage going wrong. I didn't see us drifting apart. I always thought there would be signs. Perhaps there were. I just didn't see them.

It took us a long while to work out the finances. It was difficult because John had always looked after the money side of things and we had a joint account. I was happy to hand all of that responsibility over to him. His product range was on the verge of huge success, but potential is something that is difficult to quantify on a balance sheet, let alone a divorce settlement.

Afterwards, many of my friends felt as though I should have had a stake in John's business from the beginning. John never offered and I didn't press him.

My family was pleased to see the divorce go through. They had hated the way I carried a torch for John. They had also seen how it triggered years of introspection, therapy and counselling. At the end of it all I understood who I was and why I behaved the way I did. I can talk about it today, but I couldn't for a long time.

This is also true of my relationship with Jordan. I did the best I could raising him, but I realise now that I wasn't always there for him. And even when I was there, I was tired from travelling or from rehearsals. I didn't know how to stop working. At sixteen Jordan sat his SATs in America. For months he'd been talking about what university he might go to. We had had dozens of conversations and he'd also talked to friends in the UK and America.

On the phone to me one day, he casually said, 'Mum, you know what, I'm going to university in the UK rather than America.'

I felt myself catch my breath. 'Why is that then?' I asked.

'Because I'm not American.'

Secretly I went, 'Yes!' I wanted to punch the air. Jordan was coming home!

He had already talked to John and decided to return to England to sit his A-levels before going to university here. I was over the moon.

He came to England for the summer and had interviews and sat entrance exams at a handful of top schools. He was accepted at Eton, St Paul's in London and Kings Canterbury. Westminster wouldn't entertain the idea. They were concerned that Jordan couldn't cope with going straight into A-levels after having spent three years in America.

Jordan started at Eton in 1995. Soon afterwards he discovered they were putting on a musical, which happens every four years. Ironically, it was 'Guys & Dolls'. Jordan asked if he could audition but was told the cast had already been chosen. 'Can you sing?' asked the music teacher.

'Yes, sir. My whole family can sing.'

Jordan impressed them so much that he was given the role of Sky Masterton. He certainly didn't have a problem with the American accent.

Eton arranged to borrow some costumes for the show. And who provided them? None other than the National Theatre. They were the same outfits that we had used in the 1984 production. What a small world!

Jordan and I had a lot of catching up to do. It was only when he came home that I discovered how much I had missed. I made a conscious effort to be there for him. It was a time for making amends.

When he went out with friends at weekends and came home in the early hours, he would sometimes knock on my bedroom door and want to talk. I never said no. He would sit on the edge of my bed and tell me about where he'd been and who he'd seen. I was making up for lost time.

I acknowledged what I had done and took full responsibility for what I hadn't – first with Jordan and then with John. It was time to repair the damage and allow the hurt to heal.

I am so grateful that Jordan didn't go off the rails or rebel. Nor did he succumb to drugs or try to shut me out of his life.

We all learn from our parents. I learnt from mine. I avoided repeating some of their mistakes and discovered a whole raft of new ones. Jordan will no doubt do the same when he has children. That is the nature of human beings. We are perfectly imperfect.

# 18

# *Who Do You Know in Heaven?*

My mother had never looked old. If anything she seemed to grow younger. She used to run everywhere and would very rarely sit down. She took great care of her appearance and was clothes obsessed. (You can see where I get it from.)

However, in 1995 it seemed as though her age suddenly caught up with her. For the first time she grew tired and needed to rest.

In particular, I worried because she had a weakened bladder. She was up five or six times a night going to the toilet. No wonder she looked tired.

She went to see a doctor but I don't think she asked the right questions. I had an inkling of what might be wrong. I had read an article about the problem in a magazine and knew it could be fixed by a simple operation. The article mentioned a leading surgeon, Professor Linda Cardoza, who was based in London.

Mum agreed to see her. I offered to pay for the operation, but Mum said no. 'You do enough,' she said. 'You've always done enough.'

Instead she insisted on waiting and having it on the National

Health. I spent months trying to convince her otherwise, but finally I gave up. 'I can't carry you there.'

I think she was worried about my finances. I had divorced from John. My accommodation had become more modest. Though not exactly on the breadline, I was having to pull my belt in. My trips back and forth to America had been expensive.

Eventually Mum had the operation on the NHS, but I don't think she ever fully recovered.

On Mother's Day, in March 1996, Jordan wanted the two of us to spend the day together. He was away all week at Eton and the weekends were a special time.

Edwina and her husband Barnaby and their children went to my mother's for the day. Late that night Edwina called me. 'Mum looks awful. There's something wrong. Her stomach is so distended.'

My heart lurched, but I forced down the panic. I knew from past experience that Mum was an expert at hiding her pain and discomfort. If it was obvious then it had to be serious.

It was late on Sunday night. I phoned my gynaecologist and left a message on his answering machine. 'Please, call me as soon as you get in. I'm *very* concerned about my mother. I want someone to see her quickly.'

His assistant called me at 8.00 a.m. on Monday. Edwina picked Mum up from Chingford and I met them at the Harley Street surgery shortly before midday. Mum looked pale and nervous, but had made an effort with her appearance.

Dr Tim Colthart gave no indication of what might be wrong. I tried to look for something in his eyes, but there was nothing. He arranged for Mum to have some tests done at a nearby hospital. This led to more tests, and more, in different hospitals around London.

It took about three days for the results to come back, but it felt like much longer. The wait was excruciating. I kept calling him. 'What is taking so long? Can't you rush them?'

The doctor phoned and asked me to bring Mum to see him.

'What for? She's worn out,' I said. 'You can tell me the results. I'll come in now.'

I left Mum sleeping upstairs. Amalia, my housekeeper, would look after her. I drove myself to Harley Street. Dr Colthart was a very kind and patient man. I knew immediately that it was bad news. I thought he was going to say that Mum's previous operation had created some sort of complication.

Instead he told me that she had cancer.

The word sent a chill right through me. I could feel my throat start to close, I couldn't speak. This always happens when I'm frightened or in shock. He was still talking, explaining the test results, but I couldn't get my head around the news.

'Are you all right?' he asked.

I couldn't answer. My mind had gone. I was flashing through all the possibilities and impossibilities.

'How long has she?' I choked.

'Four to six weeks.'

A voice inside my head screamed, 'No! No! It's not true. You've got it wrong.'

I felt like a high-speed lift inside me had suddenly plunged towards the basement. Everything dropped. Trying to hold myself together, I thanked the doctor and shook his hand. 'I can't accept this. I need a second opinion. Is there somewhere else I can take this?'

'Yes, of course. I'll make some calls.'

I lapsed into silence.

'Are you going to be all right?' he asked. 'Did you come alone? Perhaps I should get you a cab.'

'I'm fine.'

I had to get out of there. I wanted to run.

When I reached my Range Rover, I sat behind the wheel, unable to move. Tears started streaming down my face. I couldn't stop. Pedestrians were walking past. One of them recognised me. I saw the look in her eyes, 'Oh, it's Lulu.' She went to smile but saw my tears. She lowered her head and hurried onwards.

I don't know how long I sat in the car. At some point I pulled myself together. I tried to reach Edwina but couldn't get through to her. Instead I called Elaine, my assistant. She wanted to come and collect me, but I said I was OK.

'Listen. Something has happened. My mum is very sick. I don't want to say anything to Amalia . . . or to Mum. Tell them I've had to pick up a few things. I'll be home later.'

Finally I managed to get Edwina on my mobile. I told her the news and we both cried down the phone.

'What are we going to tell Mum?' she asked. 'We need to decide.'

Having agreed to meet at her place, she called Billy and Gordon. Edwina lived in Blackheath in South-east London. Billy wasn't far away in Lewisham. Gordon had to come from the Oval.

In a daze I drove to Blackheath. Every time I saw a flash of red hair in the crowds of pedestrians, my stomach would lurch and I would want to throw up. Mum had always walked everywhere. She was so active.

In Edwina's front room we all cried, hugged and tried to get over the shock. None of us had had any inkling this would happen. If it had been Dad it would have been different. He had lived that sort of life. He drank like a fish, smoked a packet of cigarettes a day and ate all the wrong foods. Mum didn't smoke or touch alcohol. She didn't even drink coffee.

Billy was almost in denial. He couldn't take it all in.

'We can't tell her,' he said.

'What do you mean?'

'We can't tell Mum.'

'We have to say something. We have to ask her what she wants.'

'Why?'

'Out of respect for her . . . and her faith . . .'

'What difference will it make?'

'She should be ready. She'll want to be prepared.'

'She's dying, for Christ's sake!'

'Telling her isn't going to change that.'

'Exactly. So why upset her?'

We argued about this for hours, going round and round in circles. Billy resisted all three of us. Finally we compromised. We would tell her that she had cancer, but not mention the issue of how long she had left. It was still too early. We wanted to get a second opinion, as well as investigate possible treatments if she agreed.

We all drove back to my house. Mum was in bed upstairs. She knew something was wrong when we all trooped in. Even so, I don't think she grasped how serious it was. Mum had a habit of turning off when she didn't want to hear something. She would understand what she wanted to understand and no more. To that extent, maybe Billy was right.

'The tests showed that you have stomach cancer,' I said, sitting on the bed next to her, holding her hand. 'We're not going to just leave it at that. We're going to find more doctors . . . the best there are . . .'

As I said the word cancer I saw her flinch. It was almost imperceptible, but I recognised her shock. I don't how much of the rest she took in. She showed no sign of emotion. She wasn't going to break down.

'We want to know what you want,' I said. 'Do you want to fight this? It's going to mean more tests and seeing more doctors. Maybe they'll want to operate, or give you drugs, or we can look at naturopathy.'

She said nothing.

I continued: 'If you're going to have treatment, you'll have to be very strong and positive. We'll do whatever you want. We're in this together.'

Mum didn't look at our faces. She stared at her hands and seemed lost in thought. I don't know if she was philosophical, resigned to the news, or in denial. She agreed to have more tests.

Dr Colthart had given me the name of Dr David Cunningham, a leading oncologist at the Royal Marsden Hospital in Chelsea. This led to more names and new sources of information. Edwina and I had embarked on a mission.

Receptionists and medical secretaries would say things like, 'I'm sorry, the doctor can't see you for at least a month', or 'He's in surgery all day and won't be available until late. Perhaps you should try tomorrow.'

We wouldn't take no for an answer.

'I don't care where he is. I don't care how busy his schedule is. I only have one mother and I'm going to call you until he talks to me. I am going to drive you insane until you put him on the phone. Do you understand?'

'Yes. But I'm afraid he's in surgery right now.'

'But you can get a message to him.'

'No, that's not possible.'

'Nothing is impossible.'

We were like warriors. Nothing was going to stand in our way. Some people understood our anguish and were incredibly patient and sympathetic. Others didn't seem to care, and a few were quite cold and distant. Perhaps that's how they coped.

Complacency was the real enemy. I refused to let people sit on their hands. They had to make decisions.

The second opinion and third opinion all reached the same diagnosis. The next big issue was intervention and treatment.

The hardest thing to accept – having read so many stories of medical breakthroughs and new life-saving treatments – was how limited her options were. They had given her four to six weeks, but I had to believe a miracle could happen . . . and fast.

'This is about you,' I told Mum. 'We're willing to help, but *you* have to want to do this.'

Mum had the option of drugs or natural treatments. She chose the drugs.

'She will have to be really strong,' said Dr Cunningham. 'And at the same time *you'll* need to be really strong. This will be tough. It doesn't just affect one person.'

For the next two months she was in and out of hospital. They put her on a cocktail of drugs designed to slow the growth of the tumour, as well as drugs for the pain.

She wanted to fight. She is like me. At the same time she was angry and bitter about what had happened. 'If anyone deserves to go it should be him,' she'd say of my father. 'He sits there like a lump for years, why can't he die? He's not doing anything.'

She had led such an active life. For thirty years she had shunned cigarettes and alcohol. It didn't seem fair.

When not in hospital, Mum divided her time between my house and Edwina's. She didn't want to go home. But Dad was there. Towards the very end we arranged to rent an apartment in Blackheath so they could be together.

Knowing she had so little time left, we all had long conversations with Mum, saying what needed to be said. We talked about our lives, sorted out our differences and had our questions answered.

Billy found it the hardest. He didn't know how to deal with it. Every time I phoned he seemed to be in bed asleep.

He had spent his entire life trying to be the perfect son. 'Look at me! Look at me! Love me!' he'd been trying to tell Mum. Now she was dying and he couldn't cope. He wanted to be able to protect her.

Mum was in a lot of pain, but incredibly brave. She didn't complain. She wore a bag that leaked drugs into her stomach. One of the side effects was that she bruised easily, particularly on her arms and legs.

She still looked great, despite the cancer. It had consumed her so quickly that she hadn't had time to waste away. By comparison, Dad looked like an old man. He had already had a couple of heart attacks and needed a walking stick. His eyes were failing and he was hard of hearing.

He was next to useless when it came to looking after her. Like Billy, he was lost. He couldn't believe she was going to die. He had always relied on her. They had spent their entire marriage fighting, but he had never stopped loving her.

Mum and I talked a lot about the cycle of birth and death in those few months. She had always been very religious and had gone from being born a Catholic, raised a Protestant, to becoming a Mormon. She was completely loyal and dedicated to her Church, but at the same time her mind was open. Initially, she had been very suspicious of my beliefs until she noticed the changes in me.

Eventually, she visited a Siddha yoga ashram and gained an understanding of what it was all about. She also appreciated the Eastern philosophy of celebrating life and death in equal measure, rather than swathing the latter in mourning colours and tears.

Ultimately, she accepted my beliefs. We could see God in each other.

Gordon was due to get married. Mum's only wish was that she live long enough to see it happen. That was her plan. She looked wonderful on the day. She wore a beautiful grey-blue dress that Edwina and I had gone shopping to buy. It was topped off with a very fine gauze-like straw hat.

It was a beautiful, big church wedding. All the men wore kilts. At the reception Mum danced like a whirling dervish, as though celebrating right up to the last minute. It was hard to believe she had less than three weeks to live.

Billy and I were due in Los Angeles to work with some writers on material for a possible album. We had delayed it for weeks. Our publishing company kept asking us for new dates. This went on and on until Mum asked what was happening. She knew it was important to me. She had always been ambitious for her children.

She insisted we go. I told her no, but she became quite forceful. She really wanted me to do an album of my own songs.

Billy was quite keen to go. He needed something to take his mind off Mum. We waited until Gordon and Kate returned from their honeymoon in Greece. They moved into the apartment to take care of Mum. The following day we flew to LA, planning to be away for two weeks.

Edwina and Barnaby had been putting off a holiday on a friend's yacht in the Mediterranean. Again, Mum insisted they go. She didn't want them hanging around when they could be having a good time.

I called every day from LA and spoke to her. About a week into the trip, she was too tired to talk. It happened again the next day.

I called Gordon. 'OK, what's the deal?'

'She's not good.'

'We're coming home.'

The night before Mum died, Kate sat with her and said, 'You don't have to worry about Gordon. I'll take care of him.' She knew Mum worried about us all, but there is always something about the youngest child. Gordon had been her baby. He had spent so long at home when the rest of us had gone and there was a special bond between them.

On the morning Mum died, 14 August 1996, Gordon lay on the bed next to her. She had been drifting in and out of consciousness. Suddenly, her eyes opened and her body arched. At first he thought she was trying to say something to him. Then he realised that she was looking at something far away.

'Follow the light, Mum,' he said. 'You know you don't have to worry about us. We're all fine now. You've done all you needed to do. It's time for you to go and see God . . . You have friends there. They'll be pleased to see you. Follow the light.'

She left through her eyes. That is a divine way to go.

Our plane was touching down at Heathrow Airport. Edwina and Barnaby were arriving at about the same time. A car picked Billy and I up. I phoned Gordon on my mobile. It was early in the morning.

'She's gone. She died twenty minutes ago,' he said.

We drove to the garden flat, both of us in shock. Gordon asked me if I wanted to see her. I was apprehensive. I didn't know what to expect. It felt cold in the room. There was a body that resembled my mother, but it wasn't her. My mother had been *so* alive.

She knew Kate was pregnant before she died. They named their first child Elizabeth. She would have been very proud of that.

It is a very evolved spiritual practice to put your affairs in order before you die. Mum had tied up all the loose ends and there was virtually nothing left for us to do.

She had been preparing all her life for this. She knew it was the ultimate test – not the dying, but how you deal with it. I was surprised and delighted by how far she had come.

She wanted a Mormon funeral. The Mormon tradition is to dress the departed in undergarments. I knew Mum was very particular about her hair, so I insisted that we get it just right. My aunts had come down from Scotland and Jeanie helped me. We laughed a lot. At one point Jeannie kissed Mum on the forehead, pushing her hair back.

'Oh, tut, tut,' I chided, 'You've just moved her hair. She wouldn't like that.' It made me laugh.

Each of her children put something in her coffin. I gave her a gold heart pendant that she had always loved, as well as a beautiful pink cashmere shawl.

I knew Mum was very popular, but I was still surprised at how many people turned up. The church was packed. Barry and Linda Gibb were there, along with their family.

Edwina, Billy, Gordon and I had arranged to get up and say something.

'You realise, of course, that she is here with us right now,' I said. 'Because she can feel the love in this place. And she is smiling from ear to ear because she finally got her way . . . all of her children under *this* roof.'

They all laughed.

Billy, Gordon, Edwina and I sang a song. We chose something that Mum used to sing to us when we were children. It was one of her party pieces.

> *Who do you know in heaven*
> *that makes you the angel you are?*
> *Who do you see, I wonder,*
> *that makes you just the cutest little charmer by far?*
> *Where did you get those good looks*
> *those eyes that gleam like the stars*
> *They say they made the sunshine only twice*
> *in your eyes, paradise*
> *Oh, tell me darling tell me, who do you know in Heaven*
> *that makes you the angel you are?*

True friends emerge at times like this. Many people were very kind to me. Elton was one of them. He called to find out how I was doing. His words were so heartfelt and sincere that I knew he was totally there for me.

Billy took it very hard, but eventually he recovered. The same can't be said of Dad. He didn't know how to grieve or celebrate her life. His heart was broken.

From the day my mother died he lost any desire to live. He would tell us that he wanted to die, saying it quite openly. I turned on him one day, snapping, 'How can you be so selfish? We've just lost our mother, now you want to go and leave us. Stop feeling sorry for yourself. You should want to stay and see your grandchildren grow up.'

I was acting like a wounded child and it wasn't fair on Dad. Billy, Edwina and Gordon told me to give him a break. Later, when I'd calmed down, I put my arm around his shoulders and said, 'You know what, Dad? If you want to go, you go right ahead. You don't have to worry about us.'

Edwina and Barnaby had a self-contained apartment on the ground floor of their house. They had done it up specially, planning for the day that Mum and Dad would move in there. It had lovely French doors and a view over the garden and beyond to Blackheath. Dad moved in and went through the motions of living. He was waiting for his turn.

Sometimes he would come and stay with me in Maida Vale. He really liked Amalia and would sit in my kitchen for hours, chatting with her as she ironed or prepared him a meal. Mostly he talked about Mum.

He was half deaf, or at least pretended to be. It would irritate the hell out of me because it seemed to be quite selective.

'You hear what you want to hear,' I told him. 'Well, I'm not repeating things.'

He still drank too much, which made him even more morose and sentimental. That's when he'd say that he loved me. One day I replied, 'Don't tell me that you love me when you're drunk. I only want to hear it when you're sober.'

From then on he made sure that he did just that.

*

Just before he died I took him on a trip to New York. In all my travels, Dad had very rarely come with me. Mum had always jumped at the chance, but Dad didn't like leaving home.

It was just before Christmas 1996. I lied to him when we picked him up from Edwina's. He thought he was coming to my house. Instead we were driven straight to the airport.

Jordan had finished his A-levels at Eton but was taking a year off before going to Cambridge University. He was planning to go to Australia.

'This isn't the right way,' said Dad, as we neared Heathrow.

'We're not going home,' I said firmly. 'I'm taking you to New York. You're going to spend Christmas with John, John Snr, Jordan and me, as well as John's sister Joss and her kids. It's going to be really nice.'

'Ah'm not going to New York. Och! Never been to New York. Don't need to go. What would Ah want to go to New York for?'

'Well there's no point complaining. Just sit back and enjoy it.'

Thankfully, he was quite docile by then. We took him to the first-class lounge and let him have a few drinks. He began to relax.

When we boarded the plane Jordan was ahead of us. He reached his seat and glanced down to see a very pretty blonde sitting beside him. He recognised her instantly. It was Kylie Minogue.

Jordan thought all his Christmases had come at once. He was definitely going to enjoy this flight. He looked up to see Dad puffing along the aisle, glancing at his boarding pass and the seat numbers.

'Excuse me, lady,' Dad said in a soft voice.

Kylie Minogue looked up.

'Excuse me, Ah'm sorry to trouble ye, but Ah think ye might be in mah seat.' Although he looked quite gruff, he had a very respectful and gentle way of speaking to women.

Jordan's heart sank. As much as he loved his grandfather, right at that moment he wished we'd left him at home.

John had rented a huge apartment in New York. We spent a magical Christmas day surrounded by his family. Dad enjoyed himself and quite liked being bossed around by me. It probably reminded him of when Mum was alive.

In the New Year I took him upstate to see Gurumayi at the Siddha yoga ashram. Dad had never followed any structured religion. Whenever the subject came up he would huff and puff about Bible-bashing and God-bothering. Even so, he was quite a deep thinker.

We spent a week at the ashram and Dad had the most incredible experience. He came to me one morning and said, 'Marie, Ah was talking to yer mother last night.' He always called me Marie when he was being serious. 'She spoke to me. Your mother came.'

He told me the whole story, raising his hand and saying, 'It's the God's truth. Ah'm telling you. You probably don't believe me, but Ah'm telling you she was here.' I don't know if Dad had a spiritual awakening. He was certainly moved by what he experienced. He adored Gurumayi and said he had never felt so much love in a person and in a place.

I wasn't looking to convert him. I just thought it might be nice if he understood what I believed, and that it might help him get over Mum's death. In the end he comprehended far more than I gave him credit for.

At one particular lunch a Canadian woman, who was a first-timer at the ashram, was asking lots of questions. Everybody at the table was trying to give her the answers by relating their own experience.

Dad listened in silence for a long while and waited for a pause. As the lady was about to ask yet another question he said, 'Excuse me, lady, would ye mind me saying something?' He waited patiently for her to answer.

Softly, she answered, 'No, not at all.'

'Well, Ah notice you've got an awful lot of questions ye want answered. And if ye don' mind me saying so, Ah don't think you're goin' to get all your answers here and now. Why don't ye just sit back and relax. If ye give it time, maybe yer answers will come.'

The whole table looked at Dad in wonder and delight. He'd *got* it!

After two weeks away, I took Dad to the airport for the flight home. I had to be in Los Angeles and couldn't go with him. Virgin Atlantic had promised to look after him and I knew a lot of the senior staff.

Jonathan Ross was in the first-class lounge, along with his wife and children. Typically, larger than life, he chatted away to my father, telling him jokes and making fun of his Scottishness. Dad was laughing.

'Don't worry, Lu, I'll look after him,' Jonathan said. 'Eh, Eddie, we'll break out the Chivas Regal on board.' They winked at each other.

Oh my God, I thought, he's going to be totally pie-eyed! He'll start singing to everyone. I'll never be able to fly Virgin again.

Yet a strange thing happened on the flight. Dad didn't have a drink. For perhaps the first time in his life he turned one down. He was amazed! This was a man who had been an alcoholic since his twenties and had consumed enough alcohol for a dozen poor souls.

'I just didn't want one,' he explained to me afterwards. From that moment he never touched another drop.

In October 1998, Dad had another mild heart attack. His arteries were clogged by years of smoking and eating the wrong foods, yet his body was remarkably resilient. All he lacked was the desire to live.

I visited him at the hospital and he seemed OK. The doctors

were talking about keeping him in for a few days. Edwina planned to visit him first thing in the morning.

He had another heart attack in the early hours. They called Edwina. She reached the hospital in time to see him.

'I'm sorry,' he said to her.

'Forget about it,' she answered. 'Don't torture yourself any longer. Go and meet Mum. Take her dancing.'

We cremated his body because that's what he wanted. He and Mum are together. You could say he died of a broken heart or you could say he died to be with her. Both are true.

# 19

# *We Shot Lulu. Sorry*

My mother and father died within eighteen months of each other, which I found very difficult. As always, whenever I was struggling emotionally, I threw myself into work. There is a comfort in embracing what you know. It's like slipping on a favourite sweater and an old pair of jeans.

My record company saw me as a dance diva and wanted me to carry on in much the same vein. They even suggested that I record 'It's Raining Men', which I turned down.

At that point in my life I didn't want to be a dance diva. Nor did I want to be bright, bubbly, smiling Lulu who had hits at any price. *Independence* had been a credible album which had won me a lot of respect. I wanted to build on that. In particular, I wanted to write a complete album of my own songs. And I wanted every track to be brilliant.

EMI had dropped the Dome label, so I now had to find a new recording deal. The big question was whether the songs we'd written were good enough to shop a deal.

I needed feedback, so I turned to Elton. I knew he'd be honest with me. He is very clear, opinionated and forthright when it comes to popular music (in fact, when it comes to anything). He follows the charts closely and listens to every new artist who makes a splash. In particular, I knew he'd tell me straightaway if I should stick to being a dance diva or concentrate on the rock genre.

In the lounge of his house in London I put on a CD with six of the songs. Elton jumped up and turned up the volume as the first song began playing. Halfway through, I said, 'Shall I finish it there?'

'No! No! I want to hear it all.' He began pacing up and down the room, unable to sit still. He kept raving about each song. 'This is brilliant. I love this. I'll get John [Reid] on the phone. He should hear this. We've got to do something. You need an album deal . . .' He still hadn't stopped moving. 'You can be a dance diva any time you like. You can do it standing on your head. Don't do what *other* people tell you to do. Do what *you* want.'

'So you think I can shop a deal?'

'You don't have to find a record company. I'm signing you to Rocket.'

I was gobsmacked. I knew Elton wasn't just saying these things. He didn't take passengers. He was serious. He respected the work I had put in. His excitement was infectious. Both of us couldn't stop talking. We matched each other's energy.

As I was leaving the house, he turned to me and said, 'And you know what? Your mother would want this. She would want you to follow your heart.'

He was right.

I went home on a cloud. When I rang Billy I couldn't get the words out fast enough. He made me slow down. I had to repeat everything Elton had said, word for word. I have angels in my life. Elton is one of them.

Having signed with Rocket, I travelled to America to begin

recording. Initially, I planned to stay for three to six months, but it ended up being nearly two years writing with Billy and Dave Tyson, our co-writer and producer.

Working at a studio in the Hollywood Hills, we remixed a lot of the tracks and wrote new ones. One particular day, I can remember Billy and Dave discussing things and I felt a little left out. I wandered outside and sat on the deck, overlooking a beautiful garden with huge trees. The sun was shining and it was a classic California dreaming scene.

Suddenly the skies turned grey and rain began falling. It took me back to Glasgow. I still had tremendous waves of grief over the loss of Mum and Dad.

Billy realised I'd been gone for a while. He wandered outside. 'Are you all right?'

'Yeah.'

'What's wrong?'

I tried to explain. I was thinking of my childhood and missing Mum and Dad. I said that sometimes I felt as though I was lost in a separate world, where ghosts from the past wouldn't let me go. It was a powerful image.

That afternoon I wrote a song called 'Where the Poor Boys Dance' – about my childhood and growing up in Glasgow.

> *Take me where the poor boys dance*
> *back to where it all began.*
> *I need to find out who I am.*
> *Something that I left back there,*
> *Out there in the cool night air*
> *I need to know that someone cares.*

It is one of the songs that I'm most proud of having written, and ultimately it became the title track of the new album.

\*

In February 1997 I had a call from Jennifer Saunders asking if I'd do a song for Comic Relief. She wanted me to do a spoof of the Spice Girls' song 'Who Do You Think You Are?', with all royalties going towards famine relief in Africa and other good causes in Britain.

Jennifer initially thought of playing 'Baby Spice' herself, but her daughter had said straightaway, 'Lulu has got to be Baby.'

I was in the middle of recording in LA and it was difficult to get away.

'I'll only do it if I can laugh at myself,' I said.

'That's guaranteed,' she replied.

I flew to London for two days and was taken to a theatre in Willesden, North London. The place had been set up as a mock disco, full of jugglers, snake charmers and tattooed ladies.

In the video, a spoof band called The Sugar Lumps really really wanted to be pop stars like their heroes, The Spice Girls. Dawn French dressed up as 'Posh', Jennifer played 'Ginger', Kathy Burke (Waynetta Slob in Harry Enfield's TV show) became 'Sporty', and Llewella Gideon (from *The Real McCoy*) was 'Scary'. This left me to be Baby Spice.

We began singing the song 'Who Do You Think You Are?' and halfway through the *real* Spice Girls joined us on stage. It was a lot of fun – in particular trying to mimic the mannerisms of each of our characters. Geri said afterwards that she thought I should have played 'Ginger'.


I had worked with Dawn and Jennifer before, most notably in 1995. We did a really cute sketch based on *Pulp Fiction*. I had to play the Uma Thurman character, while Dawn and Jennifer were the hitmen – John Travolta and Samuel L. Jackson.

The stunt coordinator fitted me with a special vest beneath my long-sleeved shirt. It contained tiny explosive charges that could be detonated by remote control.

Dawn's character was particularly trigger happy and kept threatening to shoot me.

'You can't shoot Lulu. She's a national treasure,' said Jennifer.

Eventually I started singing 'Shout'. That was enough for both of them. They opened fire.

For some reason the charges were far more powerful than anybody expected. I thought I'd been shot for real. I carried on and finished the scene. Then somebody said to me, 'What's that?'

I looked at my arms. There was blood everywhere. I had a large gash near my right elbow and a smaller one on my left arm. The producer and crew looked ashen. They rushed me to West Hammersmith Hospital, cancelling the rest of the filming.

I came back to BBC Television Centre the following day to finish the job. Dawn and Jennifer couldn't believe it. Lenny Henry arrived and said, 'If it had been Madonna, she'd be suing the BBC.'

A few days later a present arrived for me – a tiny, heart-shaped perfume bottle. The inscription read: *We shot Lulu. Sorry. Love Dawn and Jennifer. 9th November 1995.*

Back in Los Angeles, I carried on working on the album. One night in late August 1997 I went to the movies with some friends and saw *The Full Monty*. We were still laughing as the show finished and we came down in a lift.

A passer-by heard our accents. 'Are you guys from the UK? Did you hear the news?'

'What news?'

'Princess Diana. She's been killed in a car crash.'

I thought there had to be some mistake. Diana may have been in a car accident, but she couldn't be dead. It wasn't possible.

Back at the Sunset Marquee, I turned on the TV. Images flashed up of the tunnel and the twisted wreck of the car. They showed file footage of Diana looking bright, vibrant and young . . . sitting shyly beside Prince Charles when they announced their engagement . . . looking radiant in her wedding dress . . . proudly watching her boys play sport . . .

It was true!

The thought of those two boys hearing about their mother was almost unbearable. When someone dies it is one thing, but my mind always goes out to those who are left behind . . . those close to them.

For the next week I could hardly drag myself away from the screen. I watched the CNN and BBC World Service. I cried when I saw the funeral – particularly watching William and Harry follow their mother's coffin.

No matter what people thought of Diana and the way she conducted herself on many issues, I don't think anyone could help but be affected by her death. Yes, she occasionally said the wrong thing and made mistakes – doesn't everyone? She was thrust into the limelight, living each day with adoration and criticism in equal measure.

I remember seeing her one day in Sloane Street. I was driving my car one way as she was driving in the opposite direction, accompanied by her detective. I went home and told Mum.

'Did she see you?' she asked.

'Mum, please, Princess Diana wouldn't notice someone like me.'

The following evening I was at a charity dinner and fashion show at the Guildhall in London for Birthright, the childbirth research fund. John was doing the hair for the models. We all stood in line to be greeted by the Princess, who looked beautiful. When she reached me, she said, 'I saw you yesterday. You were driving up Sloane Street in your Range Rover.'

I couldn't wait to get home and tell Mum.

During Jordan's last term at Eton, Prince William started at the school. I knew the road well because Elton lives in the same area.

Sometimes I would pass Diana either driving in or out of the school. We'd give each other a wave.

I was always tremendously fond of her and found her to be a genuinely warm, lovely person. She had such a good heart.

Over the years I have seen far too many people destroyed by the pressures of being in the public eye. Brian Epstein took an overdose, The Beatles fought and broke up, Georgie Best fell back on drink, Karen Carpenter starved herself to death . . . (I will always remember Karen. She had a voice like honey. None of us realised, as we saw her wasting away, that she had anorexia nervosa. It wasn't a disease that any of us had ever heard of in the seventies.)

That's why I often despair when I hear young people talking of wanting fame for fame's sake. It wasn't like that for me. I just wanted to sing – everything else just came along with it.

I admit there are trappings to success. People put themselves out for you. Hard-to-get theatre tickets are found. Tables at smart restaurants are suddenly available and people return your calls. At the same time, it can be bloody tough to reach the top and stay there. You need to have the hide of an elephant and the love and support of people who will keep your feet on the ground.

I am eternally grateful for my life, but sometimes I ponder what it did to my family. At various stages of their lives, all of my brothers and sisters have worked closely with me. Billy has made a career as a manager, songwriter and publisher. Edwina is a good actress, singer and a great personality. Gordon had the best natural singing voice of all of us, but chose to become a carpenter and then a drugs counsellor.

We all, in our different ways, have addictive personalities. And each of us, at various stages in our lives, has battled addiction. Mine had to do with issues of control and co-dependency.

Most of my insecurity stemmed from the need to be loved and to be in love. You only have to look back over my diaries to see evidence of this. One week it would be Scott Walker and the next Georgie Best, or Davy Jones . . . I think I was in love with the idea of being in love.

Since the separation and divorce from John I hadn't dated anybody. I think I was afraid of getting hurt. While I was in Los Angeles, I was invited to a party thrown by the Scottish actor Brian Cox. I recognised a young Scottish actor, Angus MacFadyen, who I remembered from the film *Braveheart*.

He sat with his back to me most of the night, which I thought was quite odd. He seemed aloof, or bad-tempered. He certainly didn't seem pleased to see me, which was annoying because I thought he was goddamn cute.

A couple of weeks later, Barbara Carrera had booked a table at a typical Hollywood function and asked me to come along. 'I thought I might invite Angus,' she said.

'What a fabulous idea,' I told her.

That night I finally got the chance to talk to him. There were loads of other people at the party, but we spent all night chatting to each other almost exclusively. Rather than being aloof, I discovered that he was actually quite shy.

Over the next few weeks we saw a little more of each other and it was obvious that there was an attraction. Nothing happened. Angus already had a girlfriend. It wasn't until I returned to England that I saw him again. We saw each other a few times and it was still obvious that we liked each other. All of this seemed to take for ever.

About a year later, when Angus was next in London, I said to him, 'You know something? There was a time when I thought you and I would get together. I suppose we'll have to settle for being friends.'

That was it! It happened! It was the best sex I'd ever had. My God, he relit my fire!

Because Angus spent much of his time in America we didn't see each other that often. When we did, boy did we make up for lost time. We didn't go anywhere. Nobody ever saw us, apart from a few close friends. It was partly that we didn't want to be talked about or have to answer questions, but mostly we just wanted to be with each other. We could talk for hours, philosophising and putting the world to rights. It was intense, soulful and wonderfully romantic.

There were times when I thought I was falling in love with Angus, but it was probably just lust. I used to say to him, 'What is this connection between us?'

I still see Angus when he's in town, but he spends most of his time in America or travelling. We still talk on the phone and have a great time together. Until I met him I think I was too emotionally tied up with the past. I had always been looking over my shoulder instead of looking ahead.

Since the divorce, my relationship with John has gone through several different stages. Initially we fought each other, then became friends, and then came back so strongly together that people began to think, 'Hey, maybe they'll get back together.'

When Jordan turned twenty-one we organised a huge party in Holborn photographic and film studio in Islington. Paul Dyson from the Royal Opera House completely redesigned the studio into a fantasy land. Hundreds of people were invited, including all his university friends, along with relations and family friends like the Gibb brothers.

At one point during the evening I was sitting on John's knee and everyone was whispering, 'Oh my God, are they back together?'

In reality, the answer was no. We were just *very* cosy – to the point where it strayed into quite confusing territory. Things have settled down since then. We both want some closure and have stopped playing games.

By the end of 1997 the album had been recorded and mastered. I had trusted my instincts and not rushed. The end result was ten songs, six of which I thought were among the best things I had ever done.

Elton called me from Japan when he first heard the album. It was five in the morning, but he wanted to say how much he loved it.

Initially, the plan was to release *Where the Poor Boys Dance* early in 1998. As the months went by I began to realise that something was wrong. News leaked out in dribs and drabs. The first few delays were explained away. Then we faced a major change of personnel as Rocket Records was swallowed up by Mercury in a takeover.

Somewhere during this process, *Where the Poor Boys Dance* lost its champions. There weren't enough old-fashioned music people who recognised the potential.

When Mercury announced they were delaying the album for a year it came as a major disappointment. An excuse was offered. It was all about getting things to line up and the right campaign in place . . . blah, blah, blah.

It just didn't ring true. There is an energy that flows within every successful album launch. In this case I could see the momentum flagging.

Billy asked the key questions and began to realise that somebody, somewhere, hadn't even bothered listening to the songs.

People in the music or publishing industry will tell you that truly great albums come to the fore. That is rubbish! Truly great albums die every day, because they aren't marketed or promoted properly.

This is a tough business – and the operative word is business. Decisions are made every day, weighing up costs and offsetting losses. Good albums get ditched because the marketing budget has already been spent, or an alternative project will produce quicker returns.

Success doesn't depend solely upon talent. It's about business savvy, contacts and good personal skills. It is about beavering away relentlessly – not just an individual, but collectively. One champion isn't enough. You need an army of them.

For a long while I clung to the hope that we could rekindle interest in the *Poor Boys* album.

Billy knew how hard I would take the rejection. It wasn't just about the songs, it was a rejection of me, of who I was.

In April 1999 we released a dance record from it. 'Hurt Me So Bad' went to No. 1 in the club charts. A year later we released the single of 'Where the Poor Boys Dance'. It shot to No. 24 on the UK Top 40 within a week.

Neither single received the sort of promotional push from the label that we'd hoped for, but they were hits despite this. Some radio stations were saying, 'Give us another record. Where is the album?'

For a brief while Mercury got excited again. I was asked to host *Red Alert*, a variety show built around the live National Lottery draw. I was very cautious about going back on television – particularly into the old Saturday evening variety slot.

'No, no it's not going to be like that,' I was told. 'This is going to be different.'

Ginger Productions had been asked to produce the show. In the past it had been responsible for shows like *Don't Forget Your Toothbrush* and *TFI Friday*, both vehicles for Chris Evans. The BBC wanted the same team to transform the lottery show into a ratings winner.

They came to me with a very convoluted format, which seemed to be a cross between a quiz show and a music programme. I listened patiently to everything I was told. Finally I said, 'I think it's going to be a great show, but I don't want to be a part of it. Thank you.'

'Why not?'

'It is not for me.'

Suddenly they were scrambling around, trying to find some way to convince me. Very cleverly, someone said, 'What do you want it to be, Lulu?' It was a very seductive question.

'I'll tell you what I want, but you're not going to do it. I want a music show. I want to be able to sing new stuff. I want to work with great people. I'm definitely not a game show host. And I'm not a comedy actress. I don't want to do sketches or one-liners.'

'We want what you want,' they chorused.

I didn't believe them. TV networks don't put out pure music shows on a Saturday evening.

My record company was pushing me to say yes. They saw it as a perfect vehicle for selling records – a weekly showcase with an audience of millions. I still wasn't convinced, but I let the chorus of voices sway me.

Right from the beginning things began to unravel. It soon became clear that I was being told what I wanted to hear, while the reality was often very different.

When I was promised thirty dancers, I knew I'd get ten. When they talked of building incredibly elaborate sets, they made something that looked cheap. I was guaranteed loads of time to rehearse – it didn't happen.

The first show aired on 13 November 1999, with Paul McCartney as the guest star. It was a mixture of songs in front of a live studio audience and crosses to an outside location for lots of silly games.

The latter segments were filmed in a cavernous hangar that was too big and echoing. No matter how great the sound technician, it was almost impossible to get the sound right. Similarly, the director struggled to draw any energy from the crowd in such a large space.

People from four streets were supposed to battle it out to win an overseas holiday by playing games like 'Stand By Your Doors', 'What Are You Like', 'Happy Chimneys' and 'Pump Up Your Postie'.

It was a disaster. After one show I went into a complete depression.

I tried to talk to Ginger Productions. 'We have to change things. This isn't working. Nobody understands what we're doing . . .'

This became my mantra over the following weeks. 'Let's stay up twenty-four hours a day until we sort it out. Let's do a survey. Let's ask people what they like about the show and get rid of what they don't like . . .'

This didn't happen. The critics were merciless. The show was savaged and the ratings plummeted. I felt like the captain of a sinking ship. What was I going to do? Walk out?

Elton would call me. 'What are you doing?'

'Nothing.'

'What do you mean you're doing nothing?'

'Just what I said.'

'Are you isolating?'

'No, I'm fine.'

'I *know* you're not fine.'

He knew I was depressed. He had watched the show. I appreciated his support, but there was nothing he could do. Billy was beside himself. He wanted to go into the production offices and bash heads together. He didn't have the power.

After six shows we had a month's break over the New Year. During this time we had countless meetings to try to sort out the problems. As I listed all the things they had promised and failed to provide, people began backtracking, making denials and treating me like Alice in Wonderland. Billy leapt to my defence and furiously quoted back to them exactly what I'd told them months earlier. I wasn't trying to be difficult; I simply wanted a professional and classy show.

I was due to go to Los Angeles where Elton was receiving a life-time achievement award at a glittering showbiz ceremony. 'Let me take a film crew,' I said. 'We can bring some glamour to the show. I can do interviews. I know a lot of these people.'

Finally they accepted an idea. We were making some progress. In LA I did interviews with the likes of Stevie Wonder and mingled with Brad Pitt, Jennifer Aniston, Sting and Phil Collins.

The games on *Red Alert* were simplified and we concentrated more on the music. We had stars like Bryan Adams, B*Witched, Texas, Westlife, Atomic Kitten and the Eurythmics.

Despite the changes, *Red Alert* was probably holed beneath the waterline from the very first show. All we did was keep it afloat for a little longer.

As I'd suspected from the beginning, it didn't relaunch my recording career, as the label had hoped it would. Totally the opposite happened. It killed the *Poor Boys* album stone dead. The same record company executives who had been all in favour, suddenly acted as though it had been someone else's idea.

When the dust finally settled, I had no manager and an album gathering dust on the shelves at Mercury.

# 20

# 'Who Knew?'

*Red Alert* had been a disaster, but I managed to come out of it relatively unscathed. Rather than blaming me for what happened, I think most people asked, 'What is she doing on it?'

I was far more disappointed about *Where the Poor Boys Dance*. It had been a very expensive and time-consuming project and, ultimately, a failed dream.

Everything happens for a reason. I looked back at the previous few years and decided it had been a cathartic experience. It was part of my learning curve, as usual. I certainly had no thoughts of giving up.

Billy had started working with a young producer, Lukas Burton. Together they created a very minimalist, edgy, hip-sounding track called 'Inside Thing', which made use of McCartney's 'Let Him In' – a big hit for Wings in 1976.

We spent ages trying to get it right, mixing, re-mixing and re-writing. Lukas wanted me to play it to Paul McCartney, but I said, 'Wait. It's not right yet.'

I knew that Paul never agreed to anyone using his material, so the only way to convince him was to do something so amazing he couldn't turn us down.

Finally I sent him an almost-complete song. We all kept our fingers crossed.

On 24 January 2001 Paul wrote back:

> *Dear Lu,*
>
> *Just listened to your 'Inside Thing', which I think is fabulous. It is very catchy, radio-friendly and your singing is great . . . Maybe you'll give me a shout and let me know how you want to proceed . . . Hope all is well with you. Thanks for the cool version of my song.*
>
> *Love Paul*

Paul came in, added his voice, and the end result was on the money. Elton and I began talking about the next step. What did I want to do?

'I still want to record songs.'

'OK, well you need a manager. Someone with real clout in the music industry. What about Louis Walsh?'

Louis was managing some huge stars like Ronan Keating, Westlife and Samantha Mumba. Record companies respected him. The moment he picked up the phone or walked in the door they listened.

I had spoken to Louis only once before. Westlife had appeared on *Red Alert* and backstage during rehearsals they excitedly talked about a song called 'Heart Like the Sun', which I had written with Billy and a very talented singer-songwriter called Kavanagh. There was talk of them recording it, but not everyone at their record company could agree.

'Heart Like the Sun' was a lovely song. I first sang it publicly on a daytime TV show in the UK. I invited Kav to do a duet with me. At the time he was being managed by Nigel Martin-Smith and I was mad about his voice.

The switchboards lit up immediately after the show. From then on people kept asking to me, 'When are you going to record that song?'

Unfortunately, neither Kavanagh's record company nor mine could get their act together and the song was never released.

The idea of Westlife doing 'Heart Like the Sun' was exciting. Everything the boys touched went straight to the top spot. Backstage at *Red Alert* one of the boys was talking on his mobile as I walked by.

'Lulu, love that fucking song,' he said, calling me over. 'I've got Louis on the phone. Say hello.'

Louis was very sweet. He told me I was writing some great stuff and he'd always been a fan. It was only a short conversation, but we had made a connection.

Elton was right. Louis would be a perfect manager. But would he take me on? I called him from the south of France and asked if I could see him. He was going to be in London on the following Wednesday and we arranged to meet.

Louis had no idea what I had in mind. He thought I had some songs for him.

We made small talk until the coffee and tea arrived.

Finally I got straight to the point. 'I need a manager.'

Louis' eyes went wide. 'So this isn't about songs.'

'No. I need someone like you.'

I think Louis was flattered, but also quite cautious. 'I only like the record business,' he said. 'I hate the rest of it.' By this he meant that he didn't do all the spin-offs that Marian had once organised.

'I hate the rest of it as well,' I assured him.

'She doesn't need a nanny,' added Billy.

Louis laughed. 'No, to be sure. I saw her at the Ivor Novellos and she can work a room all right. I could learn from her.'

Louis thought for a while. 'First let me explain why it might *not* work.' He had certain ground rules and a philosophy on management and the music industry.

In particular he believed in letting record companies get on with the job of selling music, while giving them as much support as he could. He didn't believe in artists holding labels to ransom or becoming spoilt and demanding. They were record company vehicles. This is what he wanted.

Although he didn't say it, I think Louis was concerned about this. Perhaps he perceived me as having too much baggage and imagined that I wouldn't be as pliable and accommodating as a younger artist. I had to convince him this wasn't true. I was the perfect act. I was hungry. I had the songs and the experience. I just needed someone with his skill and his contacts and his power.

By the end of the meeting Louis had pretty much committed himself. I went home confident that my recording career was in good hands.

Louis spoke to Colin Barlowe, the hottest A&R man in the country. Colin worked for Polydor, which had the same parent company as Mercury. However, Universal didn't make a habit of allowing the A&R man on one label to work on an album for another. They bent the rules for Louis. He is *that* powerful.

Ten days later I had a meeting with Colin and Louis. Straightaway they put paid to any chance of releasing the album *Where the Poor Boys Dance*. Instead we talked about a duets album.

Both of them had heard the McCartney collaboration, 'Inside Thing'. They really liked it. There also seemed to be a connection between myself and Tom Jones, who had been very successful with the duets album 'Reload'. People often thought of us in the same breath. We had a similar kind of energy in our voices.

Once the decision had been made, the next step was to decide who to work with on the album. I wanted to have a healthy mixture of young and more established stars, but all of them big.

A lot of the artists who had appeared on *Red Alert* had done so because they were friends and respected me. The same thing happened again, but I have to be honest and say it wasn't just about me. Having someone like Paul McCartney on board was a huge bonus. Very few people will turn down the chance to appear on the same album as a former Beatle.

We made the calls and people said yes. Soon I had Westlife, Ronan Keating, Atomic Kitten and Samantha Mumba.

At a dinner party one night, I sat next to Sting and told him I was doing the duets album. Straightaway he said, 'So what are we going to do?'

Elton played a big role from the very beginning and became executive producer on the album. Our biggest headache was deciding which song we'd sing together.

The album took just under two years to complete. I can't even remember the chronology. Things just took on a momentum and eventually everything fell into place. During that time some people dropped out, or we couldn't pin them down. It was hard because we were dealing with massive stars, who had record companies, A&R men, managers and agents. We had to agree on songs, dates, locations and recording schedules.

Most of the tracks were recorded in London, but I recorded with Joe Cocker in New York on 10 September 2001. We worked so well together it was finished within a day. The producer jumped on the red-eye back to London, but I decided I didn't want to rush.

I spent the night in New York and organised to catch a flight in the morning. Shortly before 8.00 a.m. I was sitting on a British Airways jet on the tarmac of La Guardia Airport. Paul McCartney and his then girlfriend Heather Mills were in the seats in front. We had just left the terminal and were waiting in a queue to take off.

We waited . . . and waited. I wasn't really bothered. I had a book to read and thank-you notes to write.

After a long delay the pilot made an announcement. 'I'm afraid we are having a little problem. I can only apologise. At this stage I can't give you a reason. We've been told to wait here.'

Another half an hour passed and I sensed that people were getting agitated. Paul and Heather didn't seem to mind. They were totally wrapped up in each other.

The pilot's voice came over the intercom. 'Ladies and gentlemen, there has been an incident. A plane has crashed into New York . . .'

The news was so stunning that many people missed it. We were looking at each other. What did he say? Surely it can't be right.

He continued, 'If you look out of the right side of the aircraft you will see the twin towers. They are burning.'

From a distance the smoke billowed into the air, but it gave no indication of the scale of the outrage. It wasn't until we returned to the terminal and reached the first-class lounge that I saw the images on TV. In horror, we watched the first tower fall.

Chilled to the bone, I listened to reports of how the doomed flights had been hijacked. One of them had been a United Airlines plane. Although I normally fly Virgin Atlantic or British Airways, I had actually had been due to fly United that day. The airline had screwed up my ticket and annoyed me so much, I went to the British Airways counter and bought another one.

A political correspondent for *The Times* was on our flight. He had a mobile phone, which he lent to people. Paul called his American driver, who was still waiting at the airport. He knew not to leave until the flight had gone.

I managed to get through to John and Gail's office and talk to Gail. I let her know that everything was OK.

It soon became clear that no flights would be leaving New York (or anywhere else in America) for at least twenty-four hours and perhaps longer. British Airways began trying to find accommodation. It managed to get a handful of rooms at a Marriott Hotel near La Guardia. The airport itself was being evacuated.

We were given a few sandwiches as airline staff tried to arrange transport. Most of us were crowded around the TV screens, shocked by images of people jumping from the second tower. Soon it, too, came crashing down.

I was overwhelmed with feelings of fear, sadness and my own mortality. All those people . . . dead – every one of them with a family and friends. The ripples grew wider and wider, leaving no-one untouched.

The terminal was completely deserted as we descended the escalators and walked out the doors. There were no cars or taxis. All the airport staff had gone apart, from a handful of security officers. British Airways had managed to find some transport. I piled in beside a nice Australian lady, an Indian man and the journalist from *The Times*. We drove to the hotel through empty streets. It was like a film of the end of the world.

At the hotel we found a hundred people outside trying to find a room. My heart fluttered. What if I don't get one? Where will I go? Who can I call?

I knew that New York had been sealed off. Nobody was crossing any of the bridges in and out of Manhattan. All public transport had been closed down. The phone lines were so jammed it took hours to get a call through.

British Airways pulled some strings and found me a room. When I finally closed the door behind me I burst into tears.

I knew I had to get a message to London. I kept trying until I managed to get through. Elaine picked up the phone.

'Thank God! We've been worried sick,' she said. 'Billy is beside himself.'

'I'm OK. Tell him not to worry.'

It was an emotional call and I didn't want to hang up. I wanted to keep listening to a familiar voice.

For the next hour I tried to get through to John's office and to London. Eventually I reached Gail. 'We're coming to get you,' she said, which is typical of her.

'You can't get over the bridges.'

'Don't you worry about that. We're coming to get you.'

'I'm OK. I'm in a room. I can lock the door.'

Being able to lock the door was important. There were all sorts of rumours about looting and a total breakdown of law and order. I had visions of gangs roaming the streets. If terrorists could fly passenger jets into skyscrapers then anything was possible.

Gail and Jimmy managed to get through. Somehow they talked their way through the roadblocks and arrived with the twins in the backseat of the car. It was seven in the evening by the time they reached me.

I spent the next five days staying with them, while all flights were grounded. Gail and Jimmy both knew people who had been in the World Trade Center. It was a desperately sad time to be in New York. Everybody seemed dazed and looked at each other with disbelief.

At the same time there was a sense of shared hardship and resolve. So much so, that when international flights were restarted I didn't really want to leave. I felt as though I was somehow lending support. I didn't want to desert New York.

'Get on the bloody plane,' said Billy. 'The air is thick with danger – it scares me. Come home.'

I caught the second available flight to London. Photographers and TV cameras were at the airport. Reporters wanted to interview passengers who had been trapped in New York. I felt physically, mentally and spiritually drained.

In the months that followed I continued working on the album. Songs were mixed and re-mixed. We changed the running order and tried find the right balance.

I was very lucky to have people like Louis and Colin in my corner, but halfway through the project another champion emerged.

Lucian Grainge had taken over as the CEO and Chairman of Universal – the parent company of EMI. He was like the emperor of a huge musical empire, with hundreds of different projects and dozens of artists under his umbrella.

I had never met Lucian before, but I had read an interview that he'd given to *Music Week* outlining his philosophy on the music industry and how he planned to run the company. It was very impressive.

He called me out of the blue one day.

'I just want to tell you how much I believe in this project,' he said. 'And I'm putting a rocket up the back end of it.' That's the way Lucian talks. He is direct, very honest and tells you what he thinks – whether you like it or not. I love it! From that moment I knew the album had a chance. I had the biggest champion of them all.

A lot of work still had to be done. We spent months deciding on the right cover photographs, the title and the promotional campaign. Initially, I thought we might go in the autumn of 2001, but the juggernaut wasn't ready.

At one point I said to Lucian, 'I'm going mad. I just want this to happen. I'm getting itchy sitting around.'

'Well, you'll just have to wait,' he said. 'I am not taking this chicken out of the oven until it's cooked. I don't want just one or two planets colliding, when we release this. I want them *all* colliding at the same time.'

Everything had to be perfect for the launch. He didn't care how long it took.

Music is sold differently today. It is all about cross-marketing and finding dozens of angles to promote an artist. It takes work to have a mass-selling single even if you're a teenage heart-throb: doing every chat show, music programme and chart countdown, travelling up and down the country, never turning down an interview or an autograph hunter.

For months we'd been negotiating to do a TV special to co-incide with the launch of the album. The most likely format was *An Audience with Lulu*, which meant I could invite all my friends and sing some of the duets.

The producer Jeff Thacker was a huge fan of the idea, along with LWT's head of light entertainment, Nigel Lithgow. Ironically, Nigel had once been one of my dancers when I had my own TV series.

Despite their support, there were some in the corridors of power at LWT who weren't so sure. It became a nightmare – on one minute and off the next.

Up until only two months beforehand, we still weren't guaranteed the show would go ahead. Nigel had left, due to his success with *Pop Idol*, so Jeff continued to fight hard and eventually he won the day. For their sake, as much as my own, I wanted to pull off *An Audience with . . .*

In the meantime, I was invited to New York in April to perform in the Rainforest Concert with Elton and Sting. It is one of those things I had wanted to do for years, but hadn't been asked until suddenly it came up in conversation at a dinner party in London.

The concert (then in its eleventh year) was one of the biggest environmental fund-raising events in the world. It benefited the Rainforest Foundation – a charity set up by Sting and his wife Trudie Styler, to campaign for the preservation of the environment and tribal lands.

An amazing group of people came together, including James Taylor, Smokey Robinson, Patti LaBelle, Wynonna Judd, Jeff Beck and Nina Simone. The show was dedicated to two people who each in their own way had made a remarkable impact on the world. The first was George Harrison, who had died only a few weeks earlier. The other was Herman Sandler, one of the Rainforest Foundation's main benefactors, who had perished in the World Trade Center on September 11, along with sixty-five members of his law firm.

Elton and I did a duet of Ike and Tina Turner's 'River Deep, Mountain High'. We rocked out on stage, bumping and grinding. The energy was amazing. Afterwards, he left me in the spotlight and I sang 'To Sir With Love'.

The actress Ellen Barkin was in the audience with her husband Ron Pearlman and other members of her family. When Elton introduced me, Ellen's brother shouted out in a wonderful Jewish, Bronx accent, 'Lulu! Who knew?'

This seemed to sum up the feelings of a lot of people who hadn't seen me in years. Where had I been hiding? Why hadn't they seen more of me?'

For the next three weeks I rehearsed for *An Audience with* . . . It felt like another new beginning. The singing didn't bother me, but they expected me to answer questions and banter with the audience.

All sorts of people were going to be there from my past. At the same time, I was going to be reaching a whole new generation. Somehow I had to bridge the divide.

Despite the nerves, when I walked on that stage I felt as though I owned it. I was ready. I sang with Elton, Sting, Ronan Keating, Samantha Mumba, Russell Watson and Enrique Iglesias. Maurice had flown all the way from Miami and we did a duet of a beautiful Bee Gees song, 'The First of May'. It was the first time we had sung together in seventeen years. It was special.

A part of me felt as though I was proving myself all over again, but this didn't bother me. As far as I was concerned, I had the same raw energy and desire as that fifteen-year-old schoolgirl who burst on the music scene in 1964.

Oddly enough, I think many people in the audience felt as though they were rediscovering me as well.

Lucian Grainge said to me afterwards, 'You know what I think about tonight, Lu? Out of ten, I'm giving you an *eleven* . . . And I'll tell you something else – this is just the beginning.'

# Officially Lulu

On the long weekend in June 2002, as people filled the streets to celebrate the Queen's Golden Jubilee, I raised a glass of champagne and quietly toasted my own 'jubilee'.

Ironically, my life has been punctuated by royal anniversaries. At the age of four I sang a song from a tenement window in Soho Street, Glasgow, to a crowd of neighbours and friends who were celebrating the Coronation. And on a holiday weekend twenty-five years ago, at the Silver Jubilee, I was heavily pregnant and waiting for my baby to arrive. Again, there were street parties, but I was a little too large to go dancing between tables waving a Union Jack.

The Golden Jubilee I will remember for very personal reasons. The duets album, which we called *Together*, went straight into the charts at No. 4. It sold over 100,000 copies in a week, earning me a gold disc.

Although I had high hopes, I had no idea this would happen so quickly. The success thrilled me because I had worked so hard and been through so much. This one was special.

People were delighted to see me come back. They stopped me

in the street, waving and calling out. Taxi drivers tooted their horns and teenagers asked for my autograph.

Although excited, I felt tremendously calm. After one particular radio interview, I said to myself, 'That went really well.'

This was a big thing for me. Instead of being critical, I was positive. See how much I had changed? In the old days I would have found some fault and beaten myself up. Nowadays, if I don't quite nail a song during a performance, I tell myself, 'That's OK. I can't get it right every time.'

For the launch of the album I worked eighteen-hour days, doing television, radio and press interviews. I criss-crossed the country and answered thousands of questions and smiled for hundreds of photographs.

On the Friday before the Golden Jubilee celebrations I was in Ireland for *The Late Late Show*. Then I jetted back to London because I had to be on CD:UK on Saturday morning. It meant arriving home at 2.00 a.m. and leaving for the studio at 7.00 a.m. On Saturday evening I went to a Westlife concert. This was a pretty typical day.

Sunday was my first day off in more than six weeks and I sat around the house in my pyjamas, reading the newspapers and watching shows about the Jubilee. It was my first chance to sit back and contemplate what I had achieved.

I have been through so many ups and downs during the previous thirty-eight years that I didn't want to get ahead of myself. Instead I kept myself contained and focused on the work that still had to be done.

Elton said to me the other day, 'Just enjoy it.'

'I *am* enjoying myself. I'm loving every minute of it,' I replied.

Since then the album has continued to sell well and given me a springboard to go even further. A single – a duet with Ronan Keating – was released for Christmas 2002 and roared into the Top

Ten. I was disappointed that it didn't get a No. 1, but hey, there's always next time.

As Lucian Grainge told me, 'This is only foreplay for you anyway, Lu.' Meaning the best is yet to come.

My record company has signed me to do another album and there are great plans for the future. I'll be spending the summer of 2003 in the recording studio, hopefully working with some brilliant producers from both sides of the Atlantic.

I started the year skiing in Arizona and visiting Jordan in Los Angeles where he has based himself for a while to further his acting career. I have always been comfortable in America and Jordan feels the same way.

Bad news has a habit of breaking when I'm away from home. I was in California for the earthquake and in New York on 11 September 2001. This time Billy had been trying to reach me at the Beverly Hills Hotel, leaving message after message, until finally I called him.

'Maurice is sick. They think he might die,' he told me.

Mo had complained of stomach pains and been taken to the Mount Sinai Medical Centre in Miami on Friday 10 January. Doctors diagnosed a strangulated hernia, but before they could operate he suffered a massive heart attack.

Immediately I called Barry and Linda in Miami, where the Gibb brothers had lived since the mid-seventies. Everything had been thrown into chaos. One moment Mo had been healthy, the next he was in intensive care, having slipped into a coma.

How could this be happening, I thought. Maurice was a year younger than me. He had two beautiful children, a girl and a boy, Sam and Adam. He and Yvonne had been married for more than twenty-five years.

'It doesn't look good,' said Linda. 'They don't think he's going to make it. We're waiting for Robin. He's flying in from London tonight.'

I spoke to Barbara Gibb, Maurice's mother, who seemed to be in shock. 'I'm not sure I can go and see him in hospital,' she said tearfully. 'I don't think I can face it.'

Robin flew in to Miami that night and arrived at the hospital only an hour before Maurice died. I know he was completely devastated – the heart attack had been so sudden and unexpected. At least the brothers were together and Mo had his wife and children nearby.

Back in Britain the media were desperately trying to contact me. Television reports were running the footage of the wedding at Gerrard's Cross in Buckinghamshire, as well as the more recent footage from *An Audience With* . . . when Mo and I sang together.

Being in LA was actually a gift because I avoided the media siege. I would only speak to Billy and Edwina. Eventually Billy said, 'The calls have been almost non-stop. The press really want a quote.'

'I'll tell you what the quote is: I'm too upset to say anything.'

After I heard the news that Maurice had passed away, I waited to hear from the family about the funeral arrangements. I had a long talk with Yvonne, who sounded distraught and completely drained. She was trying to hold herself together, but I could really hear how much she was hurting.

'How are you doing?'

'I still can't believe it.'

We both cried a little and she said the funeral would be the following day.

'I would really like to come,' I said.

'It's up to you. Whatever you think is best.'

She thought I was phoning from London rather than LA.

'Whatever happens there's going to be a memorial service in England some time soon,' she said.

Yvonne very kindly left the decision up to me and my senses were sharp enough to make the right choice. I have always hated funerals and I knew that if I turned up, some of the focus would be on me. That would be inappropriate. As much as I loved

Maurice, the people who were closest to him were Yvonne and his children.

A part of me also wanted to hold on to my last memories of Mo when he came to London to sing with me. We had lots of time together during rehearsals, talking and laughing about the past and catching up with each other's lives. I will always be grateful for that.

A week or so after the funeral, as I was leaving America, I called Yvonne again and the housekeeper answered. I held on the phone for what seemed like ages, but she came back to say that she couldn't find her.

'Can you please give her a message. Tell her that Lulu called but she doesn't have to call me back. I'll phone her another time.'

I left my number and Yvonne called back twenty minutes later. We stayed on the phone for ages, talking about Maurice. The two of us laughed together and cried together, reminiscing about the man we both knew and loved.

The thing that absolutely everyone acknowledged about Mo is that he didn't have a mean bone in his body. And even Samantha, his daughter, had realised that her father could talk to anyone, from a duke to a dustman, treating each person in exactly the same way.

Yvonne said, 'I think you made amends . . .' And then stopped herself. 'No, I don't mean that . . .'

'I don't mind if you say that,' I told her.

'I think you both really made up for everything that had happened in the past.'

'I think we blessed each other.'

Five or six years ago I changed my name. I am now Lulu Kennedy-Cairns. It was just after my mother died and she was always in my thoughts. For a long time I had been Mrs Gibb and then Mrs Frieda, but now I really just needed to be me.

The name Lulu has been good to me. I'm identified by it now. It doesn't worry me that one day I'll be a little old lady who is called Lulu. I'll be this mad eccentric, who wears outrageous clothes, great shoes and is completely outspoken.

Writing this book has been a cathartic experience. At times I've been amazed at how much I've remembered and at other times stunned by things I had forgotten. I have laughed at some of the photographs and cringed at some of the headlines, particularly thing like, 'LULU TELLS US WHY MARRIAGE NO. 2 CAN'T FAIL'.

At other times, as I searched through the cuttings, I saw myself quoted as saying that I didn't care about hit records and I was happy being a family favourite doing TV variety shows. In my defence, that's what I believed at the time. We all change. We evolve. We move on.

I am fifty-three years old and I feel great. Like a lot of women, I refuse to grow old gracefully. I'll fight it until my last breath, just as my mother did. If that means jogging every day, having a personal trainer and taking advantage of science, then so be it (within reason).

In countless interviews I've been asked if I have some secret. How is it that I look so good? Every time, I say the same thing. I do yoga. I work out three times a week at the gym. I go running. I eat small portions of healthy food – always organic. I know which clothes to wear to make the most of my good points. I use stylists, hairdressers and make-up artists, who get paid to make me look good. At the same time, I don't have three kids to run to school every day. Nor do I have to cook, clean, iron or do the laundry. I am privileged.

I get halfway through this answer and I can see the interviewer's eyes glaze over. It's not what they want to hear. They want me to tell them that I have some amazing diet, or fitness regime, or better still a magic pill that will instantly shed calories, iron out wrinkles and tighten flab. The truth is it takes a lot of hard work and a lot of help. The same is true of my recording career.

I do have vices. I drink too much coffee and have a sweet tooth when it comes to chocolate. I have had Botox injections to smooth the skin around my eyes and I have picked up a lifetime of knowledge about hair, make-up, lighting and angles . . . so much so, I could probably get a degree in it.

I've said it before and I'll say it again, the real secret to looking good is feeling good about yourself – inside and outside.

At the moment I'm single and that's OK. I am no longer afraid of being on my own. Nor am I scared of having my heart broken. There are so many arrows coming at us all the time that it never happens the same way twice. As my brother Gordon, in his wisdom, said to me, 'Arrows come, they strike and they break the skin, but we all heal.'

I have had relationships since John. I don't find it easy. I can't just have a purely physical relationship. I need to connect with someone mentally and emotionally before I can commit to them or them to me.

Sometimes I wish I wasn't so choosy and could be more laissez-faire. I tell myself, 'For God's sake, you liked him, why didn't you just go for it?'

One part of me is very spontaneous, another part is still very cautious, dour and earnest. You can take the girl out of Scotland, but you can't take the Scot out of the girl.

I have had the most amazing life, full of ups and downs, triumphs and tragedy, laughter and tears. I can't complain about a single moment. I'm happy with where I am now, which means there is no reason to regret what has gone before. For me the key to life has been *learning* from the past and *living* in the moment. I'm still trying.

I have worked hard for my success. I like to think that I've earned it. At the same time, I'm aware how much goodwill, love and respect I've enjoyed. I am conscious of this and try not to take it for granted.

This is another new beginning. Let's see what happens next. One thing is for certain – anything is possible.

# I Don't Wanna Fight

There's a pale moon in the sky
The kind you make your wishes on.
Like the light in your eyes
The one I built my dreams upon.
It's not there any longer
Something happened somewhere
And we both know why.
But me, I'm getting stronger
We must stop pretending
I can't live this lie.

CHORUS:
I don't care who's wrong or right
I don't really wanna fight no more
(Too much talking babe)
Let's sleep on it tonight
I don't really wanna fight no more
(This is time for letting go)

*I hear a whisper in the air*
*It simply doesn't bother me.*
*Can you see that I don't care*
*Or are you looking right through me?*
*Seems to me that lately*
*You look at me the wrong way and I start to cry.*
*Could it be that maybe*
*This crazy situation is the reason why?*

CHORUS:
*I don't care who's wrong or right*
*I don't really wanna fight no more*
*(Too much talking babe)*
*Let's sleep on it tonight*
*I don't really wanna fight no more*
*(Tired of all these games)*

*But baby don't you know*
*That I don't wanna hurt no more.*
*(It's time, I'm walking babe)*
*Don't care now who's to blame*
*I don't really wanna fight no more.*
*(This is time for letting go)*

*Hanging on to the past*
*It only stands in our way.*
*We had to grow for our love to last*
*But we just grew apart.*

*No, I don't wanna hurt no more*
*But baby don't you know*
*No, I don't wanna hurt no more*
*(Too much talking babe)*

*Don't care now who's to blame*
*I don't really wanna fight no more*
*(Tired of all these games)*
*I don't care who's wrong or right*
*I don't really wanna fight no more*
*(It's time, I'm walking babe)*
*So let's sleep on it tonight*
*I don't really wanna fight no more*
*(This is time for letting go)*

# Index